THE CHURCH OF
THE COVENANT
1637-1651

THE CHURCH OF
THE COVENANT

1637-1651

Revolution and Social Change
in Scotland

————

WALTER MAKEY

Edinburgh City Archivist

JOHN DONALD PUBLISHERS LTD
EDINBURGH

ISBN 0 85976 035 9

285.2411
M235

Printed in Great Britain by Bell & Bain Ltd, Glasgow.

Acknowledgments

THIS book is a work of many hands and I should like to thank all those who have helped in the long process of its completion. The greater part of the research was necessarily done in short spells and at odd moments. This would have been impossible without, on the one hand, the assistance of the staffs of the Scottish Record Office, the National Library of Scotland, the Registrar General's Office, and the Edinburgh Central Public Library and, on the other, the generous lending policies of the Libraries of New College, Edinburgh and the University of Edinburgh. They are all wholeheartedly thanked for allowing me to use the materials in their custody and for the courtesy with which they always provided them. I should also like to thank my employers, once Edinburgh Corporation and now the City of Edinburgh District Council, for permission to use the records in the City Archives - with which I have more than a passing acquaintance. I am grateful to the Church of Scotland for numerous kindnesses, not least for depositing so many of its records, national and local alike, in the Scottish Record Office and thus making them generally available; my thanks are also due to the kirk session of St Cuthbert's and to the presbytery of Stirling for permission to examine their minutes before they had been so deposited. Avondale and Penicuik figure prominently enough in the theme running through this book and each disclosed its secrets through the family papers of its principal proprietor; my debt to His Grace the Duke of Hamilton and to Sir John Clerk of Penicuik Bt. is perhaps sufficiently obvious. Some of the ideas explored in this book have already been aired in a paper read to the Scottish Church History Society in 1970 and I am grateful to the Society for its permission to use them again.

Many of the issues raised in this book have been discussed, seldom heatedly but always profitably, with the members of Professor Gordon Donaldson's postgraduate seminar. It was perhaps a fortunate coincidence that several of them had sixteenth century interests; my attention was inevitably attracted to the origins of the society with which I was directly concerned. Dr Margaret Sanderson's work has had a vital influence on my own; but all concerned, whatever their period, have left their mark. Dr Rosalind Marshall shares my fascination with the Hamiltons, Edward Cowan my interest in Montrose and Argyll, Dr Michael Lynch my enthusiasm for Edinburgh, Frances Shaw my respect for testaments, and Dr Arthur Williamson my belief that argument is always productive. At one time or another, I have debated almost everything with the Reverend Dr John Todd - and many of my more extravagant notions have perished in the small hours of the morning. I thank them all; but my greatest debt - and it is a debt shared with all who are seriously concerned about the study of Scottish history - is to Professor Donaldson himself. Without his erudition, this

v

book would have been the poorer; without his encouragement, it would not have been written at all.

It is fair to say that I disagree with Dr David Stevenson about the nature of the Scottish Revolution, but I should like to record my appreciation of his work. He has produced a dispassionate narrative of the period and thus a solid foundation for research. Over the years, I have discussed various aspects of the subject with Dr William Ferguson, Dr John Moore, Professor Valerie Pearl, Dr John Imrie, Dr Ian Rae, Dr Julia Buckroyd, Lady Christian Hesketh, Elspeth Yeo, John di Folco and Richard Dell. I am similarly grateful to John Tuckwell of John Donald Publishers Ltd. for many helpful suggestions and for guiding an occasionally wayward author safely into print. Like all the others, he is absolved from the consequences of his kindness; errors of fact and absurdities of interpretation remain the inalienable property of the author.

A special word of thanks is due to all those who typed or checked the various drafts, and particularly to Ann Munro who triumphed over my hand-writing to produce an accurate rendering of the final version.

I must finally thank my wife, Phyllis, for hours of checking, for disentangling a dozen mixed metaphors and, not least, for patiently enduring a husband who periodically wandered off into the seventeenth century. There can be no higher devotion than this.

Walter Makey.

Contents

1

The Silent Revolution

THE 'Troubles' which tormented Scotland during the middle years of the seventeenth century were the final episode of a social revolution deeply rooted in a long feudal past. The previous century had experienced profound changes, some so gradual that they were barely perceptible, others deliberate enough though unpremeditated in their consequences, all of them profound in their cumulative effect. The appearance of institutional stability concealed a society in turmoil; by the early decades of the seventeenth century, Scotland was ready to explode. The Troubles were the violent culmination of a revolutionary process that had begun - where we must begin - more than a century earlier.

Feudal society, as it had been during the minority of James V, was founded on the assumption that jurisdiction, and thus political power, belonged to the King and those, his tenants-in-chief, who held land directly from him. In effect, the magnate who had the superiority of an estate also had a criminal jurisdiction over all those who lived on it. In the case of a barony, the magnate could, in theory at least, be overruled by the sheriff; but many of the larger estates were regalities in which - treason apart - neither the King nor his sheriff had any power at all. These, then, were substantial jurisdictions and they were, like the lands on which they depended, heritable. Landed power, like landed wealth, descended from father to son. The feudal magnate was almost as secure in his authority as was the King himself. Moreover, the sheriff himself was often a magnate and his office, like so much else in baronial Scotland, had tended to become hereditary. The gamekeeper was usually a practising poacher. In theory, the King was the source of power, while the magnates merely used it on his behalf; in reality, theirs was sometimes greater than his. For kings were merely mortal men and they always seemed to die before their time. The sequence was monotonously regular. The premature death of the King was followed by the accession of a minor, a long regency devoted to the interests of the magnates, a shorter period of struggle as the new King laboured to assert his power, and finally a few brief years of successful personal rule. The Crown was usually weak and occasionally contemptible.

Feudal Scotland can reasonably be likened to a mosaic of tiny fragments, each the heritable property of a magnate and each enjoying a measure of independence from the Crown. In some areas at least, the fragments were arranging themselves into simpler patterns as the larger magnates swallowed up their lesser neighbours to create 'baronial complexes' of formidable local power. (1) These in their turn periodically coalesced to form larger groups or factions sometimes professing an ideological purpose but always dedicated to the pursuit of national power. Indeed the substance of authority normally resided in the baronies and regalities of the countryside rather than in a royal bureaucracy which, though growing, was still small and impoverished. The words *in liberam baroniam* are scrawled indelibly across the pages of Scottish history.

It follows from this that the existence of the state was often threatened, but its weakness invariably proved its salvation. The appearance of a powerful, and seemingly invincible, faction would, as if by some immutable law, stimulate the growth of a counter alliance. Weakness at the centre was reflected in strength about the periphery, but division on the periphery always preserved the centre more or less intact. The semblance of anarchy concealed an institutional structure of astonishing stability. Each King, after each violent death, was followed by his legitimate successor - and the principle would live on into the seventeenth century. As Montrose was to tell his sovereign in 1641: 'Ye are not like a tree lately planted that oweth the fall to the first wind.' ([2])

But this is to race ahead of our story. The greatest 'baronial complex' of them all was the vast sprawling empire of the old church. Its estates - or temporalities - were dispersed strategically across the length and breadth of lowland Scotland; nearly all of them were held in superiority; many of them were regalities. It drew the teinds of more than five-sixths of the parishes of the kingdom and these included all the wealthiest ([3]). It has been estimated that the corporate wealth of the church yielded an annual income of £400,000 per year at a time, on the eve of the Reformation, when the patrimony of the Crown was worth a mere £17,500 per year ([4]). But, by this time, the church was a corporate institution only in a rather nominal sense. The sixteenth century, as much before the Reformation as after it, was the age of secularisation. The Crown and the factions, at odds though they may have been about almost everything else, could find common ground and common plunder in the gradual erosion of the wealth of the church. Church property, teind and temporality alike, was regularly granted to lay commendators who would eventually - as one century's parting gift to another with a different set of values - develop into Lords of Erection closely resembling the magnates themselves. Power as well as wealth gradually passed from the church to the factions and indeed the process had been hastened by the church itself. The vital office of bailie of regality had often been vested heritably in the family of a laird or even a nobleman; the trappings of power remained with the abbot or bishop concerned, but its substance had been delegated to a magnate. The old church was too tired to defend itself.

These changes made significant adjustments in the structure of feudal Scotland without undermining its foundations; blood was drained out of the first estate and transfused into the second. But the consequences, if less than fundamental in themselves, were profound in their implications. In the great days of the old church an outstanding professional man had been able to find his way through the office of abbot into a seat in Parliament and a place, secure for his lifetime, in the privileged circle of the magnates. Secularisation, by introducing the hereditary principle, could only reduce his opportunities. And, as one outlet was closed, another, leading in a different direction, was opened. Subinfeudation was, of course, as old as the feudal system itself, but the decline of the church gave it a new impetus. The widespread feuing of church land during the sixteenth century was almost a revolution in itself. The market was suddenly flooded with land; it became fairly easy for a professional man, or indeed anybody else with a moderate amount of money to spend, to acquire an estate of his own. Under the terms of a feu charter, the superior retained the rights, mainly of jurisdiction, inherent in his superiority, while alienating the produce of his land to a vassal. In return, the feuar contracted to pay an annual duty, fixed in perpetuity, and, in some cases, a capital sum which is best regarded as a composition for part of the duty. A new situation was created in the broad acres of the temporalities. Henceforth, there would be two landowners to each plot of land, the superior with his primarily judicial function and the feuar with his essentially commercial role. Their interests were different and the difference would widen with the passage of time.

The 'long upward heave' of Scottish prices during the sixteenth century is well recognised. It has been calculated, on the basis of controlled prices in burghs, that the cost of living rose at least fourfold between the minority of Mary and the death of James VI ([5]). The rather longer series available for the burgh of Edinburgh suggests that the price of ale increased sixfold, and that of bread eightfold, between the 1530s and the turn of the century ([6]). It seems likely that agricultural prices, which are more directly to our purpose, were behaving in much the same way. In Fife, where a long series of conversion prices has survived, barley sold at about 14/- per boll in the late thirties and early forties ([7]), at about 116/- per boll during the nineties and at about 140/-per boll during the 1620s and 1630s, when prices had ceased to rise rapidly ([8]). As a very rough approximation, it would seem that agricultural prices increased almost tenfold between the latter years of James V and the earlier years of Charles I.

The impact of this inexorable process on the relationship between superior and feuar, though usually imperceptible in the short term, would eventually be as violent as it was final. Rents, at least in the arable areas of the Lowlands, were almost invariably calculated in kind ([9]). They rose automatically as prices increased. The income of the feuar was protected from inflation at a time when his expenditure was effectively being reduced. Feu duties were usually expressed in terms of a currency which depreciated with each passing year; by the 1630s they were trivial. But these payments by the feuar were, or at least originally had been, a major component of the landed income of the superior. The price rise flattered the vassal and snarled viciously at his lord.

Nor is this the whole of a rather complicated story. The teind surveys carried out in 1627 strongly suggest that agricultural yields were rising fairly rapidly, at least where circumstances were favourable. On many estates, rent and teind alike were being augmented by extensive 'labouring and liming' ([10]). The rate of increase varied considerably; but gains of about a third were relatively common, presumably on land which responded favourably to lime. In St. Cuthbert's, a prosperous parish busily striving to feed a hungry city, yields seem to have been doubled by the simple, if laborious, expedient of dumping Edinburgh's

inexhaustible supply of dung on the fields around its boundaries ([11]). It would be
absurd to conjure up an agricultural revolution from the evidence of a scattered
handful of parishes - not to say dung; but it is fair to conclude that prosperity was
increasing and that the profits from it were shared between the titular of the
teinds, the feuar and his tenants. The superior, passively collecting his devalued
feu duties, did not necessarily participate.

It is sometimes possible to measure the extent of the superior's loss. In the
1630s, the total income from rents and teinds in the Lordship of Coupar
amounted to rather less than £40,000. The income actually received by Lord
Coupar was, by contrast, just over £7,000, of which nearly £6,000 came from
teinds. This in its turn was reduced by the various burdens upon it - mainly
ministers' stipends - to £5,400. To look at the same question in a slightly different
way, the collective income of the feuars, less the teinds which were drawn from
their lands, was rather more than £30,000; the feu duties paid by them to Lord
Coupar totalled a mere £1,100. The loss may modestly be described as
catastrophic. If Coupar can be regarded as fairly typical, the smaller Lordship of
Culross provides an interesting extreme case. It would seem that most of the lands
had been feued with the teinds included and that the income from teinds had
depreciated with the feu duties. An estate, which had once, in 1561, been worth
£1,600 and which would now, in the withered pounds of 1617, have been worth
nearly ten times as much, was 'super-expendit'. The Abbacy of Culross had been
cruelly violated ([12]).

It is clear enough that the feuing of church land, operating as it did in a period of
rising prices, eventually brought about a vast transfer of wealth from superior to
vassal - and vassals were of several kinds. A recent study, as exhaustive as it must
surely be definitive, has classified all the charters known to have survived
according to the status of the grantees. The results are startling enough. Only 2%
of the vassals were noblemen. A further 20% were already landowners of one kind
or another, but some of these held from subjects-superior and many were far from
wealthy. Another 9% were the kinsmen of landowners, but nearly all of these were
previously landless and some at least were farmers. The proportion of burgesses
was, at 8%, surprisingly low, while the lawyers and the courtiers were merely a
handful. It seems unlikely that more than a fifth of the charters were granted to
tenants-in-chief or that more than a third went to the affluent. On the other hand,
44% of the vassals are known to have been of lower status, while 13% are not
identifiable at all - and most of these must have been tenant farmers. Indeed nearly
two-thirds of the lands named in all these transactions went to the men who had
previously possessed them and, in the vast majority of these cases, to the farmer
who had previously worked them. Furthermore it is evident that some of the
wealthier vassals were merely middlemen who sub-feued their lands to the sitting
tenants as soon as they had acquired them ([13]). The feuars thus fell into two fairly
well defined groups. A relatively small number of gentlemen operated their
substantial estates through tenants, while a much larger number of yeomen
became the owners of their farms. In both cases, land, and eventually most of the
income from it, was transferred from the feudal classes to other social groups

outside the privileged circle of the old order.

This huge transformation was not confined to the temporalities. The same sequence was reproduced at more or less the same time on the estates of the Crown - and these were similarly impoverished in consequence. At a very conservative estimate, a third of the agricultural land of Scotland, measured in terms of its productive capacity, was feued during the early stages of the price revolution. A rather similar situation obtained on some, though by no means all, of the lands of the civil magnates. It seems likely that the barons of the sixteenth century had resisted the temptations of feuing fairly successfully; but subinfeudation was as old as the feudal system itself. For centuries, the magnates had been granting land to their dependants and their relatives and they had done so at rents which had nearly always been nominal and which would eventually become meaningless. The superior had effectively alienated his entitlement to the produce of the lands concerned. Once more, the grantees fell into two well recognised groups: they were either 'gentlemen' with substantial estates or they were 'yeomen' working their own farms. The parallel with the kirklands was plainly fairly close. But the rest of the magnates' lands were, like the proper lands of the temporalities, worked through tenant farmers of one kind or another. Of these, the rentaller had almost total security; his lease extended to the grave and often beyond it; his rent was, to all intents and purposes, a fixed quantity. At the other extreme, the tenant at will had no formal security at all and his rent could lawfully be increased at any time. But many, and probably most, of the farms concerned were worked on limited leases and the rents attaching to them could, at least in theory, be raised at intervals.

These distinctions were largely irrelevant in the arable regions of eastern Scotland where rents were normally calculated in victual; they adjusted themselves to the price rise and there was no urgent need to increase them. But elsewhere it was often otherwise. In the west of Scotland, in Galloway, in the Borders and along the Highland line, a moist climate combined with heavier soils to produce an agricultural economy with a pastoral rather than an arable bias and a range of products which had traditionally been sold in the seaport towns of the east and indeed further afield. For centuries they had produced for the market as well as for local consumption. Their rents were sometimes paid in wedders, butter, cheese or, in favoured localities, in victual; but they were often calculated in money. There was no automatic adjustment for inflation and the landlord, whether superior or gentleman, could only maintain the real value of his rents by deliberately increasing them - and this may often have been difficult. Long years of relatively stable prices had yielded a rigid rent structure with the power of custom, as well as the conventional wisdom of Rome and Geneva, behind it. Rack renting was probably almost impossible on lands occupied by rentallers, for no court could lawfully evict them; but there seems every reason to suppose that the ordinary husbandman was only less favoured. On church land at least, leases seem, during the crucial middle years of the sixteenth century, to have been getting longer rather than shorter and they were often renewed to the same tenant or his heir ([14]). It is difficult to be certain that the civil magnates were similarly generous;

but they were subject to the same constraints. Evictions for one reason or another were not unknown, but they were relatively rare. It will be argued that money rents commonly remained static for a long period before being violently increased in the rather different social climate of the seventeenth century. It is at least reasonably clear that money rents nearly always lagged a long way behind prices and that the eventual increases were so belated, and thus so sudden, that they could only seem rapacious. The tenant farmer was gradually enriched and then suddenly impoverished. The traditional relationship between landlord and tenant was distorted beyond recognition. The western experience was not merely different from the eastern; it was - or so we shall claim - opposite to it.

It would not be impossible to find parallels in other parts of Europe; inflation, like money itself, knows no frontiers. But the price rise was much greater in Scotland than it was anywhere else. The impoverishment of the Crown, of the Lords of Erection, the bishops and, for the time being at least, the barons of the west was more than an inconvenience; it was a catastrophe. The consequent transfer of wealth from superior to vassal was gradual, but it was eventually so large that it eroded the foundations of feudal society. Seventeenth century Scotland was still, to all outward appearances, a land of baronies and regalities surmounted by a Parliament of tenants-in-chief. But everywhere, except on the lands of the eastern magnates, history was slipping away from the feudal superior. His rights of jurisdiction were not his to alienate; but the income, which alone could lend them substance, had almost gone. The basic assumption of any feudal society - that landed power springs directly from the heritable possession of landed wealth - was denied. Charles I inherited a social structure that his great-grandfather would scarcely have understood. The intervening years had witnessed the gradual unfolding of a revolutionary process that was unobtrusive and thus almost unobserved, unpremeditated and thus imperfectly understood. But the eventual impact, silent though it may have been, was as final as it was fundamental. The Scotland of Charles I wore feudal clothes - and it carried them somewhat uneasily.

Neither Calvin nor Knox understood inflation. They accepted that rents, like the profits of trade or interest on lent money, were justifiable in the sight of God; but they denied that any of them could ever be excessive. In effect, they assumed a static economy in which rents and prices, profits and interest would be stable and predictable and they condemned excess as extortion born of avarice. The rack renter, like the monopolist, was quite simply a sinner. It is scarcely surprising that the *First Book of Discipline* should have urged landlords to rest content with their customary rents. These attitudes were in no sense peculiar to Calvinism. The old church had often said much the same thing; so had Lindsay and indeed the Three Estates themselves. Scottish theory, like that of Europe as a whole, emerged reluctantly from the Middle Ages. The voice of Bodin was soft and somewhat lonely; but anybody could hear the ministers, many of them from a great distance [15]. It would be absurd to suggest a causal relationship between inflation and Calvinism - and yet the persistence of the one nourished the triumph of the other. It can reasonably be argued that the revolutions of later years could scarcely have happened without the distortions inseparable from the price rise. A revolutionary movement, which had drawn its social theory from medieval models, would eventually feed on their destruction. But the revolutionaries themselves were only dimly aware of this. They found their inspiration elsewhere.

The ideology of the revolution, the distilled essence of a theological system of almost infinite subtlety, was far from inappropriate. Mankind, it was claimed, was totally corrupt - and John the Commonweill would not have dissented from this. But some, though not all, had been chosen for salvation by a God who was as omnipotent as he was inscrutable - and were not the Scots, for all their sins, a chosen people? It followed inescapably from this that no man could shape his own eventual destiny, that his behaviour in this world was, in the last analysis, irrelevant to his salvation. It is not difficult to understand the profound emotional impact of this appeal on a society which had for centuries been riddled with doubt and insecurity. The situation seemed to demand a strong King - whom Lindsay called Divine Correction - and godly preachers - like Lindsay's Doctor of Divinity - to expound the new doctrine. In the absence of the one, the others became doubly desirable. The individual - who might willingly have been ruled had there been a monarchy strong enough to rule him - could only seek consolation elsewhere and he found it in the doctrine of predestination; he was caught up in a scheme so majestic in its vastness that his own difficulties, whether personal or political, dwindled into insignificance. The merely factious were nerved to make rebellion in the name of God.

Calvinism was at once simple and complex. Good works might not be sufficient in themselves, but they were to be expected nonetheless. It was the duty of the elect to pass their brief span in this world in the service of God. The process of salvation could only manifest itself in a society that was consciously godly in its principles: 'There is no entering into life unless the church conceives us in her womb, brings us to birth, nourishes us at her bosom and preserves us by her guardianship and discipline' ([16]). It became the business of the church to regulate the behaviour of every citizen from the King to the cottar.

Calvinism thus made its appeal on two levels which, however closely related they may have been, were nonetheless distinct. On the one, it was proudly aloof from mundane affairs; as such, it was not necessarily revolutionary and it discovered an eager audience among the political classes. On the other, it was almost obsessively concerned with human conduct and this would inevitably lead it into collision with the state; it would indeed justify the construction of a new apparatus of government founded on different principles from the old and operated by ministers and elders who would, or at least could, be drawn from different social strata. In this - its second - guise, Calvinism would, as the price rise wrought its silent havoc, become subversive in more than the obvious sense of the word. Indeed the political circumstances of Scotland would virtually force the church into the centre of a stage left vacant by the weakness of the Crown. And a new estate - the feuar and the farmer in the countryside, the lawyer and the lesser burgess in the towns - was waiting in the wings. The bosom of the church was as ample as it was inviting. It is not perhaps surprising that Knox should have contributed so much more to political theory than he did to theology.

The call to revolt was suitably ambiguous. In the summer of 1558, Knox issued his famous appeal to the nobility and the Estates of Scotland, to the heritable jurisdictions of the realm, to the inferior magistrate 'with his lawful powers of God' and this, while it was plainly an incitement to rebel, was not the blueprint for a social revolution. It merely demanded that one part of feudal Scotland, the Lords of the Congregation, should redeem the sins of the other, the Queen Regent and her supporters among the magnates. It was directed, with a superb sense of political strategy, at the very heart of the Scottish tradition. It embroiled the protestant cause in an old-fashioned faction fight on the implicit understanding that victory would produce an aristocratic church. The new church would be impeccably protestant in its doctrine, but it would be reluctant to challenge the existing values of a feudal society. Above all it would approach the delicate issues surrounding the ownership of church property with caution.

But, at the same time, Knox also appealed to 'his beloved brethren of the Commonalty of Scotland'. In so doing, he was addressing the network of illegal congregations that were springing up, certainly in the towns but probably in rural areas as well, all over Lowland Scotland. It is perhaps important that these protestant cells - the privy kirk of Knox's *History* - were, at least in theory, classless organisations. They might, or they might not, include the inferior magistrate; but, even if they did, he would not enjoy an automatic, let alone an hereditary, right to positions of power. Moreover, the privy kirk would eventually become the public kirk and, once this had happened, the commonalty would come to embrace, however nominally, the whole of the population. Seen in this light, the *Letter* becomes a revolutionary document of the highest significance. When Knox declared: '. . . it doth no less appertain to you, beloved brethren, to be assured that your faith and religion be grounded upon the true and undoubted word of God, than it does to your princes and rulers', he was hacking away at the foundations of the feudal order. When he went on to assert that the people might, if their 'superiors' were 'negligent', justly 'provide true preachers' for themselves, he was looking forward to a new society in which the church would be totally independent not only of the royal administration but of the inferior magistrate as well. He foresaw the appearance of an entirely new form of government([17]).

It might fairly be objected that these radical notions existed only in the fertile imagination of Knox himself and it may readily be conceded that they were relatively insignificant in their own time. It was obvious enough that Scotland was politically unstable; a rebel with a cause could hope to succeed. The price of victual was probably at least twice as high in the late sixties as it had been in the late thirties; inflation was already noticeable but its worst excesses were still to come. Scotland was not yet ripe for revolution. The aristocratic revolt was so successful so quickly that the real revolution was almost stifled at birth. But the radical ideas of the *Letter* formed a very real part of the potential of the Reformation and they would grow luxuriantly enough as a changing climate began to favour them. The privy kirk would be revived as a vehicle of protest. It would become an explosive force in the 1590s, during the insurrectionary years of the late 1630s and, above all, during the radical revolution of the late 1640s. Indeed it was to show itself in the conventicles which would meet 'in times of persecution' throughout the seventeenth century.

Nonetheless the church actually established during the 1560s was, at least at a national level, essentially a feudal organisation. The 'Lords and Barons professing Christ Jesus' - a phrase which somehow contrives to epitomise the crowded history of an eventful decade - developed from an alternative government into a provisional government and then again into a general assembly ruling over a protestant church. The new structure consisted of a scattered multitude of kirk sessions, each individually retaining some of the characteristics of a privy kirk, linked through salaried superintendents to a central governing body on which lay politicians were influential. The resemblance of this body to a Parliament was close and enduring and it was re-affirmed at the end of the century, when the assembly itself described its lay members as barons and commissioners of burghs. The Reformation thus gave birth to an aristocratic church which faithfully reflected the eternal verities of a society commonly dominated by the inferior magistrate.

But neither church nor state was unchanging. The advent of a Godly Prince ruling through a series of Godly Regents added a new dimension to the argument. For it could now be claimed, without violating fundamental Reformation principles, that the logical guardian of the new faith was less the inferior magistracy than its titular head, the King. The distinguishing features of this trend were a marked disinclination, apparent during the administrations of Morton and Arran, to hold general assemblies and, more subtly, a growing skill in the manipulation of their composition - and this was the peculiar achievement of James VI.

It is at least arguable that the two trends, the aristocratic and the royal, were not mutually exclusive. They shared a common reluctance to meddle with teind or temporality and thus a common interest in a dependent church. They shared a common mistrust of the aspirations of the professional churchman and thus a common erastianism which manifested itself in a common determination to involve the laity at all levels of church government. In the last resort, the one could live in the same society as the other. The first originated in the unique circumstances of the Marian interlude and was appropriate to a minority, when the royal standard tended to look like the ensign of the over-mighty subject. The second was better suited to a period of successful personal rule, when a restrained display of royal power, or royal dexterity, was not unacceptable.

The early reformers were able to adapt themselves, with every appearance of an easy conscience, to any or all of the trends which emerged from the inspired confusion of the Reformation. They believed, as Calvin himself had believed, that it was necessary to establish the godly society; but they shared his indifference to the exact shape of the framework surrounding and supporting it: this could be left to the accidents of time and place. The church, as it was originally reformed in Scotland, was able to merge itself into society as a whole[18].

This indifference was dismissed as naive by Andrew Melville, a second generation Calvinist who returned to Scotland from Geneva in 1574. The *Second Book of Discipline* rested on the assumption that the godly society had failed and the assertion that its failure had sprung from the futility of the lay church of the reformers. Instead it postulated a church of dedicated professionals which, far from reflecting society, would seek deliberately to transform it. The new church would separate itself from the debilitating grasp of a decadent state, purify itself by the intrusion of a carefully indoctrinated elite and sustain itself from the patrimony of the old church, before re-emerging to dominate the state which it had so recently deserted. To this end, the conquest of the universities, which would train the new generation of ministers, elders and deacons, was essential. No less so, since this vast bureaucracy would have to be paid, was the reclamation and rationalisation of the revenues of the old church. The conversion of any part of this vast wealth 'to the particular and profane use of any person' was held to be a 'detestable sacrilege before God' ([19]). To the Melvillians, everything and nothing was sacred. It is obvious enough that the idea threatened the commendator in his superiorities; it called in question the charters granted to his vassals; it at least opened up the possibility that feu duties would be renegotiated on an economic basis. The church was surely seeking to release itself from the twin tyrannies of the feu charter and the 'long upward heave'. But it was also seeking to control an empire of baronies and regalities and it is perhaps reasonable to assume that these would not simply have been dissolved as they might have been in a pure theocracy. Melville proposed to retain the civil magistrate, if only in a subordinate capacity. Would the bailies of the ecclesiastical regalities have become the local hangmen of their local kirks?

The question is in a sense an idle one, since the sixteenth century disdainfully ignored it; but it would pose itself again during the 1630s when another professional church would challenge the basic assumptions of feudal Scotland. But these were also, in the nature of things, being challenged by the royal administration. The Crown and the Church, whether as one kingdom or as two, shared a common interest in reducing the regalities to order and a common incentive to create new systems of local administration. The pretext was not far to seek. Church and Crown alike could reasonably concern themselves with the desperate social problems presented by the army of the poor. *The First Book of Discipline* committed the church to the care of the 'aged, impotent and lamed, who neither can nor may travail for their sustentation'; but it declined to support 'stubborn and idle beggars who, running from place to place, make a craft of their begging'; these were criminals 'whom the civil magistrate ought to punish'. True to Reformation theory, it left the sturdy beggar to the heritable jurisdictions and the earliest legislation, passed in the Convention of 1574, respected the distinction. But the vagabond, who made a craft of his begging, was a responsibility which the heritable jurisdictions were uniquely unable to discharge. A band of thieves, hounded out of the territory of one magnate, might find a ready welcome on the lands of his rivals. A problem, which had assumed the proportions of a national scandal, demanded a unified apparatus of repression and it is scarcely surprising that the Morton administration should have sought to devise one. The famous statute of 1579, besides authorising assessments for the deserving poor, entrusted the major problem to an entirely new jurisdiction, plainly suggested by the English Justices of the Peace. The new Justices would hold office at the King's pleasure; they would not necessarily have hereditary power - indeed, they might be feuars; their area of jurisdiction would be the parish, which thus became a civil, as well as an ecclesiastical, unit. It was a revolutionary proposal and this, together with a series of weak governments in the vital early stages, probably explains its failure. Indeed the last provisions of the act virtually confessed its impotence; it entrusted the oversight of the system to the Sheriffs, Stewards and Bailies of Regalities - to the very jurisdictions that it was designed to supplant [20].

A further act of 1592, passed at a time when the Melvillians were strong, repeated the earlier statute, while adding a corollary which totally changed its meaning. If the Justices were negligent, as frequently they were, the 'ministers, elders and deacons' of the local kirk session would name magistrates, whom the Crown - apparently without question - would appoint as Justices. Kirk's local hangman indeed. But James retreated only to advance along a parallel path of his own choosing. Two further acts of 1597 and 1600, perhaps a trifle unexpectedly at first glance, turned the entire problem over to the kirk sessions. The first was too short to reveal the King's mind, but the second was explicit enough. It ordered the presbyteries not only to assist their kirk sessions, but also to 'take diligent trial of (their) obedience' and to report their findings to the royal administration - which would punish negligence. The English Justices were the antennae of the monarchy; James seems to have seen the Scottish elder in the same role. The two kingdoms were merging themselves into one [21].

It is perhaps scarcely surprising that Justice and elder alike should have failed to solve a problem which was neither peculiar to Scotland nor confined to this period. Their failure merely reflects the platitude that it was impossible to cure unemployment by whipping the unemployed. But, quite apart from this, both approaches had obvious defects. Little is known about the Justices, but it seems likely that they were often local magnates thinly disguised as royal administrators. The kirk sessions were, however nominally, gatherings of the godly rather than the rich or the powerful. The one already had too much power; the other did not have enough. It is interesting that the next experiment should have involved the creation of a new kind of kirk session. In 1635, when King Charles seemed even stronger than Melville had been in 1592, the session clerk of the parish of Dundonald recorded a local act, not particularly remarkable in itself, against the entertainment of the sturdy beggar. But it was passed by a body that the previous century would surely have found strange. It included the minister and the elders and it obviously resembled the kirk session; but it also included the 'gentlemen' of the parish, whether they were actually elders or not. This augmented session, gathered somewhat informally together to perform a function which the *First Book of Discipline* regarded as civil rather than ecclesiastical, was built into a highly centralised church, linked through its bishops to the Crown. It was a High Commission in miniature, deliberately confusing the Sword with the Keys, and it is significant that the revolution would use it as much as the bishops [22]. For the implications were perhaps even deeper than this. The augmented kirk session was able to reflect, as the old feudal courts could not, those gradual changes within the landed class which had followed the feuing movement of the middle sixteenth century. The 'gentleman' was the child of the price revolution and the kirk session was his nursery.

The heritor - another old word that was assuming a new meaning - similarly represented the new view of land ownership. He was quite simply the proprietor who drew the rents of the lands concerned, irrespective of the nature of his tenure and whoever his immediate superior may have been. In the feued lands of the temporalities he would be the feuar; in a civil barony, he would be the baron except in respect of land which he had feued or mortgaged; in a royal estate, he would be the freeholder. The heritor was a landowner in the commercial rather than the feudal sense and it is important that he was a central figure in the rather obscure story of the revocation of Charles I.

The earliest version, concocted at Court and broadcast throughout an unsuspecting Scotland soon after the King's accession in 1625, would have revoked all grants of church property made to private individuals for nearly a century. There was no hint of compensation and it was possible to believe that the temporal lordships, erected with the approval of Parliament only two decades earlier, would be reduced to empty shells. It is scarcely surprising that rumour should have foreseen a chain of royal estates or the re-endowment of a monolithic church. There is no reason to doubt Balfour's opinion that the revocation was the 'groundstone of all the mischief that followed after' [23].

The truth, as it slowly unfolded itself, was less dramatic, rather more reasonable, but scarcely less radical. The Lordships were to be surrendered to the Crown on the understanding that they would be granted back to the original holders on different, and much less secure, terms. The Lords of Erection owned three more or less distinct forms of landed wealth. The proper lands, which they held in both superiority and property, yielded the rents paid to them by their tenants; in arable areas at least, these were normally calculated in kind and were thus preserved from the inroads of inflation; but, in some cases, they represented only a small proportion of the original temporality. The feued lands, of which they held only the superiority, were, by contrast, often huge in extent; but the income from them, being a fixed sum of money, had been decimated by the price rise. The most important element of their revenues consisted of teinds and pre-eminently of the rich victual teinds of the appropriated parsonages.

The Decrees Arbitral of 1629 laid down the terms in all their menacing detail [24]. The Lords would retain their proper lands, though they would hold them for a feu duty, re-calculated in seventeenth century terms. This might involve a modest financial loss, but it fell far short of confiscation; it was the least damaging part of the settlement. On the other hand, the superiorities of the feued lands were in jeopardy. The Lords would retain them for the time being; but the Crown reserved the right to buy them, at a price equal to ten times the annual yield of the feu duties, whenever it wished. The deal was not unreasonable in a narrowly financial sense and it applied in any case to the least valuable element of the whole.

But money was not the vital issue. The Crown would be buying jurisdictions as well as entitlements to feu duties and it would be doing so at a price ludicrously cheapened by inflation. Indeed the price may well have seemed even lower when viewed from a distance, since it is almost certain that land values were higher in southern England than they were in Scotland. The mere prospect of a resurgent Crown buying Scottish power with English money at bargain prices was enough to shake baronial Scotland to its foundations. We need not doubt Balfour's judgement.

The revocation also embraced the teinds, the richest assets of the lordships. The teinds had always been regarded as a first charge on the harvest and the tenant had been legally compelled to leave his crop in the fields until the teind sheaves, traditionally a tenth of the whole, had been collected - an evident inconvenience in an uncertain climate and an invitation to blackmail where the titular was at odds with the heritor. Charles, ambitiously enough, sought to rectify this and to augment the stipends of the ministers of the erected kirks at one and the same time. The sequence envisaged, and indeed largely accomplished, was as follows. In the first instance, the teinds would be valued by Commissioners with the object of establishing their yield in an average season. This done, the teinds would cease to exist in their previous fluctuating form and would be replaced by a fixed annual levy, expressed either in money or in kind, according to the valuation. This would be collected by the heritor as a part of the rent, and would be paid over to the titular after the deduction of an allowance for the minister's stipend. But this was not all, for the heritor would be allowed, if he wished, to buy out the titular's share at nine years' purchase. In the meantime, the minister's stipend would be augmented, usually from the titular's share, and it followed that this would rapidly diminish. In a small parish, it might easily disappear altogether - and this was much closer to confiscation.

The augmentation of ministers' stipends, and the corresponding impoverishment of the titular, was successfully accomplished by Commissioners established on the one hand by Charles during the 1630s and on the other by the radical government of 1649 - a coincidence so interesting that it cannot be dismissed as merely coincidental. The diminishing remainder of the teinds passed more slowly into the hands of the heritors, perhaps because so many of them already had tacks of their own teinds. Charles himself moved slowly in the acquisition of superiorities, although there is no reason to doubt that the process would have continued had it not been violently halted in 1637. But the aspirations of Charles I are in a sense more important than his achievement. The teinds would cease to be a distinct form of property. The concept of superiority, the distinguishing mark of feudal Scotland, would disappear from the lordships. In many of the temporalities, there were three property owners to any given plot of land. There was the superior passively drawing his ravaged feu duties while dispensing autocratic justice through the bailie of his court. There was the titular of teinds who enjoyed a much larger income protected from the impact of inflation. And there was the feuar drawing his prosperous rents while languishing in the lowly status of a sub-vassal. Now, in the new society of Charles I, there would only be one - and this one the least. The King did not disguise his intentions. He wanted to 'free the gentry . . . from all those bonds which may force them to depend upon any other than upon his Majesty'. This was revolution ([25]).

This reading of the King's revocation is consistent with his policy towards heritable jurisdiction in the wider sense and his re-establishment of the justices. A more general assault on feudalism as such was clearly implied and we may guess that, given favourable circumstances, he would eventually have proceeded with this. But this, his personal approach, reveals only one side of a many-sided King, and Archbishop Laud stood insistently, and sometimes clamorously, at the other. The statute of 1633 abolishing ecclesiastical regalities displays the dilemma; for the episcopal jurisdictions were ostentatiously excluded from its scope ([26]). The line between Lordship and Bishopric could scarcely have been more harshly drawn and it inevitably posed a further question: might not the monastic temporalities themselves, once purchased by the Crown, be granted back to the church? It is certainly true that all the superiorities actually acquired by the Crown were either used or earmarked for the endowment of bishoprics. The rumour, that titular abbots would enjoy the remainder, must have seemed more plausible to contemporaries than it does to us ([27]). True or false, it was undoubtedly damaging to the interests of the Crown. It extended the threat from the Lord to his vassals. The 'gentlemen', released from the servitude of the lordships, would find new, and perhaps more irksome, masters.

There can be no doubt that this was the predominant element in the King's policy during the middle thirties. The bishops were gradually gaining an ascendancy in the Council at the expense of the civil administration of the Crown; the Bishop of Ross, or so it was thought, would shortly supplant the Earl of Traquair as Treasurer; the Archbishop of St. Andrews was already Chancellor. The Bishops were the vital element in the Crown's control of Parliament. Spottiswood had once remarked that the King was 'Pope now and so shall be' ([28]). But who was the 'Pope' of the Canterburian church of Laud and Maxwell? Was it the King or was it a bishop? Would this new and revitalised church break free of its creator? Would it eventually become as independent in practice as Melville's had been in theory? It is not without interest that Melvillian and Canterburian alike eagerly claimed the entire patrimony of the church, that both would have used its revenues to sustain a huge bureaucracy manned by a professional elite, that both wanted to reduce the ordinary administration of the Crown to a subordinate role, that both were anti-aristocratic and indeed that both saw the church as an instrument of social change. This is not, of course, to deny the differences. The two churches were built on different, indeed on opposite, theological foundations; their organisations, though similarly bureaucratic, were contrasting in construction, and the difference between them was emphasised in 1636 with the publication of a Code of Canons which omitted all mention of kirk sessions, presbyteries, synods and general assemblies. Melvillian and Canterburian were born to fight and to fight each other; but they were drawn by the nature of the Scottish predicament into rather similar historical roles.

The prehistory of the revolution was as long as it was devious; but its actual onset sprang from recent innovations which were largely symbolic in their importance. Laud's Liturgy served to encapsulate the essence of the Canterburian system and thus to focus the opposition against it. The feudal classes, the civil administration of the Crown, and the vast majority of the ministers were totally ignored in its composition and virtually ignored in its adoption. The bishops had sufficed and it almost seemed that they were imposing a caricature of the English way of life on the ancient kingdom of Scotland. But, if the opposition was partly inspired by patriotic motives, it was also a reaction against the sheer radicalism of the Canterburians and the subtly different radicalism of the King they had captured. Charles was trying to do in a decade what his father had failed to do in a lifetime - and the Tudors had actually done in a century. The revolution would eventually unleash a new radicalism of its own; but the present mood was reactionary. The phrase 'Religion and Liberties' would soon prove elastic enough; but, for the time being, its meaning was unambiguous; it quite simply stood for the preservation of the Scottish constitution in church and state. The Canterburian church seemed as foreign as it was arrogant and as arrogant as it was new. It was the tree lately planted.

2
The Supplicants, 1637-38

THE preamble to Rothes' *Relation* depicted the revolutionaries as they chose to see themselves. The upheaval of 1637 was traced back to the 're-entering of bishops into this kingdom' and, above all, to their 'neglect' of the 'caveats' and 'conditions' imposed on them by the Assembly of 1610 and 'purposely omitted' from the statute of 1612. Since then, the bishops had 'encroached so by degrees' that they had obtained an 'uncontrollable dominion over the church'. In the end, they had 'loosed the flood of illegal violence to overthrow the truth of religion and liberties' ([1]). Indeed the bishops were everywhere. They managed the Parliament; they dominated the Privy Council; they dictated policy at Court. One bishop was Chancellor and, unless rumour lied, another would soon be Treasurer. The Liturgy, important though it may have been, was merely the outward manifestation of the system which the bishops had created. But, if this was so, the Supplicants did not reject episcopacy as such. Their words were consistent with the possibility - no more - that episcopacy might eventually be removed as a matter of expediency; but there was no hint that it would ever be abjured. There was a Melvillian element in the revolutionary party from the first; but most of its members found their inspiration elsewhere. They rather conspicuously refrained from blaming the King for their troubles. He was the legitimate head of his feudal kingdom and as such he must remain; but he had been seduced by his upstart bishops - and they must not remain. They must be dislodged from the state and reduced to their proper place in the church. The revolutionaries had two main objectives. They wanted to restore the traditional government of the King and his tenants-in-chief; they wanted to renew the previous subjection of the bishops to an aristocratic general assembly. They looked backwards towards their own version of a feudal past.

The immediate grievance was a recent innovation which would disappear as suddenly, though not as silently, as it had come. It is probably fair to say that Laud's Liturgy was misunderstood by a nation utterly determined to misunderstand it. It was tragically ironic that its authors, shortly to be accused of anglicising their own church, should have laboured so mightily - and yet so stealthily - to meet the inevitable Scottish objections to it ([2]). It may even be true, as Hamilton and Traquair both believed, that it could have been accepted, however grudgingly, if it had been introduced through the normal machinery of church and state. It is at least probably true that an assembly and a Parliament would have accepted it if they had been free to amend it. But this is mere hypothesis. In fact, it was composed by bishops and, to all intents and purposes, it was imposed by them as well. Parts of it appeared briefly in the autumn synods of 1636; a draft was read to the spring synods of 1637 ([3]). But these brief glimpses only served to inform the committed opposition without reassuring the moderate majority. Scotland knew little about the Liturgy when it made its first public appearance in the summer of 1637 and the Supplicants, so called from the petitions that they would soon be presenting against it, could do what they liked with it.

The Liturgy sounded English enough, could be presented as popish enough and was in fact unfamiliar enough to generate an antipathy that was at once classless and, a few Canterburian enclaves apart, universal. It was neither difficult nor particularly dangerous to provoke an apparently spontaneous uprising against it. For the time being, the illusion of spontaneity was carefully fostered. The tumult in St Giles, the petitions of August and September and even their riotous sequel of mid-October were not, or so it was implied, really organised. The revolution was neither conceived nor born; it was found under a gooseberry bush.

The opposition was indeed almost as secretive as the bishops themselves had been. The evidence, almost all of it second-hand and some of it written down long after the event, is nearly always defective. Much of it is rather wild; some of it is malicious; but there is an obvious element of truth at the heart of it. There had long been an aristocratic opposition to the revocation. Canterburian policy, especially in the extreme form which rumour attached to it, had always, as we have seen, had a decidedly anti-baronial flavour. Many of the magnates had been disaffected for some time and, in 1637, they found a new grievance. The names suggested, most of them from Fife or the West, are all plausible enough. Rothes, Loudoun, Lindsay, Balmerino, Coupar, Lothian, Cassillis and Eglinton would all figure prominently enough in the early stages of the revolution and Glencairn would at least sympathise with it. The other four - Hamilton, Traquair, Lorne and the Lord Advocate - belong in a slightly different category ([4]). They were all, in one way or another, members of the royal administration; but they all saw the bishops as rivals and they all sought to diminish episcopal power. Traquair invited suspicion by his conspicuous absence from the capital when the Liturgy was introduced. Hamilton, a powerful figure in the anti-Laudian faction at Court, used the same channel of communication between London and Edinburgh as did the Supplicants themselves ([5]). There is no reason to suppose that any of the four actively contrived the riot in St Giles; but it is unlikely that any of them were surprised or indeed distressed by it. There were two oppositions from the first. One, operating within the royal entourage, whispered its grievances into the ordinary channels of political communication; the other, acting outside it, hammered noisily on the door; each fed upon the other.

The ministers as a group advanced somewhat timidly into rebellion; but their leaders, some of them inspired by the distant memory of Melville, were forward enough; there was a strong clerical element in the opposition and it was closely organised from the first. Indeed a meeting held early in July actually recorded its proceedings - which were somewhat unspectacular in consequence - and named

ten of the ministers present. The list was headed by Alexander Henderson, a
natural leader of men who already towered above his comrades. Once a young
protégé of Gladstaines and now an old enemy of Spottiswood, he had come rather
late to presbyterianism. His ideological roots are obscure and are perhaps as
unimportant to us as they probably were to him. Henderson was sometimes a
patriot, sometimes a Melvillian and always a superb politician. The kirk would be
safe as long as he was there to lead it. Robert Douglas, often as sarcastic as
Henderson was usually inspired, was a brilliant organisation man who would
eventually succeed him. But, in the summer of 1637, he was still a young man
making his determined way. For the time being he was overshadowed by David
Calderwood, whose arteries were only beginning to harden, and David Dickson, a
radical Melvillian who was already making the acquaintance of Johnston of
Wariston [6].

This particular gathering commissioned a tract against the Liturgy and advised
the godly to boycott it. But not all the meetings were recorded and at least one of
the others was less cautious. In April, if Henry Guthrie is to be believed,
Henderson and Dickson, who often acted for the ministers of Fife and the West
respectively, had come to Edinburgh to enlist its famous mob. They first
consulted Balmerino and the Lord Advocate and then made their way to Nicolas
Balfour's house in the Cowgate to meet the matrons of the privy kirk - and it was
they who would let loose their serving maids on the fateful 23rd of July. The story
is entirely plausible. Nicolas Balfour was the daughter of a Melvillian minister of
St Giles, a known opponent of the Perth Articles and the known possessor of a
house off the Cowgate; her landlord was the Lord Advocate and her immediate
neighbour was his radical son. This meeting almost certainly took place and the
results would be plain to see [7].

The new Liturgy made its first public appearance in the cathedral of St Giles in
the impressive presence of the Dean, the Bishop of Edinburgh, the Officers of
State, the rest of the Privy Council and the City Fathers. The absence of Traquair
was conspicuous; but it must have seemed, as the bishop undoubtedly hoped it
would seem, that the civil power would enforce the Liturgy. Appearances only
contrived to deceive. A gang of serving maids hurled abuse at the Dean - 'a son of
witch's breeding and the Devil's get' - and one hurled her stool as well. The stool
missed its target, but the demonstration did not. The service dissolved in an
uproar which the magistrates could scarcely quell. The performance was
eventually completed, though the clamour continued off-stage. As the
congregation dispersed, 'a little man in a gown . . . got his back bones and belly full
of no small buffeting distributions' and the bishop himself had to run for his life.
He was back again in the afternoon with an armed guard; but he was stoned as he
emerged and only reached the safety of Holyrood under the protection of the Earl
of Roxburghe. The civil power had at least saved the bishop's neck [8].

The sequel was revealing. The bailies of Edinburgh arrested a few rioters, went
through the motions of questioning them and then let them go again. We shall
never know for certain that the riot was contrived, for the very good reason that
nobody really wanted to find out. The Canterburian bishops were suddenly alone

and the balance of power was already moving against them. The laymen of the Privy Council, backed by the cautious Spottiswood, prudently advised the suspension of the new service book, and the old one as well, pending further instructions from Court ([9]).

The rather evasive voice of the lay Councillors was heard again towards the end of August. They considered a petition from Henderson and Dickson against their act of the previous June ordering every minister to buy two copies of the Service Book for the use of his parish on pain of horning. The ministers were supported by letters from their friends among the magnates addressed to individual Councillors. The impression of spontaneity was preserved. The wording of the earlier act had been somewhat ambiguous and the Council chose to argue that the penalty applied to the purchase of the books and not to their use. They insisted that the ministers must buy the books - and, for all we know, some may actually have bought them - but they allowed the point that the petitioners really wanted to make ([10]).

The brilliant tactical victories of July and August were engineered by two small groups of determined conspirators. In the short term, the ministers and the magnates were united by a common hostility to the bishops and their Liturgy; but their differences were already beginning to appear. Samuel Rutherford, cut off from his colleagues by his confinement in Aberdeen, was an intellectual rather than a politician and, despite his love of metaphor, he seldom concealed his purpose. He too had his contacts among the nobility and, unlike Henderson, he seldom spared their feelings. He quite cheerfully invited Cassillis to lay down his earldom in the service of the kirk: 'Ye hold your lands of Christ; your charters are under his seal.' Rutherford's imagery was as often legal as it was sexual; but this was more than mere metaphor. He was seeking the support of a magnate who was known to be cautiously sympathetic, but his contempt for the old order was barely concealed: 'I am sure that many kings, princes and nobles, in the days of Christ's Second Coming (will) be glad to run errands for Christ even barefooted through fire and water. But in that day, he will have none of their service.' Rutherford already seemed to be planning an assault on the feudal system as such - and this was a thought that Henderson could never have committed to paper. The alliance was brittle; only the bishops held it together ([11]).

And the bishops were doing exactly this. The King's first considered reaction to the tumult plainly carried their mark. He roundly condemned the vacillations of a 'very slack Council' and commanded it to stay in the capital until the Liturgy had been 'settled'. It was also ordered to see that the burghs - and especially the burgh of Edinburgh - elected conforming magistrates to assist in the process. If the capital conformed, the kingdom would follow. But it was to be otherwise. The City Fathers, perhaps remembering that King James had once removed his capital to Linlithgow, promptly obliged by choosing Sir John Hay - once their Town Clerk, now the Clerk Register and a prominent Canterburian - as their Lord Provost. But the response of the kingdom, or at least a substantial part of it, was more threatening. When the Council met on 20th September, it was deluged with petitions all asserting the illegality of the Liturgy and demanding, with varying degrees of asperity, that the King be informed of it. As the Councillors came up to the Tolbooth, they found the High Street thronged with the Supplicants. There were twenty noblemen, who did nearly all the talking, a 'great many barons especially out of Fife', nearly a hundred ministers and, no doubt, a great mob of attendants. The mood was outwardly courteous, but the atmosphere was heavy with menace. The balance of advantage on the Council tipped back towards the laymen, most of whom substantially agreed with the Supplicants. After a nervous day, it resolved to transmit a sample of the petitions, toned down but essentially unaltered, to the King. They persuaded the Duke of Lennox, who chanced to be in Scotland for his mother's funeral, to take them to Court. The Supplicants, for their part, obediently dispersed in the belief that their cause was in good hands at last. The voice of the bishops would be silenced and the King would listen to a Duke.

The petitions originated from a broad area extending from Ayrshire through Clydesdale, Stirling, the Lothians and Fife to the more accessible areas of Perthshire and Angus. They all said much the same thing; they all arrived at the appropriate time; they were all accompanied by commissioners of some local standing. It is obvious that a remarkably efficient organisation had contrived them and Baillie, minister of Kilwinning in the presbytery of Irvine, leaves us in no doubt about its character. After a brief consultation with his friends among the ministers of Glasgow, he told the Earl of Eglinton, the patron of his living and the superior of the greater part of his parish, that he intended to 'have a session for to send a commissioner to supplicate the Council'. The initiative, it should be emphasised, came from Baillie and not from Eglinton, who was merely asked to allow his son to be nominated. The Earl, after some debate, cautiously agreed. But Baillie's travels took him beyond the bounds of his own Kilwinning. He went on to approach the ministers of seven other parishes, sometimes urging that they in their turn should solicit their neighbours. He also drew up a list of suitable commissioners: Hunterston or Waterston for Kilbride, 'old Skelmorlie' for Largs, Caprinton for Dundonald, and so on. He must surely have been satisfied with his journeyings; at least seven of his ten parishes sent petitions to Edinburgh (12).

Most of the petitions emerged from the kirk sessions of individual parishes. Each was the work of a body consisting of a professional minister and a group of elders who - or so we shall argue - were mainly feuars or tenant farmers. In some cases, as for example in Cumnock, Stewarton and Dundonald, the session was augmented to include the 'gentlemen' of the parish; while the petitioners from the landward area of Culross described themselves as the 'heritors and feuars' of the parish - that is, the landowners of the Lordship of Culross irrespective of whether they were elders or not. The Supplicants, like the Canterburians before them, were using a device which built the new estate of the landed vassal into the machinery of the church. In 1635, the elders and gentlemen of Dundonald had passed an act to exclude the sturdy beggar from their parish. In the spring of 1638, they subscribed a local covenant to perform the same, essentially civil, function. In the early autumn of 1637, this same body elected a commissioner, and possibly an armed guard to go with him, to present a petition against an ecclesiastical innovation. It is evident enough that the kirk session was becoming an instrument of local government in rather more than a narrowly ecclesiastical sense and furthermore that the superior was playing a relatively minor part in it. In the late 1630s this was still unimportant; but times would change ([13]).

Most of the September petitions were sent in from kirk sessions and, as such, they were the responsibility of the session as a whole. But, as Baillie's account shows, the minister himself had a special role. Baillie took all the original initiatives and most of his contacts were ministers. The official machinery of the presbytery of Irvine was denied to him, since the archbishop was still actively attempting to rule his diocese; but it is evident that an informal presbytery, consisting of ministers willing to risk his displeasure, was beginning to emerge and that Baillie was its 'moderator'. Elsewhere the process had already been carried one stage further. The presbyteries of Dalkeith, Haddington, Cupar, Stirling, Perth and Auchterarder, presumably acting with the consent of their constant moderators, all submitted collective petitions on behalf of their constituent parishes ([14]). There may well have been some discussion with some of the kirk sessions concerned; but the presbytery itself was still, at this early stage, a purely clerical body. Then, as indeed at other times, there was a marked tendency for parochial feeling to express itself through the minister or - to put the same point in almost the same way - it was often possible for the minister to interpret popular feeling to his own advantage. We shall argue that the Supplicants were dominated at the centre by the feudal classes; but the minister was clearly vital in the localities. For the time being at least, the linking machinery was largely his.

The King's answer to the September petitions turned out to be no answer at all. A series of proclamations from Court drew the rest of the Privy Council, and thus the Supplicants, back into Edinburgh; but their content was disappointing to everyone except the bishops. There was to be no discussion of the petitions; the petitioners were given twenty-four hours to leave the capital; the Council and the Session were to move elsewhere. The King had adopted a policy which only the laymen on his Council could enforce - and they had rather conspicuously left their retainers at home. They duly passed the necessary acts and did very little about them. The Supplicants, for their part, ostentatiously chose to stay and grasped the earliest opportunity of showing that they could not be ejected. The occasion was not far to seek. The Town Council of Edinburgh had, under the influence of its new Provost, ignored the Supplicants on the 20th of September; then, a few days later, it had submitted a belated and rather half-hearted petition while the Provost's back was turned. Now, in mid-October, Hay was back again brandishing the King's threats. As the Council met, a 'multitude flocked' to the Tolbooth 'in a high mood'. The Edinburgh mob, almost certainly stiffened by units from the Supplicants, raucously demanded the appointment of commissioners and threatened to lynch the Council if they were denied. Hay cajoled, bribed and threatened by turns; but the King was far away and, beyond the doors, the mob was clamorous. The City Fathers, most of them sympathetic in any case, voted almost unanimously to join the Supplicants. John Cochrane, once a bailie and recently Dean of Guild, and John Smith, a future Lord Provost, were promptly commissioned to attend them. The capital had caught up with the kingdom.

Shortly afterwards, the Bishop of Galloway, the least popular of the Canterburians, was preparing to leave the Tolbooth. As he emerged, he was greeted by the same mob which had tormented Hay. Traquair appealed for order and was jostled for his pains; but he at least knew what to do. He hastily despatched a messenger to the leaders of the Supplicants, who were in conference nearby, and sought their protection. They eagerly obliged and conducted the bishop down the High Street to the safety of his lodgings. It was a remarkable display of disciplined violence and it showed, as it was surely meant to show, that the Supplicants could rule Edinburgh as long as they chose to stay in it ([15]).

The conference which Traquair had interrupted was almost certainly considering the draft of a new petition, different in kind from its predecessors. The National Petition demanded the withdrawal of the Book of Canons, 'tending . . . to the overthrow of our church discipline established by Acts of Parliament', as well as the Service Book itself and then went on to seek the trial of the bishops who had introduced both. The petition did not actually say any more than this; but it obviously envisaged a general assembly to try the bishops; it looked beyond the transient issue of the Liturgy and attacked the Canterburian system itself. Samuel Rutherford, still locked away in Aberdeen, put the issues clearly enough in another letter to the doubting Earl of Cassillis: 'When such a bastard, pretended step-dame as our prelacy is gone mad, it is your place, who are the nobles, to rise and bind them. At least the law should fetter such wild bulls as they are . . .' Cassillis agreed with this - though the words 'at least' may have bothered him a little ([16]).

There was nothing in the petition itself to disturb the tacit alliance between the Supplicants and the laymen of the Council and they were able to resolve their tactical differences amicably enough. The Councillors wanted to restore order in the capital and the Supplicants wanted to avoid the expense of a long stay. It was obvious that some form of surrender was necessary and it is interesting that Hay and Galloway, both Canterburians and both demoralised by the mob, were deputed to negotiate it. They would have to give in and they would both be compromised; there would, or so it was hoped, be no repercussions from the south. Provost and bishop complained bitterly of the violent hordes that had taken over the city and begged that their numbers should be reduced. The Supplicants, taking 'much vantage' of the opportunity thus presented to them, willingly agreed to disperse on the understanding that they would return in mid-November for 'choosing of Commissioners'. Thereafter a small delegation would remain to await the King's answers to their petitions. The numbers would be reduced - but a permanent executive, capable of becoming an alternative government, would be formed with the approval of the Privy Council. It is as unlikely that Hay and Galloway intended this as it is certain that they could not prevent it. Indeed the Lord Advocate smilingly assured them that it would all be perfectly legal.

The Supplicants punctually returned in strength on 15th November; but this time their bearing, like their purpose, was different. Violence was now pointless; it could only embarrass their allies on the Privy Council. The multitude remained quietly in the background, thus demonstrating the fact that it was an army rather than a mob. In the meantime, its leaders quietly negotiated the remaining formalities with Lorne and Traquair. The elections could commence.

The influence of the Parliamentary example is fairly obvious. The Supplicants first divided themselves into four groups broadly corresponding to the four estates of a Parliament. The Noblemen simply selected a few of their number to sit in Edinburgh, perhaps in rotation, for as long as was necessary. The Barons, who were present in much greater numbers, split up into their shires to elect two representatives from each and these, in their turn, chose a smaller delegation to remain in the capital with the nobles. The burgesses exactly followed their example; a large meeting consisting of one commissioner from each burgh with the usual two from Edinburgh authorised a smaller standing committee to act in its name. Thus far, the parallel with Parliament was close. The organisation, which came to be known as the Tables, was similar to a Convention of Estates from which the clerical estate had been removed; it clearly anticipated the Parliaments of the 1640s with their three secular estates and their Committees of Estates entitled to act on their behalf in the intervals between Parliaments ([17]).

To this extent, the Supplicants can be regarded as a feudal body feeling its way back into an idealised version of the past. But the elections to the Ministers' Table, though organised in a rather similar fashion, revealed an interesting contrast. A minister, unlike a bishop or an abbot, was a landless stipendiary with no assured place in the feudal order; he held no superiorities. His constituency belonged to the seventeenth century rather than its predecessors; it embraced those elements of society which - or so we shall argue - found an outlet in the kirk session rather than the privileged world of heritable jurisdiction.

Indeed the Tables were an organisation of a new kind and they were not bound by precedent. It seems quite likely that the local foundations supporting the Barons' Table were only incidentally feudal. The National Petition had been signed by over three hundred landowners of one kind or another and, despite the inevitable difficulties of identification, it is clear that some of these were gentlemen. Again the central committee was served by a network of local agents extending from Angus to the Borders and from the Lothians to Ayr. Upwards of forty heritors, each representing the district in which he lived, were charged with the duty of acting on the 'advertisements' of the Barons' Table. An early list indicates that nearly all these local agents, and indeed all of those who served on the committee itself, were freeholders with a baronial jurisdiction. But it is clear from the profusion of terms - barons, shire commissioners, gentry and, occasionally, gentlemen - used to describe them that there was no formal definition of their status ([18]). The Barons' Table spoke with the voice of feudal Scotland, but its constituency was larger or at least capable of enlargement. Indeed, in one sense at least it was about to grow. Early in March, soon after the Covenant had transformed the Tables into an alternative government, this organisation would be used to invite and collect voluntary contributions from the landed classes. These contributions, which would eventually develop into a new system of taxation, were paid, on the basis of the free rent yielded by their estates, by all heritors whether they were superiors or not. The logic of the situation demanded a new structure in which the landed vassal could claim his place. The same combination of circumstances was simultaneously producing a new unit of administration. The shire was often too large to perform the function efficiently, while the sheriff might be unwilling to perform it at all. The civil parish - which was much too small - would soon be surmounted by the civil presbytery [19].

The civil presbytery was a new device arising out of the necessities of the moment and its ecclesiastical counterpart, now long established, was gradually falling to the Supplicants. In September only five presbyteries had been under their control, but the numbers must have increased during the autumn. The signatories of the National Petition included well over a hundred ministers from 35 presbyteries - 28 out of the 35 presbyteries in Scotland south of the Tay, a small fraction of those beyond it, and those of Argyll. But nearly all of these attended as the representatives of their parishes. They arranged themselves informally in presbyteries for the purposes of the elections to the Tables; but this did not necessarily imply control of the machinery. The conquest of the presbyteries as such was a slow process largely depending on the attitude, and indeed the determination, of the constant moderator. The case of Lanark, which had a high proportion of opposition ministers, is revealing. Only two of its ministers had signed the National Petition and nothing seems to have happened at all for most of the winter. It was alleged that the moderator - John Lindsay, minister of Carluke - had rarely called meetings and seldom informed his opponents when he had held them. The 'wonted unity' of the brethren had been 'broken'; the presbytery had in a sense been 'deserted'. But this was to change. On 8th February, the brethren met 'more frequently'. They urged the moderator 'in a calm and loving manner' to 'concur and run course' with the Supplicants. This was probably standard procedure and it had already been effective elsewhere. But Lindsay, though not a Canterburian, was less co-operative. He would neither agree nor resign and the majority simply left him and set up a new presbytery of their own. They formalised the procedure which Baillie had improvised in Irvine and they would eventually be recognised as the true presbytery of Lanark [20].

Once the Covenant had been signed, the presbyteries began to usurp the functions of the bishops. In April Kirkcaldy admitted George Gillespie, the radical thunderer of the 1640s, to the parish of Wemyss, and the example was followed in other vacant parishes in the presbyteries of Haddington, Dumfries, Dunfermline and no doubt elsewhere. Indeed the Supplicants were gradually assuming the government of church and state alike [21]. The new church of Scotland would consist of kirk sessions, occasionally augmented, and of presbyteries without constant moderators. These would be surmounted by the Tables, which included ministers but were dominated by the magnates. But the Supplicants also had a civil organisation thrusting its tentacles down into the localities and this too was not confined to the feudal classes. The analogy with the reforming Lords and Barons professing Christ Jesus is tempting, defensible and, in some important respects, misleading. The Supplicants were a seventeenth-century phenomenon; they reflected the silent revolution of the years between.

But, as autumn hardened into winter, a good deal of this was still in the future. The Supplicants could still persuade themselves that they were merely organised to protest against legitimate grievances. The Tables were still a potential government rather than a government in fact. Their programme (though not their methods) was shared by the laymen who had come to dominate the Council. They could still convince themselves that they would disband as soon as success on the Council had been followed by success at Court. Traquair's January journey to the south was thus vital. Its failure, which was also the failure of the Councillors themselves, was even more so. He was discredited; they were paralysed; the Supplicants expanded into the vacuum. The revolution was silent no longer.

While these great events were being determined, the structure of the organisation was quietly and almost casually completed. On 8th December, Loudoun - the Lord of the ecclesiastical regality of Kylesmure and second only to Rothes at the Noblemen's Table - invited Archibald Johnston - a rather obscure Edinburgh advocate and the feuar of Wariston in the shire of Midlothian and the barony of Renfrew - to become Clerk to the Tables. Wariston accepted through a shower of tears precipitated by fears, as genuine as they were unjustified, of his own inadequacy. He had already, with remarkable foresight, pondered the list of statutes which were soon to figure in the National Covenant - and this would please the magnates well enough. But he had also read, and obviously approved, George Gillespie's recent rendering of the theory of the two kingdoms - and this would please them less. There were indeed two Waristons. He was outwardly an industrious advocate with a compendious knowledge of statute law, a man who could produce a vast protestation or a vital paper at a moment's notice; as such, he was, as Baillie was to point out in an only slightly different context, a 'nonsuch' for a clerk. But the inner Wariston, concealed though he was behind a cloak of private anxieties, was a man of a different calibre; he had already succumbed to the revolutionary vision which alone gave his doubting life meaning and coherence. Without it he was useless; through it, he would almost conquer the tormented heart of Scotland. For Wariston would use his position as clerk to change the direction of the revolution. He would become the leader of the radical presbyterians [22].

3
Another Step of Reformation, 1638

LINDSAY'S *Satyre of the Three Estates* presents a complex but entirely convincing picture of the Scottish monarchy. *Rex Humanitas* is carefully portrayed as a callow youth looking on, almost silent and totally bewildered, as the business of the nation goes on around him. In sharp and plainly calculated contrast, Correction is a truly magnificent, almost a divine, figure dispensing impartial justice with an authority so absolute that the magnates themselves dare not question it. Indeed it never occurs to them to question it. The one is the King as he so often actually was; the other is the King as he always ought to have been. The subject owed a highly qualified allegiance to the one - who was fallible reality - and an absolute obedience to the other - who was abstract perfection.

The same distinction was implicit in the Negative Confession which was later to form the hard core of the National Covenant. The Confession committed the subject to uphold the King's authority, but only 'in the defence of Christ his Evangel, liberties of our country, ministration of justice and punishment of iniquity against all enemies within the realm or without' ([1]). If *Humanitas* assumed the role of Correction, he would be obeyed. This concept, ambiguous though it may seem to have been, was not anti-monarchical. It had been formulated for the benefit of another - and more precocious - youth who had been presumed to be the creature of his courtiers. Good advice made a good King; bad advice merely brought new advisers. The monarchy was intrinsically as blameless as the King himself was usually useless. It was a concept that feudal Scotland accepted easily enough; it emerged quite naturally from a period of long minorities and weak governments. The sixteenth century's only serious advocate of divine right was a King sensible enough to ignore his own reasoning, however convincing it might sound.

The seventeenth century asserted this dual conception of kingship as compulsively as its predecessor had done, despite the differences in the surrounding circumstances. The King, once so weak that he could scarcely protect the liberties of the subject, now seemed so strong that he could hardly avoid infringing them. But the answer was still the same. Scotland eagerly embraced the half-truth that King Charles was the innocent victim of bad advice. Shortly after the riot in St. Giles, the Earl of Traquair, in a letter to the Marquis of Hamilton, attributed the tumult to the 'folly and misgovernment of our clergymen'. He did not blame the King, a 'wise and judicious master' who would have his way if he listened to his 'faithful subjects'. Traquair wanted Charles to silence his bishops and to hear his magnates instead, and the Supplicants said much the same thing. They had first sought the withdrawal of the bishops' work and they had gone on to demand the trial of the bishops themselves ([2]).

The King's answer, so anxiously awaited, was finally published at Stirling on the 19th of February. It was a momentous document. The Liturgy, it claimed, was consistent with the 'true religion'. He, King Charles, had personally 'seen and approved' everything in it. The autumn petitions had thus been a direct assault on the royal authority. Past transgressions might be forgiven, but future gatherings were forbidden on pain of treason. The Tables must disband and the Supplicants must disperse ([3]). Charles rejected the concept of the evil counsellor and uttered a threat which only an English army could implement. He had always suspected treason and, in suspecting, he made it so. The Supplicants were forced, only half unwillingly, up a further 'step of reformation'. Almost immediately, they swarmed into the capital at a signal from the Tables. Nobody tried to stop them; it was obvious that Edinburgh was theirs. A riot had grown into a rebellion which was soon to become revolution.

The pretence of legality was now absurd, and the Supplicants hastened to justify themselves anew. The National Covenant, whatever else it may have been, was an oath binding its signatories to defend the revolution and, in doing so, to extend it. The original initiative seems to have emerged from a meeting of the Noblemen's Table held on 23rd February. The other Tables were given a 'little inkling' of the plan, but only Henderson and Dickson seem actually to have been consulted. Wariston almost certainly attended the meeting as its clerk and he was invited, along with Henderson, to prepare a provisional draft. There can be little doubt that Wariston was chosen for his compendious knowledge of the statute law, and even less that he intended to use his position to secure a radical text if he could. But the ultimate responsibility was neither his nor Henderson's; it resided in a sub-committee, consisting of Rothes, Loudoun and Balmerino, appointed from the Noblemen's Table on the following day. The three Lords saw the first draft on the 26th after an interval long enough to suggest some disagreement among its authors. If this was so, their next move strongly suggests that Wariston had been more successful than Henderson. For the draft was then circulated among a number of selected noblemen and ministers, nearly all of whom were moderates. In consequence, two changes, both vital and neither to Wariston's advantage, were made to the original text. The modified Covenant was then submitted to all four Tables and accepted without serious disagreement; it was generally subscribed on the 28th of February and the 1st of March ([4]).

The National Covenant was composed by a minister and an advocate, but its shape was fashioned at the Noblemen's Table. It was, as will emerge, ambiguous in some respects, but the general drift was conservative; it was at once a call to rebellion and an appeal to the past. The text consisted of three distinct, if closely coupled, elements. A verbatim reproduction of the Negative Confession of 1581 was followed by a long inventory of statutes ostensibly designed to show that it had been consistent with the civil law. This in its turn was followed by a bond which, though it was based on the Confession, modified its meaning to fit the 'corruptions of the time'. In a sense, the new Covenant was assembled round the old Confession and its essentially traditional rendering of the relationship between the King and his subjects. It respected the ancient distinction between *Humanitas* and Correction - between the King wrongly counselled and the King rightly advised. Charles may have said that he was personally responsible for the innovations; but this, if true, was trivial. If he had said this, it was merely because the bishops had advised him to say it. Indeed, if he had really committed such a crime, he would have violated the oath, solemnly sworn at his Coronation, to protect the religion and liberties of his subjects. He could only be deposed. But this was scarcely conceivable. He was not a 'tree lately planted', but the legitimate King of feudal Scotland. He was also the King of England and thus the embodiment of Scottish foreign policy as it had been since the Reformation. Scotland must be distinct from England and yet closely allied with it. The Supplicants wanted a Scottish King - rightly advised - on the English throne. King Charles was essential to all their purposes, internal and external alike. The February proclamation must have been the vile work of *Humanitas;* Correction was not only untainted but incapable of taint.

The bond of 1638 thus pledged the Supplicants to defend the King as long as he defended them and this was conventional enough. Thus far, the Lords of the Council were at one with the Lords of the Covenant; the King himself would be saying as much before the summer was out. But the bond, unlike the Confession itself, went further than this. It bound its signatories to the 'mutual defence . . . everyone of us of another against all sorts of persons whatsoever' endangering the cause and to the collective support of 'any such resolutions as by common consent shall be found to conduce to so good ends'. The meaning of these phrases was clear enough. 'Mutual defence' and 'common consent' could only mean the recognition of the Tables as a provisional government. 'All sorts of persons whatsoever' could obviously include the royal government and, in practice if not in theory, the King himself. The Confession had been a declaration of conditional obedience; the Covenant was an oath of positive defiance. The petitions of yesterday became the demands of tomorrow.

There is every reason to suppose that Wariston's original draft,which does not survive, was more specific and that the phrase 'all sorts of persons whatsoever' was a euphemism introduced to satisfy the constitutional qualms of the moderates. If this was so, the second alteration was no less revealing. The bond obliged the subscriber to oppose all the innovations introduced since the Union of the Crowns and it seems likely that Wariston's draft abjured them all. He almost certainly proposed to tack them on to the list of popish horrors condemned in the Confession. But the final text conspicuously did not do this. It carefully divided the innovations into two categories. The Articles of Perth, the 'corruptions of the public government of the kirk' and the 'civil places and powers of kirkmen' were all deemed offensive, but they had all been recognised by Parliaments or Assemblies or at least by long usage. The subscriber was merely asked to forswear the 'practice' of the first and the 'approbation' of the other two until they could be 'tried and allowed in free assemblies and Parliaments'. In a sense they would continue to be the law until the law itself had reconsidered them. On the other hand, the Liturgy and the Canons were, as they had been in Wariston's draft, forsworn as evil in themselves and the signatory was obliged to 'detest and abhor them amongst all the other heads of papistry' abjured in the Confession. The first set of innovations had been properly introduced through the traditional channels; the others had been slipped in through the back door. It was the kind of distinction that a conservative constitutionalist would have wished to have made.

The bond was separated from the Confession by a long list of statutes, 'all . . . for our Confession against popery'. The official record remarked, with a disarming candour, that it also favoured 'our present way'. The Parliament of 1592 had annulled the episcopal acts of 1584, which thus excluded themselves; but the omission of all the seventeenth century legislation in support of episcopacy was plainly calculated. It was implied that the Scottish tradition knew little of bishops - and this was the interpretation that Wariston, the compiler of the list, placed upon it. But in this, as in so many other respects, the Covenant was ambiguous, and there is another explanation. It is obvious that most of the Supplicants merely wished to exclude the form of episcopacy which had actually emerged from the 're-entry' of bishops in the earlier years of the century.

The list, selective though it was, included two of the Black Acts left unrepealed by the Parliament of 1592. Both of these had suggested the supremacy of the King in Parliament - rather than the King in person - over the church. It was implied that the church should be, in one way or another, subordinate to the traditional, as distinct from the existing, power structure - and the Melvillians can have taken little comfort from this. It was perhaps even more significant that the Covenant relied entirely on statute law rather than the law of the church. In a sense, this can be explained away by the fact that the lost records of the sixteenth century assemblies had still to be rediscovered. But the *Second Book of Discipline* had been published, along with the acts of assembly approving it, in 1622 ([5]). The law of the kirk as it had been in Melville's day was at least known in general terms. It seems certain that the most powerful elements among the Supplicants had already decided that the new church would in some way be subject to a feudal state. Would they, wanting this, have sworn to its opposite even if the records had been available?

This essentially conservative reading of the Covenant is confirmed by the nature of the programme which accompanied it. The Eight Articles, which were despatched to the King in March, demanded a general assembly for the trial of the bishops. It would presumably have deprived some of them and it would have established the vital principle that their successors would be responsible to the assembly rather than to the Crown. The ultimate meaning of this would depend on the composition of the proposed assembly and this was not specified. But its likely form was suggested by the parallel demand for a Parliament which would ratify the work of the assembly as well as re-opening the customary channels of civil government. It is obvious that the Supplicants were seeking to rebuild the ancient government of the tenants-in-chief. The new assembly would be penetrated by

But the Articles were less ambiguous than the Covenant itself. The phrase 'corruptions of the public government of the kirk' was so vague that it could mean almost anything. Wariston, knowing that Rothes and Loudoun would never allow a radical text, must have been pleased with this. He may have guessed that he would eventually find support outside the feudal classes. Revolutions, he may have reflected, are easier to start than to stop. The Covenant, whatever its text may have seemed to have meant, was introduced, in a highly emotional atmosphere compounded more or less evenly of fear and fine defiance, to a background of rhetoric reminiscent of the Melvillian years of the 1590s. In one sense, it was a statement of a profoundly conservative purpose. In another, it was the opening salvo of a radical cannonade which would soon leave the conservative position, if not in ruins, at least in outward disarray. The Covenant was both these things, but it could not ostensibly be either of them. Radical and conservative needed each other; neither could afford the truth. Each was compelled to resist a King who, however clumsily, accused both alike of treason. Ideologically they were poles apart, but they struggled along united by common perils and common antipathies.

In the spring of 1638, the conservatives were still the stronger force and the Eight Articles reflected their dominance. The opposite view was, by contrast, seldom publicly expressed. Sermons tended to be vaguely inflammatory rather than specifically radical. George Gillespie's famous *Dispute Against the English Popish Ceremonies* had, on the King's instructions, been burned by the common hangman in the previous autumn and the Supplicants, busily protesting about almost everything else, had rather conspicuously failed to protest about this. It seems to have sold well, partly perhaps from the curiosity aroused by the censor; but its influence was small. Baillie, who often reflected the views of his friends among the nobility, admired the author but 'misliked much of his matter'. Wariston was naturally more impressed; but, for the time being at least, he kept his thoughts for his diary (7). Indeed his celebrated denunciation of episcopacy was uttered, as the Supplicants anxiously awaited the King's response to the Articles, in strict secrecy to an audience of two. Radical presbyterianism was still a conspiracy whispered in dark corners. But no corner could contain Wariston for long. His day was coming and he already, with a truly remarkable perception of the turmoil around him, sensed how it would come: 'at every step we would have stooden at, (the Lord) has made our adversaries to refuse and forced us to go up another step of Reformation'. As clerk to the revolution, he had drafted the Articles; now, as its prophet, he earnestly prayed that the King would reject them. Then, 'instead of these cautions and limitations of prelates . . . (we shall) speak plain truth according to the will of God, that is the utter overthrow and ruin of episcopacy, that great grandmother of all our corruptions'. The radicals, as Wariston realised, were still weakly represented at the summit of the revolutionary edifice. They were driven to rely on the violence, or rather the threatened violence, of the King's displeasure to force their conservative comrades back into the mainstream of the revolution. The period was dominated by a force which Wariston described, appropriately enough, as the 'worker by contraries'. The process had been tested by experience and the prospect was as limitless as it was alluring. The new radical church, triumphant in Scotland, would become a 'pattern to other nations'. It would spread to England and thence to Ireland. There would be a vast theocracy extending from Shetland to Munster and beyond until the papacy itself, 'that chair of antichrist in this world', collapsed in ruins before it. Then, in the final phase and the ultimate perfection, the visible church, its task completed, would wither away. The conflicts of a troubled world would disappear in a limpid pool of universal virtue - and this was rather different from the Eight Articles ([8]). Radical and conservative differed fundamentally from each other, and the National Covenant reflected the tension between them.

4

The Worker by Contraries, 1638-41

KING Charles, presented with an ambiguous challenge, contrived a typically tortuous response. After long and conflicting deliberation with bishop and magnate alike, he decided to send the Marquis of Hamilton as his Commissioner to Scotland; but he appointed Laud to act as his secretary for Scottish affairs at Court. Hamilton's despatches would be read by Laud; the replies to them would be drafted by Laud on advice tendered by Laud. Hamilton would arrive in Scotland as the King's delegate rather than his plenipotentiary. He would have tactical control over the negotiations, but the substance of power would lie elsewhere. His instructions fell into two groups, the one designed to please Laud - and thus incidentally Wariston too - and the other to placate the magnates on the Privy Council and, indeed, Hamilton himself. The first group offered the bare minimum of concession, and brusquely demanded the surrender of the Covenant. It dismissed the Supplicants as traitors. In the event of defiance, the Commissioner was ordered to declare that, 'if there be not power (in Scotland) to force the refractory to obedience, power shall come from England and . . . myself shall come in person with them, being resolved to hazard my life rather than to suffer authority to be condemned'; there would be a 'kingly way' with rebels. This was plainly the voice of Canterbury. The second group, in astonishing contrast to the first, authorised Hamilton to drive a private bargain with his friends among the Lords of the Covenant. Broadly speaking he would concede the substance of the Articles, including the subjection of the bishops to the general assembly, in exchange for the surrender of the Covenant; he would persuade the Supplicants to disband by offering everything that their baronial component had demanded. He would isolate the radicals and then, if necessary, assemble Scottish force to smash them (1).

It is perhaps just possible to reconcile the two approaches. Under certain circumstances, Hamilton might have been able to use the threat of overwhelming English strength to reinforce the argument for a bargain; indeed he would be driven to attempt this. But the argument was in a sense self-defeating. The Lords of the Covenant were in rebellion; they could not afford to surrender. It might have been possible for Hamilton to reach a voluntary agreement with them on the basis of the concessions which he was authorised to offer; but the threat of force could only poison an atmosphere already polluted enough.

In many respects, the Marquis must have seemed an obvious choice as Commissioner. He had his enemies among the factions - for he was never at ease with Montrose or Traquair, even when he was agreeing with them - but his friends were as numerous as they were powerful. He was related by marriage to several of the Lords of the Covenant; he had a close political friendship with Lorne, the most formidable of the Councillors; he felt an instinctive sympathy for Rothes, the most accomplished politician of the revolution. He was at once a personal friend of the King and a genuine, if usually distant, ally of the Supplicants. It is important that he did not - and that we should not - see any contradiction in this. Hamilton spent much of his life in a predominantly English court, but his view of the monarchy remained essentially Scottish. He believed in the cause of religion and liberties and he saw it as his role to enlist King Charles in their service. His conduct as Commissioner is only comprehensible on the assumption that he was deeply in sympathy with the aims of the Noblemen's Table - and that he had bluntly, if privately, advised the King to come to terms with them.

Hamilton has too often been dismissed as a court jester frivolously juggling with the fate of two kingdoms and their King. Contemporary Scottish opinion nearly always admired a man who was widely regarded as a political wizard - 'if the King have many such men, he is a well served Prince' (²). Events too seldom justified this confidence - for Hamilton was perhaps unlucky in his period - but his political skill cannot seriously be questioned. His aims seemed practical enough and he pursued them assiduously enough; but he was indecisive in an age when indecision was nearly always fatal and he was timid at a time when boldness might have saved his cause and incidentally his King as well. In 1638 he allowed himself to be imprisoned by his instructions; he did not betray King Charles; he passively allowed King Charles to betray himself.

The sources of his weakness are fairly obvious. His long absences at Court left the control of his Scottish estates in the hands, at once capable and ruthless, of his mother. It may be thought that she shared his aristocratic view of the nature of Scottish society and the place of the church within it. But, if she did, her approach was different; she mistrusted the Court while he revelled in it; she was in league, as well as in sympathy, with the Supplicants. As the Commissioner crossed the Border, she was careful to make her point. He summoned his dependants to meet him and very few actually came. It was a vital moment. Hamilton now knew that he had little Scottish force at his disposal; he could only buy it with the King's concessions. In the Court itself, he was haunted by the memory of his ancestors. His claim to the throne was, thanks to the multiplying progeny of James VI, remote; but it was just close enough to justify the suspicion that he was an usurper. Hamilton could never feel quite certain that Charles would not believe the insinuations of a Court that had seldom been scrupulous - and the danger was doubled as soon as his back was turned. He was vulnerable to blackmail and possibly too conscious of the fact. In consequence he seldom committed his private thoughts to paper; his despatches from Scotland were nearly always ambiguous; they usually represented his unenthusiastic estimate of a dutiful Commissioner's appropriate thoughts; they read like the work of a Wentworth who had lost faith in himself. It is at least possible that the Commissioner, if he had been bold enough to tear up the other half of his instructions, could have returned to Court with a binding agreement that neither Laud nor the Lord Deputy would have dared to destroy.

But Hamilton did not wholeheartedly do this. For a time he was able to conceal his instructions and the proclamation that was inseparable from them. We find him in affable, if strictly private, conversation with Rothes - and Wariston's consternation is evidence enough that a bargain was on the way. But Wariston's answer was obvious enough. Was it safe to give up the Covenant to a Commissioner who could not show his proposals in the clear light of day? He drove Hamilton to equivocation and Rothes to mistrust. The Marquis, in his turn, suggested an ingenious compromise which would later prove important. Instead of surrendering the Covenant, the Tables would compose a preface to it which would describe it, after the fashion of the original Confession, as an oath of conditional obedience rather than an obligation to positive defiance. The original text would survive in all its revolutionary purity, but it would be used as such only in cases of emergency. And, as Hamilton asked a little disingenuously, was there an emergency now? Was not the King offering an assembly? Would not the bishops 'wag on a widdy'? Once more the magnates were tempted and once more Wariston reclaimed them. The Commissioner decided to return to England, hoping to turn the deadlock to his own advantage at Court ([3]).

But the worker by contraries had further twists to unfold. Laud insisted that a proclamation be published before Hamilton's return, and Wariston delightedly penned a protestation against it. At about the same time, the English Council met to ponder the possibility of a 'kingly way' with rebels.   They decided against it - for war meant taxation and taxation a Parliament - but the damage was done. Rumour clattered up the Great North Road like a regiment of horse. The Commissioner, armed with new and less ambiguous proposals, followed it to find the Supplicants entrenched behind a Melvillian rampart. The pulpits of the capital had been cautiously expounding the 'extirpation' of episcopacy for some time, but now they were cautious no longer. Indeed the magnates themselves were considering it. Even more significantly the revolution went on to assert 'that which was before but in the minds of some very few, our right from God, which the Prince may not in law or reason take from us, to keep a general assembly'. The threat from the South had restored the unity of the Supplicants; the conservatives, from motives that were essentially patriotic, joined the radicals in a total rejection of any link with the Court. The revolution was now at Wariston's command. As if to emphasise the point, the Tables began to organise elections for an assembly of their own as soon as Hamilton had left for his final journey to the South ([4]).

The Commissioner returned to a King who, in the absence of English force or any considerable Scottish support, had lost the power to govern his northern kingdom. In consequence, the balance of power in the Court itself swung back in his favour. The Laudian policy had collapsed and its author was banished, if only for a time, into the shadows. On 9th September the Commissioner was granted all the powers which he had so desperately needed at the beginning of June. The Eight Articles, which still formed the official programme of the Supplicants, were now granted in their entirety. The surrender of the Covenant was no longer demanded; instead, a new Covenant of the Commissioner's own devising would be enjoined by Act of Council. This would consist of the Negative Confession, together with a bond of 1589 which defined the allegiance of the subject in similar terms. This was a gesture of profound significance; King Charles, if only under pressure, had embraced the concept of religion and liberties.

The September Proposals had a twofold purpose. They were designed to create a royalist party and this was swiftly achieved; they were unanimously approved by the Privy Council at the first time of asking. But they were also intended to disarm the revolution. They must satisfy its baronial component; they must isolate its radicals. There followed a period of probing during which individual Councillors tested the reactions of their opposite numbers among the Supplicants. The noblemen of the revolution had tasted power and they were acutely aware of the dangers of relinquishing it. Could they, technically in rebellion, trust a King with a Scottish Covenant in one hand and an English sword in the other? The brief interval, which preceded the actual proclamation of the King's pleasure, produced two compromises both calculated to make the new Covenant look as much like the old one as possible. Somebody, probably Lorne, revived the idea of a loyal explanation of the February Covenant, and it may well be that Rothes and Loudoun would have accepted this as an integral part of a larger settlement. But, if they would, the Commissioner, whatever his personal feelings, could not; he did not know that the King would accept it and there was no time to find out. This notion was stillborn and the other, pressed by Lorne and the Lord Advocate and accepted by the rest of the Council, turned out to be ineffective. The February Covenant had included a long list of ecclesiastical statutes implying by its omissions that the government of the kirk had normally been without bishops or at least that its bishops had been responsible to the general assembly. The King's Covenant, by contrast, said nothing about church government at all. To supply the deficiency, the Councillors stated that they - and thus everyone else - were subscribing the Confession of 1580 in the belief that it defended religion 'as it then was professed in this kingdom'. In saying this, they merely meant that they were not defending all the changes - and especially the notorious statute of 1612 - made since that time. They were seeking to soothe the natural fears of the Noblemen's Table and indeed of the Council itself. But the gesture was ambiguous. In 1580, the church had actually been governed by bishops, while its general assembly had declared that episcopacy was contrary to the word of God. It would now be possible to argue - as the Commissioner eventually would - that the proposed assembly must approve episcopacy or - as Wariston might - that it was bound to abjure episcopacy with the approval of the King's Privy Council.

But these were mere devices. Robert Baillie, who often reflected the views - and the doubts - of the Noblemen's Table, was not really concerned about the substance of the proposals. They were, as he freely admitted, 'extremely gracious to most of our desires'. But they were mistimed; 'if they had been a little before used or yet, if we could be persuaded of the sincerity of (them), matters might go well'. But the Commissioner was asking them to accept a new and weaker Covenant at a time of 'continual rumours of the King's preparation for war'. It was really a matter of trust. It was all very well for the Lord Advocate to tell Rothes, as he would a fortnight later, 'I dare not deny obedience to my sovereign where he commands that which is lawful and agreeable to God's Word.' Hope, sympathetic though he had always been, had not, as a Privy Councillor, been asked to take the Covenant. He was not a rebel; he could afford to trust King Charles. But Rothes, though ideologically less radical than Hope, was in rebellion. He had to fight and he had to win. In a few brief moments of frantic haste and total confusion, the Tables resolved to greet Hamilton's proclamation with another of Wariston's now famous protestations. Nobody trusted anybody any more. Scotland was in a revolutionary situation (⁵).

As Wariston rejoiced, so did Laud. The King could now withdraw with honour if he wished, and it was soon obvious that he had done so. On the 2nd of October, as Hope was reprimanding Rothes, the Tables, acting within the terms of the King's recent concessions, sought the Commissioner's formal consent to the trial of the bishops - which he 'delayed verbally but refused really'. The refusal was indirect; Charles did not deny that bishops could be tried, only that they could not be tried by the kind of assembly now in prospect. He insisted that he must nominate the judges; he denied the right of the Lords of the Covenant to nominate any of them; he determined to dissolve the court as soon as he found positive evidence that they had done so. This was a different but no less contentious argument. The magnates of the Council suddenly discovered not only that their proposals had been withdrawn, but that magnates could only influence the resulting assembly if the King allowed them to do so. For some time a 'poor damsel' with delusions that passed for raptures had been holding forth, perhaps under Wariston's guidance, to doubting supplicants. Now she began to acquire a wider circle of admirers. The Lord Advocate attended at the end of October and he was followed a fortnight later by Archibald Lord Lorne, now, on the death of his father, the eighth Earl of Argyll. The 'worker by contraries' had laboured long and lovingly; it was predictable that Wariston would pass the winter in an ecstasy of immoderate delight (⁶).

The principal objective of the Supplicants had been, almost from the first, the calling of a general assembly which would be more than the governing body of a church. The 'Lords and Barons professing Christ Jesus' had been an alternative government as well as the predominant element in the earliest general assemblies of the reformed church and the managers of the assembly which would open at Glasgow in November were sufficiently conscious of the precedent. Their new assembly could wield executive power only for the few brief weeks of its existence and it was not intended to supersede the Tables. Instead it would legislate for them and, in so doing, it would give them the air of respectability which they had so conspicuously lacked. The Glasgow Assembly was not an alternative government, but it came very close to being an alternative Parliament, and it followed from this that its composition was vital. It must reflect the realities of power within the revolutionary movement.

The matter had first formally been discussed on 26th June when the King's Commissioner had mentioned it in one of his secret meetings with Rothes. The reply, if strictly inexact, was unequivocal enough. The Assembly would consist of 'two ministers and one lay elder chosen out of every presbytery'; it would comprise a series of delegations, part clerical and part lay, sent up from the lower courts of the church. Rothes did not explain the term 'lay', though it is likely that both men understood it well enough. The Crown would - or so Rothes quite sincerely hoped - be represented by the Commissioner himself; but, this apart, there would be no nominated element. Hamilton, possibly reflecting that this would suit him personally better than it would suit his master, prudently allowed it to pass without comment, but he discussed it with the King during his first return to Court in July. The royal response was quite simply a royal refusal: 'strive to draw it as near as may be to the former assemblies of my father's time'. It was clearly impossible to insist on the presence of the bishops themselves - except of course as penitents - but the assembly must include the constant moderators, whether they were actually commissioned by their presbyteries or not. The attendance of lay-men was not specifically denied; indeed it was assumed that some laymen would be nominated by the Crown - but it was insisted that 'no lay person whatsoever' could 'meddle' in the elections and, above all, that they could not participate in the choice of ministers. The King saw the projected assembly as an essentially clerical body, to which a sprinkling of Councillors and Officers of State might be added. The Supplicants, by contrast, wanted an assembly in which laymen would not only be powerfully represented but actively consulted at every stage of a rather complicated electoral process(7).

If Charles looked back to the first two decades of the seventeenth century, it was no less inevitable that the Supplicants should have sought, and perhaps have found, their precedents in the last two decades of its predecessor. They were clearly tempted by the *Second Book of Discipline*, with its seductively symmetrical assembly of representatives from below; but the Melvillian elder was not a layman and they found the practice of the church more useful than its theory. The rediscovery of the proceedings of the assemblies concerned allowed them to argue that laymen had, at least in particular cases, taken an active part in presbytery meetings. They claimed that 'barons' and 'gentlemen' had appeared as elders at the first erecting of presbyteries and that they were subsequently recalled for special, though unspecified, purposes. They asserted that, from 1588 onwards, the presbyteries had chosen certain 'barons' and 'gentlemen', sometimes including 'Lords and Earls', to go with their ministers to the assemblies of the period. These claims, which were openly propagandist in character, are no longer verifiable; but there can be no doubt about the act of the Dundee Assembly of 1598 which sought to define the membership of assemblies with some precision. According to this act, the 'commissioners to every assembly' were to be 'three of the wisest and gravest of the brethren from every presbytery at the most', together with one layman 'in name of the barons' and 'one out of every burgh' with the inevitable exception of Edinburgh, which would have two. This act was publicly distributed by the Tables to the presbyteries at the end of August (8). It was held to be definitive; it was the founding charter of the assemblies of the period.

But the act, definitive though it might seem to have been, was vague in detail. It failed to describe the mechanism which allowed a clerical body, as the presbytery had usually been, to send a 'baron' to the general assembly. The newly rediscovered records of past assemblies, which so conveniently noted his arrival, did not disclose how he had got there. The Tables, starved of the precedents which they so clearly loved, were forced back to first principles. The solution thus devised was embodied in a series of papers, some more or less public, others restricted to 'trusty persons', circulated to the presbyteries late in August. Three phases were envisaged. In the first, 'barons' of the right persuasion would be introduced into their local kirk sessions if they were not already members. Once there, they would secure their own election as elders to a presbytery meeting which would send commissioners to the assembly. In this, the final phase, the electorate would consist of an equal number of clerical and lay members less those who had actually been nominated to the leet. But the typical delegation would include two or three ministers and only one layman; it followed from this that the ministers' leet would normally be the longer of the two. The assembly itself would have a majority of ministers, but the elections to it would, or at least could, be dominated by laymen.

The management of the election in each presbytery was delegated to a carefully selected minister and a 'baron' who must usually have been the local agent of the Barons' Table. These, the 'trusty persons' of the secret instructions, were authorised to use force; if any session proved recalcitrant, they were to 'put themselves in possession notwithstanding any opposition'. Once the session elections had been completed, the chosen laymen were to be enjoined 'on their oath' to vote in the presbytery for 'none' but those who were 'named already at the meeting in Edinburgh'. This was not to be a nominated assembly in the Jacobean sense of the term; but it was nominated nonetheless; indeed it had largely been nominated already.

The selection of candidates was not an accidental process. If a suitable nobleman lived in the presbytery concerned, he was to be chosen; where there was none, the choice should fall on a 'baron or one of best quality and he only a Covenanter'. Where a nobleman's territorial interests were distributed among several presbyteries, he should be elected for the one with the 'greatest scarcity of able men'. In the short term, the main consideration was the fidelity of the candidate. The conspiratorial aspects of the system were primarily intended to exclude Councillors who had not taken the Covenant and could not therefore be trusted; the future Earl of Argyll was already regarded as a sympathiser, but he was not invited to participate in the elections. In the Glasgow Assembly, political reliability was vital, but aristocracy was only less so. Noblemen were preferred to barons, barons were preferred to gentlemen; the unlanded were never considered at all. It was obviously hoped that elders would be magnates. For the time being at least the civil presbytery, which was now a living reality, would be a feudal organisation. It had now joined, and indeed had come to dominate, the ecclesiastical presbytery ([9]).

The reluctance of most of the ministers was open and unashamed; they were quite simply bullied into a system which they did not, and could not, want. But their leaders, moderate and radical alike, struck different attitudes. Their reluctance, though no less real, was seldom openly expressed ([10]). The magnates were a shield against the bishops; it was impossible to do without them. In the Glasgow Assembly, they were welcomed into the church with a smile that was just a trifle bilious. As Wariston, who shared the regrets of his clerical comrades, rather grudgingly admitted, 'ruling elders (would) hold episcopacy at the staff'. By and large the alliance would hold as long as the emergency lasted ([11]).

The term 'ruling elder' had normally been used to draw a distinction between the elder and the minister. Now Wariston was using it in an entirely different sense. He was distinguishing the presbytery elder and the assembly elder from the ordinary elder who sat from week to week in his own kirk session - and this was entirely new and highly significant. The assembly was founded on an act which had described its laymen in feudal terms as 'barons'; the system laid down by the Tables indicates that the term was far from inappropriate. And yet the nominal role of the assembly would describe them in ecclesiastical terms as elders, while their commissions would testify that they had arrived there by an impeccably ecclesiastical route ([12]). Direct evidence is lacking, but this was surely a compromise between layman and minister. The present dominance of the layman was not seriously contested, but the ministers succeeded in carrying the general principle. The elders concerned were, however nominally, ecclesiastical persons. There would be no clerical assembly, but it would at least be disguised as an assembly of churchmen.

It is possible to trace the progress of the elections as they occurred; though the typical kirk session, no doubt conscious of their novelty and doubtful of their legality, failed to record them. The sequence had really begun early in May, shortly before the King's Commissioner arrived in Scotland. In Kilconquar, the session, augmented to include the 'gentlemen' - that is the heritors - of the parish, drew up a rota, consisting entirely of landed proprietors, to attend the 'weekly meetings of the presbytery' of St Andrews according - as they alleged - to the 'ancient and laudable custom before observed in this kirk of Scotland', and this presumably continued for the rest of the summer. Then, on 9th September, Forbes of Rires, with the consent of the 'gentlemen and elders' of the parish, was appointed to attend a presbytery meeting a few days afterwards, there to vote as he should think 'most expedient for God's glory and the good of the kirk'. The phrase is vague and it was obviously meant to conceal the fact that it was intended to hold the assembly elections before the Commissioner's return, that is, before it was known whether he would proclaim an assembly or not ([13]).

On the 13th of May, Falkirk elected a new session more or less in the normal fashion. Lord Almond was re-elected, thus continuing a long tradition which had regularly placed the Lord of the large civil regality of Callendar at the head of the roll of elders. There he was joined by a newcomer in Sir Thomas Hope, the second proprietor of the parish and holder of the barony of Kerse. Almond was a Councillor who would prove his sympathy with the Supplicants by recognising the Glasgow Assembly as soon as the Commissioner tried to dissolve it; Kerse was an outspoken Supplicant who almost certainly enjoyed the favour of the

Tables. Neither attended at all regularly; indeed neither was actually sworn in until 9th September when, as in the case of Kilconquar, the elections to the assembly were discussed for the first time. The session, almost certainly under pressure from Almond, decided to postpone their choice 'until the return of His Majesty's Commissioner'. Neither attended again until the 23rd, when Hope appeared but Almond did not. The election was postponed again, though only until the 25th, when a rather poorly attended meeting, lacking both the principals, considered a letter from Almond and promptly elected him. It seems possible that Kerse was not informed of the meeting. Almond's bailie, Livingston of Westquarter, who had attended throughout and who may have stage-managed the whole affair, was appointed to go to the presbytery in the absence of Almond himself. The result was at once a defeat for the Tables and a triumph for the system they had created ([14]).

The response of the parish of Stow, where the minister would shortly be deprived, was noticeably less enthusiastic, and the election to the presbytery of Earlston was deferred until the 30th. Once more, the session was augmented to include the 'gentlemen', who were for the most part the feuars of the Archbishop of St Andrews. They drew up a short list of seven, six of whom were heritors. The issue, surely somewhat oddly, was decided 'by drawing of seven figures'; six of the candidates were Pringles; perhaps it did not matter. However this may be, 'it befell to . . . John of Cortilferry', a small feuar, who took the hill road to Earlston a few days later, safe in the knowledge that he need go no further ([15]).

It is possible to build up a more complete picture for the neighbouring presbytery of Haddington. On the 9th of September - a date that recurs too often to allow of accident - the session of Pencaitland added three new elders - two heritors and the son of one of the two - to its number. A week later, a few days before the assembly was proclaimed, one of the three - Belsches of Belsches - was chosen ruling elder. The session of Bothans can have had few doubts. Lord Yester, an original Supplicant who was already an elder and the only large magnate in a rather small parish, was unanimously, and surely automatically, elected on the 18th. In the presbytery as a whole fourteen of the fifteen parishes participated in the election, and the fifteenth probably did not have a minister. Eleven of the fourteen sent a proprietor as ruling elder, the remaining three - Bolton, Morham and Athelstaneford - being small, unimportant and largely in the hands of absentee landlords ([16]).

On the opposite shore of the Firth of Forth, the ruling elders from the rural parishes of the presbytery of Kirkcaldy were all proprietors. Lowland Perthshire presented a rather similar picture. Nineteen parishes sent ruling elders to a presbytery meeting in Perth on 26th September; of these, thirteen were landed proprietors; one - the Earl of Wemyss - was a nobleman; three others - Moncrieff of Moncrieff, Ruthven of Frieland and Blair of Balthayock - would serve as shire commissioners in the Parliaments of the next decade or so; at least five had a baronial jurisdiction; another was bailie of the regality of Abernethy which was held by an absentee; yet another was a feuar in the Lordship of Methven, which was held by the absent Duke of Lennox; two more were feuars of the Lordship of

Scone. Five of the thirteen were the wealthiest proprietors in their parishes, three more were the second wealthiest and one of these was the wealthiest resident; most of the remainder were typical feuars in parishes divided among many relatively small proprietors. The impression remains that one or two of the feuars and some at least of the tenants appeared as substitutes for other and wealthier men. The bailie of regality is an obvious example and there were almost certainly at least two more. Ruling elders began to attend the ordinary, as distinct from the election, meetings of the presbytery during the following January and the first list included two notable additions. Dron was represented by Auchinlek of Balmanno, the wealthiest heritor in the parish and the son of a former shire commissioner who had recently died, while Scone sent Viscount Stormont instead of one of his vassals ([17]). By and large, the elders who appeared in the presbytery of Perth, and indeed of Haddington as well, were the wealthiest Covenanters in their parishes; and they included a significant sprinkling of magnates who probably dominated the elections.

The peripheral presbyteries of Strathbogie and Chirnside display an interesting contrast. In the former, where the Gordon influence was powerful, thirteen parishes mustered only eight ruling elders and the remaining five quite specifically refused to send them. The presbytery elected one of the eight, but he did not go, while the two chosen ministers returned to Strathbogie as soon as the Commissioner had left the Assembly. In Chirnside, where the presbytery had been similarly unenthusiastic, lay intervention brought a sudden and dramatic reversal. The Earl of Home, himself an early Supplicant and future signatory of the Bond of Cumbernauld, was chosen, one imagines without much difficulty, 'for the seculars' by his own kirk session. He then proceeded to the presbytery, where he threw out the moderator and engineered the election of - to quote a hostile source - three 'ignorant' and 'malicious' ministers as well as himself ([18]).

Baillie tells us a good deal about the elections in the south-west. In his own presbytery of Irvine, two of the three ministers, including Baillie himself, were unanimously elected, but the most obvious candidate for the remaining place was passed over 'for his wilful opposition to the lay elders' in favour of a reliable nonentity. In the neighbouring presbytery of Paisley, where the presence of elders was not recorded in the minutes, a parallel situation found a parallel solution; but the most obstinate struggle took place in Glasgow. The levers of local power had traditionally been operated by the Archbishop, who was hostile but demoralised, and the Duke of Lennox, who was friendly but aloof. It was a situation which had clearly been anticipated by the Tables. In the spirit of their instructions, they proposed to import the Earl of Eglinton from the presbytery of Irvine with its enviable surplus of Covenanting magnates. But the ministers, mindful of a long local clerical tradition and fortified by the proximity of the Commissioner, declined to elect any ruling elder at all. The election was hastily postponed and a powerful delegation from the Tables, headed by Loudoun, harangued the ministers into submission. Eglinton was duly elected and Loudoun rounded off his triumph by securing the election of a ruling elder in the Commissioner's presbytery of Hamilton, although here a group of ministers signed a formal

D

protestation against the elections and the part played by laymen in them ([19]).

The conflict in Clydesdale had been between two contrasting concepts of the nature of the General Assembly. The Commissioner had sought, on behalf of the Crown, to achieve a clerical assembly elected by clerical presbyteries. The Tables, on the other hand, were striving for an assembly, which would indeed consist predominantly of ministers but which would, nonetheless, be dominated by the feudal classes. We may speculate that the Marquis of Hamilton would personally have preferred to turn the system to his own advantage by actively participating in the elections themselves. However this may be, it is reasonably clear that Almond had already done this in the kirk session of Falkirk and absolutely certain that two other Councillors, Southesk and Traquair, were actually doing it in the presbyteries of Brechin and Peebles. These were struggles of an entirely different kind, since both parties accepted the general principles underlying the instructions issued by the Tables.

In Brechin, a meeting attended by a chosen few yielded a commission for Erskine of Dun, a descendant of the reformer and the nominee of the Tables; but a second meeting, better attended than the first, elected Lord Carnegie, the heir to the greatest magnate in the region, the Earl of Southesk. Southesk himself, as a Councillor, had not taken the Covenant; but he had allowed, and perhaps encouraged, his son to do so. Carnegie was thus, under the rules laid down by the Tables themselves, the obvious candidate. But the Tables no longer trusted Councillors or their sons. Their own choice was a relatively small laird, almost certainly supported by the Earl of Montrose who held the barony of Old Montrose in the parish of Maryton. There is no evidence that Montrose actively intervened - indeed he was the designated ruling elder for the presbytery of Auchterarder - and it seems obvious that the first meeting was carried by stealth rather than confrontation. However this may be, the name of Montrose headed the list of signatures which attached the imprimatur of the Tables to Dun's commission and denied it to Carnegie's. The conflict between them was left to be decided in the assembly itself ([20]).

The election in Peebles brings the same issues into sharper focus. The story really began on the 2nd of August, when Gavin Mackall replaced the previous moderator. At first glance, he was a strange choice; he had served the same cure since 1603 without attracting much notice from anyone; in 1638 he was old, ailing and obscure. But it may be significant that he was the minister of Traquair and that James Stewart, 1st Earl of Traquair, Councillor and Lord High Treasurer, was the patron of his living and the largest proprietor in his parish. The election was originally intended for 27th September, when the brethren duly attended with their ruling elders. The Earl of Traquair was also present, ostensibly to discuss the vacant living of Kailzie, of which he was also patron. He affably offered to fill the vacancy or alternatively to divert the stipend to 'pious uses'. This was generous enough, but it did not give him a voice in the election. He had taken the 1598 act literally and had attended as a 'baron', and this was disallowed. Not to be deterred, he procured, presumably with the connivance of the moderator, the postponement of the election until 1st October and used the interval to some purpose. The ruling elder for Traquair - who was probably one of his tenants - had not had a written commission from his session. The King's Treasurer hastily substituted himself and cheerfully presented himself in the presbytery as an ecclesiastical person. It was predictable that this second meeting would be less affable than the first. The ruling elder for Lyne was none other than Lord Yester, who had been chosen commissioner for the presbytery of Haddington a week or so earlier. At first, the meeting took its normal course. Five of the more articulate ministers were nominated to the leet and duly removed; they included Gavin Mackall and John Bennett, both supported by Traquair. Three lairds - Stanhope and Blackbarony for the Tables and Posso for Traquair - followed their example, leaving the two magnates to maul among the minnows. The election itself was punctuated by protestation and counter-protestation. The two principals angrily contested each other's commissions. Traquair had intruded himself at the last minute; Yester was neither resident nor had he - or so it was alleged - the support of the residents. Yester objected to Cardrona as ruling elder for Kailzie, which had no minister. Traquair retorted that the elder for Glenholm was a rebel at the horn. Yester complained that Nasmyth of Posso had helped to vote himself onto the leet, and so it went on. At some point in the debate a lonely clerical voice had whispered a protestation against lay elders; one can see his point.

The result was a paper triumph for Traquair. Posso was chosen ruling elder, while Mackall and Bennett were among the three chosen ministers; but neither Mackall nor Posso would reach the assembly. The moderator, who would be dead before the winter was out, pleaded his infirmity and resigned his commission. The whole delegation was suspended by the assembly, pending a decision on the inevitable protestation against the election. The protestation was eventually rejected; but by this time Hamilton had left the assembly, taking Traquair - and thus Posso - with him ([21]). It is perhaps fair to add that this might not have happened. Traquair, like Southesk, had challenged the Tables under their own rules and he had won. If the rest of the Council had followed their example, the resulting assembly would surely have followed a rather different course. That most of them did nothing at all possibly reflects their reluctance to assist a King who seemed determined to exclude the feudal classes altogether, if he could. They declined to engineer their own destruction.

One election stands apart from all the others of which records have survived. Moray, the most determined of the bishops and the only one to use his civil power to any purpose, was still in control of part at least of his diocese and he continued to attend the presbytery of Elgin until the following February. On the 25th of October, he held an election quite unlike anything envisaged by the Tables. There were no laymen present at all. Two commissioners were elected and both were ministers; one was the bishop's son; both would soon be deprived ([22]). In Elgin at least, the King's concept of a clerical assembly was respected and it can be inferred that Elgin was not entirely alone. Out of a total of 61 active presbyteries, 53 were represented in the assembly as it was after the King's Commissioner had left it. One of the others - Brechin - had its commission disallowed, while the remaining seven - Chanonry, Aberlour, Fordyce, Ellon, Strathbogie, Arbroath and Elgin -

had either been unrepresented from the first or had withdrawn their delegations with the Commissioner. In eight presbyteries, all of them north of Tay and most of them north of Dee, the principle of lay participation was challenged more or less successfully ([23]).

The burgh elections were, for the most part, uneventful. They were based on the same act of 1598 which had determined the shape of the assembly as a whole and this had entitled each royal burgh to send one commissioner, with the exception of Edinburgh which was allowed two. As in the case of the barons, the act had made no pretence that these commissioners were ecclesiastical persons and it was presumably this which led the Tables, no doubt under pressure from their clerical wing, to place their own interpretation on its meaning. Possibly looking back to an even older act of the Assembly of 1568, they insisted that burgh commissioners should be elected with the 'consent' of their kirk sessions. There was no suggestion that the commissioners must themselves be elders - although many of them probably were; but it was implied that the church, acting through the local kirk session, was entitled to a veto on their selection. In fact all the surviving commissions definitely accepted by the assembly stated that the delegates concerned had been elected with the advice or consent of their sessions; while two others, from Annan and Sanquhar, in which consent was not signified, may, though the evidence is not entirely clear, have been rejected ([24]).

The practical meaning of this advice is difficult to assess. In Edinburgh, nineteen Magistrates and Councillors were joined by two ministers and thirty-seven sessioners for the purpose of the election. But it is far from clear that the churchmen actually voted and it seems rather unlikely that they did so. It is almost certain that the Town Council merely chose a merchant and a craftsman, exactly as they would have done in the case of an election to Parliament, and that the kirk sessions then gave their consent. Whether this is so or not, it is evident that the Commissioners, once elected, saw themselves as the representatives of their burghs. The Edinburgh delegation sent back regular reports to the Town Council - not to the session - while the Glasgow commissioner, who was also the Lord Provost, was bound to seek the opinion of his Council before casting his vote - and this is surely remarkable.

The Glasgow election is well recorded, but the Minutes of the Town Council do not mention the kirk session at all. On the other hand, the commission, which was made out a week later, does state that the session was consulted. It seems evident that the session was subsequently invited to confirm the election and that it actually did so. This may well have been a fairly general practice, but it is fair to add that Glasgow was a special case. At a time when most of the southern burghs had fallen to the Supplicants, Glasgow placed itself at the disposal of the King's Commissioner. The Archbishop, using his civil power at Hamilton's prompting, successfully procured the election of Patrick Bell as Provost and four of his friends as magistrates and this was a minor triumph, since Glasgow had already been chosen as the site for the assembly. As it transpired, the eventual outcome was unfortunate. Bell was duly elected as commissioner to the assembly; but he stayed on after Hamilton had gone, solemnly sat in judgment over the Archbishop who had appointed him, and then, as if to make betrayal doubly sure, voted for the abjuration of episcopacy as well. No doubt he was mindful of the hordes of armed men that surrounded the assembly; but there may also have been an element of cold calculation in this. Glasgow escaped from the clutches of the bishops, who were usually demanding and nearly always there, into the gentler grasp of a distant Duke too idle to use his power oppressively [25].

It is scarcely surprising that Aberdeen should have been another exception. The Councillors seem to have contemplated sending a commissioner; but, if they did, they were soon dissuaded. A petition, supported by Huntly and clamorously presented by a 'great number of neighbours', demanded that the assembly be ignored. To send a commissioner, it was urged, would force them to choose between a King, to whom they had every reason to be grateful, and the other burghs, with whom they had to live. The burgh resolved to stay away from the assembly unless it was specially summoned to it by the King, as it probably had been for the later assemblies of James VI. There is no hint that the kirk session played any part in the argument.

But neither Aberdeen nor Glasgow was typical. In most burghs there was no conflict and the consent of the session was important only for the precedent it created. Thus the burgh of Stirling had joined the Supplicants with some alacrity a year earlier. The presence of the session at the election, which is recorded in the Town Council Minutes, must have seemed natural enough and it certainly did not affect the result. The chosen commissioner was Thomas Bruce of Welden, Provost of Stirling, and this was also typical enough [26].

Fifty-five royal burghs would send a commissioner to all or some of the Parliaments of the period and forty-four of these appeared in the roll of the assembly, as did Stranraer which was not represented in Parliament. Of the remaining twelve, only three - Arbroath, which probably withdrew before the roll was made up; Elgin, where the bishop was still a powerful force; and Aberdeen itself - would regularly appear in subsequent assemblies and the remainder were too insignificant to count. The burgh elections were a triumph for the Tables [27].

There were thus forty-six burgh commissioners, two from Edinburgh and one from each of the rest. Sixteen of them had already sat in a previous Parliament; twenty-eight, including many of the sixteen, would be elected to the next Parliament of 1639. In all, thirty-six of the forty-six attended one or more of the Parliaments of the period. Again at least thirty-two either had been, were, or would be magistrates of their burghs, while at least seven more were town clerks. Only four members - for Jedburgh, North Berwick, Inverkeithing and Wigtown - did not fall into one or other of these categories, and it seems quite probable that two of these are cases of mistaken identity, and that Wariston - who was perhaps too busy or too excited to bother with details - entered the wrong christian name in the roll. However this may be, it is obvious that the burgh members were, in almost every case, prominent members of their local burgh oligarchies. They were ecclesiastical persons only in the rather nominal sense that their kirk sessions had consented to their election. The parallel with the barons is almost exact. Two examples may perhaps serve to make the point. Gideon Jack, who represented the small burgh of Lanark, had been elected to Parliament for the first time in 1621 and he attended every Parliament from 1628 to 1649 with the exception of those of 1640 and 1641 - when he must surely have been seriously ill. He also regularly sat in the Convention of Royal Burghs as well as at least four of the assemblies from 1638 to 1646. He was Bailie of Lanark in 1629 and 1639 - and probably much more often than this. Mr Robert Cunningham, Bailie of Kinghorn, did even better: he contrived to sit in nearly all the Parliaments from 1612 to 1661, as well as several assemblies. These were local worthies of modest affluence and modest horizons; but some of the others were national figures. Mr Robert Barclay, Bailie of the small port of Irvine, not only represented his burgh in Parliament, Convention and Assembly, but was also a regular member of the Committee of Estates and of Commissions appointed to deal with the English, notably in the negotiations concerning the Solemn League and Covenant [28].

If the origins of the typical burgh commissioner are reasonably clear, those of the ruling elders are almost too obvious. Forty-nine elders remained in the assembly after Hamilton had left it and all of them were landed proprietors of one kind or another. Seventeen of these were noblemen and one of the others was the brother, and probably the representative, of the Earl of Sutherland; twenty of the remaining thirty-one had been or would be members of Parliament. To look at the same question from another angle, at least thirty-eight had a baronial or a regality jurisdiction. Only five, a mere tenth of the whole, cannot definitely be placed in one of these two categories [29]. One or two of these may have been feuars, but it is sufficiently clear that the ruling elder was essentially the 'baron' envisaged in the Dundee Act of 1598. He was the voice of the heritable jurisdictions.

But the laymen in the assembly were exceeded, at least in a narrowly numerical sense, by its clerical members and these had emerged from a totally different setting. The origins of eighty-six, out of the total of one hundred and forty-one ministers remaining in the assembly, are known. The largest single group, of thirty-four, were the sons of earlier ministers, while two others were the sons of notaries. Seventeen - about a fifth of the whole - came from a burgess background, while thirty - rather less than a third of the whole - came from landed families. The remaining two were the sons of tenant farmers. A full analysis of the origins of the ministry must await separate treatment in a later chapter (see chapter seven); but the bare statistics are misleading in some respects and they can hardly be left as they stand. It is not unreasonable to assume that most of the unknown ministers were of relatively humble origin; many of them were quite probably the sons of farmers fortunate enough to have been born into a parish with a school. Again, the sons of proprietors consisted predominantly of younger sons with no reasonable expectation of a landed inheritance at the time they entered the ministry; only one is definitely known to have been the heir of his father's estate, although two others seem eventually to have inherited. Similarly, the ministers of burgess origin did not, for the most part, emerge from the upper reaches of the burgh oligarchies; they were usually the sons of craftsmen or of small merchants.

It is not difficult to find apparent exceptions. Patrick Hamilton, minister of Innerwick, was a son - but only a natural son - of the Earl of Haddington. The great Robert Douglas, who would follow Alexander Henderson as the undoubted leader of his church, was distantly related to the Earls of Morton and occasionally - in his few lighter moments - claimed descent from Mary; but his father may well have held no land at all. Henderson himself descended from a cadet branch of the family of Fordel, but his father was possibly a farmer, and at best a feuar. David Dickson was the son of a wealthy Glasgow merchant and inherited a small estate from him; but Samuel Rutherford came from farming stock. The ministers were drawn from a much broader social range than were the ruling elders or the burgh commissioners; but it is evident that very few of them came from the feudal classes. They were almost innocent of inherited wealth and totally innocent of heritable jurisdiction. Two kingdoms, not entirely unlike those envisaged by Melville, met in the Glasgow Assembly and, at least to the casual observer, it seemed that they met as one ([30]).

But it would be misleading to present the ministers of the assembly as a gathering of radical zealots. One hundred and fifteen of them would still be alive in 1648; of these, nineteen would support the Engagement, while five more would have been involved with Montrose or Huntly; one in five would eventually strike a conservative attitude, compared with about one out of every nine of the ministry as a whole as it would be in 1648. The statistical pitfalls built into these calculations are reasonably obvious, but the conclusion is confirmed by the scarcity - only five out of a possible ninety-two - of future Protesters and by the high proportion - twenty-eight out of forty-one survivors - who would conform at the Restoration. Indeed one of the ministers, who abjured episcopacy in the Glasgow Assembly, became a bishop at the Restoration.

The chosen venue for the assembly was Glasgow and this was evidently a compromise. The King would have preferred Aberdeen, while the Supplicants were attracted to Edinburgh, where the City Fathers were cautiously friendly and the mob noisily obedient. Glasgow was a different matter. The west of Scotland was already covenanting territory, but Glasgow itself emphatically was not. The presbytery and the university had both objected to lay participation in the elections and both, together with the burgh itself, had wanted to embrace the King's Covenant. All of them had been dissuaded on both issues; but the doubts of the Supplicants were understandable enough. Glasgow had traditionally been under the influence of its bishops and the Dukes of Lennox, while the Hamiltons themselves were not far away; indeed the magistrates of the burgh had recently been chosen to please the Commissioner. Armed intervention was perhaps unlikely; the Bishop was in disgrace; the Duke was in England; the Marquis would have to ask his mother. But the possibility remained and it was just strong enough to justify counter measures. The Tables instructed each presbytery and each burgh to send six assessors with its delegation. They were described as advisers, but they all came armed and it was obvious they were there either to protect their own commissioners or to threaten the King's. But this was not all. Eglinton and the other Ayrshire magnates brought their tenantry with them. The little town of Glasgow was crowded enough as the assembly foregathered. Wariston, perhaps with his mind on weightier matters, wasted a day seeking lodgings for Henderson and himself ([31]).

The assembly met on 21st November in an atmosphere of violent confusion that may well have been carefully rehearsed. If Hamilton had ever had any illusions about his ordeal, they were soon dispelled: 'my soul was never sadder to see such a sight . . . many swords but more daggers, most of them having left their pistols in their lodgings.' After an hour's jostling, the throng finally distributed itself into its various elements. The Commissioner occupied a raised throne, with his Councillors around and below him. In front of them was a table for the Moderator and the Clerk. Before them again were long tables about which the Lords of the Covenant and the rest of the ruling elders were seated. They, in their turn, were flanked by the burgesses and the ministers 'sitting on good commodious rooms rising up five or six degrees on either side'. At the far end was a gallery for distinguished visitors, 'with huge numbers of people, ladies and some gentlewomen in the vaults above' ([32]).

It is interesting to speculate on the Commissioner's private thoughts as he peered down from his throne. His duty was clear enough. It was notorious that the Tables had begun to organise the elections to the assembly before the King had authorised it; it was obvious that laymen had intervened at every stage of the process and that they had participated in the election of ministers. He must therefore dissolve the assembly as soon as it decided to try the bishops. But duty was dictated by bishops and the Marquis was a nobleman. Neither he nor his Councillors objected to baronial intervention in the elections nor to a baronial presence in the assembly itself. He was being asked to dissolve the assembly in a cause he believed to be bad and he felt that the practical impact could only be worse. Dissolution would be seen as an act of war. The assembly would be compelled to go on without him. Its members would be driven, in most cases unwillingly, into Melvillian attitudes that would profit nobody but the Melvillians themselves. The argument for remaining can only have seemed compelling. It may have been true that the abolition of episcopacy was now inevitable, but its abjuration was not. The moderates were content to 'remove' it and the Marquis must surely have wanted to support them. Another Melvillian triumph might be avoided. Rothes, Argyll and Hamilton could all agree on this - and they surely did so.

The facts are consistent with an informal, though almost certainly unspoken, compact between the Commissioner and the Lords of the Covenant; he would remain with them, albeit with a carefully assumed air of reluctance, as long as they did not embarrass him by parading the irregularity of their elections. He welcomed with all sincerity the choice of Henderson as moderator; he opposed the appointment of Wariston as clerk and allowed himself to be over-ruled because he knew that he could not prevent it: Wariston, as even the moderate Baillie believed, was a 'nonsuch' for a Clerk. The assembly then attempted to complete itself by approving the commissions of its members. Hamilton dutifully replied by attempting to introduce the Bishop's Declinator which, with its objections to lay management of the elections, effectively questioned them all. In doing so, he pleased the bishops without seriously damaging the compact, since he knew that the assembly would refuse to receive it. The commissions were finally considered in the fourth session and it is significant that Hamilton did not seem particularly interested. He reserved his right to object to them later on, but there was no suggestion that he would scrutinise them there and then. It seemed that the comedy could be indefinitely prolonged. The Commissioner would stay in the assembly, leaving a minefield of protestations behind him to mark the line of his retreat. Each one would pay a gold piece, but very little else, to the Clerk. This would not be a Melvillian assembly - or so the moderates may have thought ([33]).

At first the session promised to be unusually uneventful; even the inevitable protests against the commissions from Peebles and Glasgow University barely disturbed the calm as the Clerk droned his way interminably through the list. The eighty-second commission related the impeccable qualifications of the Provost of Forfar and the assembly yawned its silent consent. But the eighty-third came from Brechin which had, as we have seen, sent two rival delegations. One, which seems mainly to have been elected by ministers, had Lord Carnegie, the son of Southesk, as ruling elder; the other, probably elected by a majority of laymen and certainly supported by the Tables, had Erskine of Dun, a friend of Montrose, as its elder. There was still no hint of drama as the Clerk innocently intoned Dun's credentials, though Carnegie may have flicked over the pages of a protestation. Then, with a superb sense of theatre, Wariston turned over the commission and solemnly read out the 'back writ' which not only mentioned lay participation but also bestowed the favour of the Tables; not content with this, he mercilessly ploughed through the list of forty signatures appended to it. It was an indiscretion so huge that it must have been calculated. We may imagine that the Marquis paused for a moment as he pondered the implications of a disclosure that he might personally have preferred to ignore. But he had just been presented with the evidence that the King's Commissioner could not possibly ignore. He rose majestically from his throne and demanded a copy of the commission 'back and fore'. For once Henderson was at a loss; he implausibly protested that the back writ was merely a 'private thing'. Rothes, seeing that the game was up, intelligently suggested that the 'ingiver' should withdraw his commission and thus everything in it; better lose Dun than lose the King. But Montrose, seeing his protégé in danger, angrily swore to 'avow the least jot that was in it'. Henderson desperately claimed that the back writ was 'accidental'; whereupon the Marquis, who was beginning to enjoy the confusion around him, sarcastically retorted that the accident had 'forty hands' to it. Henderson hastily changed his tune and suggested that both commissions be withdrawn, but this only made bad worse. Southesk, speaking from the foot of the throne and believing that his son's commission was valid, 'unreverently roared out his wrath'. Loudoun, no more reverently, sprang to the moderator's defence and suddenly everyone was shouting at once. They had fortunately left their pistols at home. It was, as Wariston's official report testified, 'like to have drawn to a great heat if the Commissioner had not prevented them by commanding them to silence'. For a few brief moments, the Marquis was moderator of the Glasgow Assembly ([34]).

Wariston had torn the assembly apart. He had exposed the divisions between moderate and radical, between magnate and minister, between the Lords of the Council and the Lords of the Covenant, between Montrose and the rest of the revolutionary establishment. But he had achieved his purpose. The compact was shattered. The Marquis would have to go and, once he had gone, the Supplicants would re-form themselves around the Clerk. In the seventh session, as the assembly was pondering its right to try the bishops, the Marquis rose and announced his farewell: 'I find an absolute determination to maintain the lawfulness of lay elders . . . to vote here and of the election of ministers by lay elders; I can acknowledge nothing . . . done by the vote of such men.' This had been composed for the benefit of a more distant audience, for his manner betrayed his reluctance; he 'acted it with tears and drew by his tears water from many eyes'. His compromise had collapsed and he left the assembly to its own, now necessarily Melvillian, devices; he became a mindless robot punctiliously publishing proclamations inspired from the Court and ignored by the kingdom (35).

As he left the assembly, his old ally attached himself as firmly to it. There is no evidence that Argyll stayed with Hamilton's approval, but it seems clear that he wanted to follow a similar course. His status was equivocal enough. He had come to the assembly as one of the Commissioner's assessors; he stayed in it as a guest without a vote or even the right to speak. And yet there can be no doubt that he was welcome. The Supplicants regarded him as a sympathiser who was slowly becoming an adherent; he saw himself as an adherent who would soon become a leader. Either way, the moral support of the most powerful magnate in the kingdom could only lend confidence to an enterprise that still seemed rather desperate. Nor did he come alone. Seven more Councillors, all incidentally friends of Montrose, declared their support for the assembly at the same time. The possibility of effective opposition in Scotland receded even further into the distance.

It is arguable that the Glasgow Assembly, despite its occasional riotous informality, was as carefully managed as its Jacobean predecessors or indeed its covenanting successors. The agenda was controlled through a committee called the Moderator's Assessors; the most contentious issues were thoroughly prepared in the Committee for the Confession and presented to the full assembly as almost accomplished facts. There was little debate on the floor of the assembly and most of the votes were unanimous or nearly so. An assembly in which ministers outnumbered laymen by about three to two naturally tended to elect committees with a clerical majority; but the most striking feature of these two committees was the predominance of laymen on them. The Moderator's Assessors included five noblemen, three lairds, three burgesses and only four ministers; the Committee for the Confession, although showing a truer balance, consisted of the moderator and nine other ministers, three barons, three burgesses and four noblemen to whom Argyll was added. The Clerk attended both by virtue of his office - and did his full share of the talking. If the elections to the assembly were managed by magnates, so was the assembly itself.

The noblemen among the Assessors were Rothes, Loudoun, Balmerino, Lindsay and Montrose. Rothes was a moderate who would fix his sights on an

English dowager with £4,000 - Sterling - per year; he would die, tragically enough, just as he was bringing her to the point of acquiescence; we shall never know for certain that he would have been tempted by the Engagement. Loudoun was aiming at the Treasury and would eventually settle for the Chancellory and a pension; he did not die, would be tempted and would finally be reclaimed. Balmerino, who was at once the most irreconcilable and the least active of the leading Lords, would consistently oppose the Engagement; but Lindsay would as consistently support it. Montrose speaks for himself. These men can only by an abuse of language be described as radicals. It seems just possible that the omission of Lindsay and Montrose from the Committee of the Confession was politically inspired; but, if this could have been so, it is equally true that the only two barons to serve on both committees - Stirling of Keir and Douglas of Cavers - were friends of Montrose.

Only three ministers - Henderson, Dickson and Rollock - served on both committees. The moderator himself had been an episcopalian at a time when bishops had not scorned general assemblies, and he had found Melville rather late in life. He was a moderate by inclination and the assertion that he would have favoured the Engagement is not implausible. But Henderson was essentially a conciliator who regarded the radicals on the one hand and the magnates on the other as an integral part of the church; they were both essential to it. He gained the respect of the magnates because he was never overawed by them; indeed he would retain the trust of Argyll and Montrose alike - and this was unusual. He was at once the leader of the kirk and the solvent of its differences. David Dickson, his comrade in rebellion, was a friend of Wariston who would eventually become a Resolutioner; in 1638 he was still a radical but no firebrand. Henry Rollock had once angled for a bishopric and was now running as furiously in the opposite direction; his present prominence probably reflected the fact that he was the more pliable of the two surviving ministers of Edinburgh; it would not last. The rest of the committee men were a mixed bag. John Adamson was a confirmed moderate who shared Baillie's dislike of abjuration. Andrew Cant was an angry radical who would spend the period thanklessly preaching the Covenants in Aberdeen, but his near neighbour from Belhelvie would accept the Restoration as cheerfully as he now accepted the assembly. Above and beyond this, the great radicals of the forties - Guthrie, the Gillespies and Rutherford - had still to penetrate the inner councils of the kirk. The guiding spirits of the Glasgow Assembly embraced several opinions, but their collective image was one of moderation driven by circumstances into a radicalism that was none the less determined for being feigned ([36]).

. The proceedings of the Committee for the Confession are poorly recorded, for Baillie was not a member and Wariston was too busy to keep a detailed diary. But it seems certain that Argyll attempted a twofold compromise under which episcopacy would have been removed rather than abjured and the rebellious bond of 1638 reconciled with the 'loyal' bond of 1589. If this was so, he was outmanoeuvred and indeed routed by the radical Wariston. The first phase of the argument burst briefly on to the floor of the house on 8th December when the assembly formally abjured episcopacy. Argyll was invited to deliver his opinion as one who had 'taken pains to be clear therein'. The response was scarcely a model of radical clarity. Though normally a fluent speaker, Argyll rambled through the pros and cons like a man in a trance. If the assembly had hoped for a lead from him, it was disappointed and perhaps a trifle bewildered. This was not the real Argyll, but the voice of a man already defeated. Like Loudoun and many others, he wanted to support the opinion which Robert Baillie delivered much more coherently to the assembly later in the debate: 'episcopacy such as it was in the ancient church and in our church during Knox's day in the persons of the superintendent ought for many reasons to be removed but not abjured'. Baillie, and surely Argyll as well, declined to dismiss as a popish error the government of the church as it had been reformed in Scotland. But this appeal was rejected and the triumphant Wariston heard a 'wonderful' chorus of 'abjuring and removing' as the assembly recorded a vote that was unanimous apart from Baillie's lonely dissent.

On one level, this extraordinary result can be explained away as a rather shabby deception. Everybody in the assembly wanted removal and the question was framed in such a way that it was difficult to remove episcopacy without abjuring it as well. But the assembly as a whole was willing to be deceived. The final blow to the moderates seems to have been a rumour - later to be confirmed - that the Commissioner would shortly issue an interpretation of the Negative Confession describing it as an oath in favour of episcopacy. The 'worker by contraries' was busy still. But this was merely a symptom. Scotland was on the brink of war with its King; the church was assuming a vital part in the alternative government that was opposing him. It could only seem absurd to leave its administration in the hands of a foreign, and now potentially hostile, power. The embattled kirk was sensitive to the presence of traitors in its entrails. In the violent atmosphere of the Glasgow Assembly, mere removal seemed inadequate; the Word of God sounded more final than an act of assembly. Episcopacy, along with the Perth Articles and the civil powers of kirkmen, was quite simply tacked on to the other 'heads of popery' abjured in the Confession. It could now quite plausibly be asserted that they were all invalid whatever the King, his Council, the Parliament or even a subsequent assembly might think about them.

In these circumstances, the rest of Argyll's compromise was foredoomed, though he clearly pursued it energetically enough in the privacy of the committee. Argyll, as the Lord Advocate had done before him, cheerfully opposed *Humanitas*, but he insisted on obedience to Correction. But Charles was *Humanitas* now and his Commissioner hastened to prove the point. Rumour had it - and as always the Tables were well informed - that the Assembly would soon be branded as seditious. This, as Wariston said with quite unusual restraint, cleared 'My Lord Argyll's mind' and the assembly duly set the seal of its approval on the bond of 1638 in all its revolutionary purity ([37]).

Wariston had confided his dreams to his diary at the beginning of the assembly. He would, he claimed, 'declare unto all the royal prerogative of King Jesus . . . above all prerogatives and extend his kingdom through all the borders of the earth'. Now, as the assembly drew to its close, it must have seemed that victory was in prospect. The complex web of conflicting interests that made up the Supplicants had been dragged up several 'steps of reformation' at once. But this, if true, was scarcely the whole of the truth. Bishops might be abjured, but ruling elders were holy still. The magnates, albeit in ecclesiastical disguise, had been formally invited into the government of the kirk. The assembly, for all its Melvillian rhetoric, had merely adapted the proposition that the church was independent of the state to mean that it was independent of the Crown ([38]).

Indeed the advantage was already swinging away from the Clerk. The penultimate speech of the assembly brought the Earl of Argyll, hitherto a doubting guest at its deliberations, firmly into the ranks of the revolution. Soon afterwards he took the Covenant, perhaps in a form of his own devising, and immediately climbed on to a throne which would soon seem his by right. He would lend dignity and wisdom to a cause which had often been lacking in both. Argyll had chosen his moment well. The transition from a hostile peace to a war that would prove strangely friendly was marked by a wave of patriotic fervour stimulated by fear of an English invasion. Henderson, in a tract on defensive resistance to kings, captured the mood faithfully enough: 'We would put a difference between the King, resident in the kingdom opening his ears to both parties and rightly informed, and the King far from us in another kingdom, hearing the one party and misinformed by our adversaries in the other - between the King as King proceeding lawfully according to the laws of the kingdom against rebels and the King as a man, coming down from the throne (at the foot whereof the humble supplications of the subjects do yet lie unanswered) and marching furiously against his loyal disposed people.' Henderson was drawing the traditional distinction between Correction and *Humanitas*. The mood was now conservative and it reflected a decisive change in the balance of power. The regiments of the new army, a formidable and a disciplined force, were commanded by the Lords of the Covenant under the benign direction of an ageing general with his eye on an earldom. The Tables were no longer a box of tricks with Wariston pulling the strings. The Pacification of Berwick would be managed by Rothes and Henderson, acting on behalf of Argyll, and neither would protest very loudly when Charles banished Wariston from his tent. The skeleton of an agreement was reached easily enough. There was indeed no irreconcilable difference between a King who was listening to Hamilton instead of Laud, and a revolution that was led by Argyll rather than Wariston ([39]).

The alliance between Hamilton and Argyll rested in the last analysis on a common view of the Church of the Covenant. The Marquis, on the eve of his fateful assertion that the Glasgow Assembly could not try the bishops, had told the King, as bluntly as he had ever told him anything that Laud did not want to hear, that the bishops ought to be tried. They had 'abused their power by bringing in these (innovations) in this church not in the ordinary and legal way'; their 'pride was great and their folly greater'. Argyll, immediately before the assembly had dissolved itself, had warned it against a similar danger latent in its own ranks. He had told the ministers there to purge themselves of the 'pride and avarice' that had ruined the bishops; they should 'shun these rocks as they would eschew ship-wreck'. Argyll's metaphors - which were heavy enough to sink a Spanish galleon - concealed a profound insight into a revolution which he was about to make his own. Scotland had just been saved from one radical dictatorship engineered by professional churchmen. He was wondering - and for once he wondered aloud - whether he could save it from another one. The alignment of forces was complex. The circumstances of the moment thrust Hamilton into an alliance with Laud, and they both found it uncomfortable enough. Similarly, Argyll and Wariston developed a political friendship which was outwardly close in periods of danger; but their ultimate objectives were fundamentally different. Hamilton and Argyll, divided though they were by the necessities of war, shared the attitudes of an essentially feudal society and their friendship would endure for a decade. Laud and Wariston, who never met and probably never wanted to meet, at least agreed in their antipathies; they both sought the destruction of feudal Scotland ([40]).

The acts of the Glasgow Assembly left no permanent mark on the law of the church; they were superseded by the work of the legal assembly which met in Edinburgh at the end of the summer. In the euphoric atmosphere of the Pacification, it had even seemed possible that the gathering at Glasgow would be dismissed as a 'pretended' assembly, but the radicals still had strength enough to prevent this. According to the new dispensation, the Glasgow Assembly was neither pretended nor real; it was simply ignored. Its Melvillian precedents would still be inscribed in Wariston's compendious registers and they could be used if events made them useful, but there was no present intention of following them. The ambiguity which had allowed moderate to live with radical and which could allow both to live with the King was carefully restored. The meaning, though not the immediate impact, of the Acts of Glasgow was also changed. The Glasgow Determination had boldly 'abjured and removed' episcopacy and the Perth Articles; but it had been content more hesitantly to condemn the civil places and powers of kirkmen as unlawful. The Edinburgh Assembly greatly extended the area of hesitation; it declared all three of them to be 'unlawful within the kirk'. A good deal turned on the meaning of the word 'unlawful'. It could, since it was used in the context of a Confession of Faith, still mean contrary to the law of God - and the Lord Advocate, privately at least, construed it in this sense. But it could merely mean contrary to the law of the church, and the addition of the phrase 'within this kirk' plainly suggested that only this was intended; sin can know no frontiers. Episcopacy was more than merely removed but less than totally abjured. The Covenant thus modified was enjoined by Act of Council, with the King's presumed consent, on a petition from the assembly which would describe it as a loyal undertaking after the fashion of the bond of 1589. If the pattern of events allowed, an oath of positive defiance would become an oath of conditional obedience. The revolution would only be radical if the King chose to make it so.

The compromise of 1639 was fashioned by Traquair, who had recently replaced Hamilton as Commissioner, and Argyll, who left his mark all over it. It would eventually receive the royal assent in the legal Parliament of 1641, but this was still one more war away. Traquair had been persuaded to exceed the letter, though not perhaps the spirit, of his instructions; he gambled and he lost. He was forced to repudiate the settlement in the Parliament which met as soon as the assembly had dispersed. The King's reasons were perhaps English rather than Scottish. He would almost certainly have accepted the removal of episcopacy as contrary to the constitution of the kirk; for constitutions, as he understood them, were the work of fallible men; they could change from time to time and from kingdom to kingdom. The mere removal of the Scottish bishops did not imply the abolition of episcopacy in England. But the word 'unlawful', qualified though it might be and ambiguous as it was intended to be, was a different matter. It sounded like the Word of God. It could only strengthen the puritan opposition in England in a matter which simply did not permit of compromise. The peace was lost. The bishops, now strengthened by the return of the Lord Deputy from Dublin, had gained their last triumph. Charles once more became the 'King far from us in another kingdom' ([41]).

The Parliament which met in 1640 duly reverted to the insurrectionary attitudes of the Glasgow Assembly; but, in doing so, it adopted grounds that were feudal rather than Melvillian in character. A private meeting, attended by Argyll and Montrose as well as Wariston, solemnly pondered the deposition of kings; but it resolved to depose King Charles only if he chose to invade his own kingdom with a foreign army and thus to break the contract which bound him to uphold the religion and liberties of his Scottish subjects. This was essentially a traditional position and it indicated that the moderates were still in control. The armies were on the march again and the Lords of the Covenant had force at their disposal. It seems possible that the decision to launch a pre-emptive invasion of northern England was taken at this meeting and that one of the several motives behind it was a desire to save Charles from deposing himself. For this was a consequence that only Wariston could welcome. Indeed the Parliament of 1640, rebellious though it may have been, was in no sense anti-monarchical. It would send its acts to the King in the hope, obviously fragile until the war had been won, that he would agree to them. It deposed the King in Whitehall, but it sought to restore the King in Parliament ([42]).

The Parliament of 1640 granted the civil sanction to the ecclesiastical settlement negotiated in the Edinburgh Assembly and it went on to pass a rescissory act repealing all the Jacobean legislation in favour of bishops; it left the Golden Act of 1592 to define the government of the church - and this is surely revealing. The Golden Act had not condemned bishops; it had merely left them out. Moreover it had, in its selective rejection of the Black Acts, implied the continued supremacy of the King in Parliament over the courts of the kirk. The Parliament repudiated the Melvillian notion, advanced half seriously in argument with Charles at the Pacification, that an act of assembly could overturn an act of Parliament. It willingly confirmed the abolition of episcopacy, but it questioned the idea that episcopacy was sinful. In 1640 it was still possible to argue that Wariston's registers described a Melvillian church, but the statute book told a rather different story.

Indeed the Parliament of 1640 implicitly redefined the relationship between state and church. It established a Committee of Estates, largely fashioned in its own image, to act as an executive while it was not in session. It supplanted the Tables as the effective government of Scotland and thus replaced an institution in which ministers had participated with another from which kirkmen of any kind had just been excluded. It divided the state from the church and then proceeded to argue, albeit somewhat hesitantly, that the one was superior to the other [43]. The Parliament of 1641 insistently emphasised this superiority. Many of its members were ruling elders of the assembly which had met, if only to adjourn, at St Andrews on 20th July. The Estates suggested that it should move to Edinburgh to allow its elders to attend both bodies. The ministers had little choice but to agree to an arrangement which was obviously intended to allow the management of the assembly by politicians. And yet the Parliament had already rejected its opposite. A petition from the church, conveyed by Wariston himself, had asked that 'some ministers (as) Commissioners from the General Assembly' should attend the Parliament for 'hearing'. This was immediately denounced by Argyll 'with storm' as 'making way for churchmen's voices in Parliament', and no more was heard of it. The policy of the Lords of the Covenant was clear enough. They intended to use their presence as ruling elders to dominate the kirk and they were equally determined to preserve their own independence from the ministers. In 1641 it still seemed likely that a relationship of this kind could survive if only because the leading ministers seemed content to preserve it. Soon afterwards the Estates, preoccupied as always with the feud between Argyll and Montrose, chose to ask the church whether the Bond of Cumbernauld had been a 'divisive motion' in breach of the Covenant. The kirk duly delivered a rather evasive opinion which at least served to renew its claim - later to be of vital importance - to be the sole arbiter of the Covenant; but it went on to offer mediation in the dispute itself and this was turned aside. The ministers had sought to penetrate the inner mysteries of a faction fight and they were rebuffed with the careful courtesy that conceals contempt. Indeed the most powerful elements among the Supplicants had regarded the Covenant, and thus the Tables too, as means to an end rather than as ends in themselves. They were really seeking to restore their own version of the ordinary processes of feudal government. In 1640 they had captured the Parliament; in 1641 they captured the King as well [44].

In a sense, the logic of the situation suggested the abandonment of a Covenant which, modified though it might have been, was now an embarrassment. And yet this was never seriously contemplated. The revolution seemed to be over; but this could be an illusion; the rebellious bond of 1638 might still be needed. Quite apart from this, the Covenant had been signed by a broad cross-section of the community, from the nobleman down to the cottar; it had seemed to foreshadow a society in which vassals mattered. It was almost impossible to disown a concept which had promised so much and delivered so little. At the same time, the necessities of war and revolution had created a new range of local and regional institutions. The civil parish had been surmounted by the civil presbytery entrusted with the vital duty of levying men and money to pay them. These new units of administration, like the shire committees which would be appointed by subsequent Parliaments, had usually included a strong baronial component; but there had always been room for a landed vassal of the right persuasion. Furthermore they taxed their landowners on a basis of income rather than status; superiority was irrelevant; a feuar was the equal of a baron of equivalent wealth. The feudal Parliaments of the period were perched, perhaps a trifle uncomfortably, on a series of local cells of a different character [45]. The church itself had been caught in a similar contradiction. It was certain that the barons had penetrated the kirk and arguable that they had come to dominate it. But its constitution gave them no exclusive rights; in theory at least, they came as ruling elders and not as barons. Indeed, the Tables had regarded a 'well affected gentleman' as an acceptable substitute for a magnate. The franchise of the Parliament was restricted and immutable; but the franchise of the kirk was neither. It could reflect social change - and we shall argue that it eventually did. The Covenant, if only symbolically, represented aspirations still unfulfilled.

As the King intrigued with his magnates in the Parliament of 1641, all this was half known but almost wholly forgotten. In effect, he came to terms with his tenants-in-chief. He swallowed all the legislation of the previous year in a single gulp and he went on to enact the principle that the executive must be appointed by the King in Parliament rather than the King in person. He accepted the inevitable corollary that his government would be dominated by magnates. He became the kind of King that Hamilton had wanted in 1638 and his difficulties immediately began to melt away, or at least to change their shape for the better. The Edinburgh mob had burnt the effigy of Traquair, now ironically the symbol of *Humanitas,* as he had entered his capital; but Correction was respected and was not without resource. The feud between Argyll and Montrose developed into a full-scale faction fight over the control of the new executive. Feudal Scotland divided itself between the nobles of the Campbell-Hamilton connection and their rivals led, if only from the rear, by the Duke of Lennox. Charles, for once the true son of his father, strove, not entirely unsuccessfully, to hold the balance between them. The struggle, complicated as it was by a constitutional argument between the nobles and the two lower estates, occupied the whole of an unusually long Parliament. In the end, the office of Chancellor went to Loudoun, who had coveted the better emoluments of the Treasury; while the Treasury itself was temporarily placed in a commission of four nobles from the connection. These appointments pleased Argyll well enough, but the price of the Duke's consent was as high as it was significant. He insisted that the third vacant office of Clerk Register should go to his protégé, Gibson of Durie, rather than to Wariston, who would dearly have liked it. Argyll, forced to compromise, did so at the expense of the zealots. Scotland, or so it seemed, was no longer groping for the millennium [46].

The settlement of 1641 was merely a brief pause in the rush to revolution, but there is no reason to doubt that the consenting parties expected their work to last. Its conclusion had been hastened by reports of the Grand Remonstrance and the Irish Rebellion, but it was still far from certain that England would dissolve into civil war. It was easy enough, in the deceptive calm of the day, to believe that the **revolution was** over. Laud had been routed and Wariston thwarted; the bishops had gone and the ministers were quiet. In practice if not in theory, the church seemed to have accepted the supremacy of the state; in both, the substance of power had been restored to the feudal classes. Thus far, or so the settlement seemed to say, the seventeenth century had been an aberration; Scottish politics had resumed their normal course.

There was perhaps a hint of something different in an incident that had occurred shortly after the King's arrival at Holyrood. He had heard Henderson preach in the morning; but, possibly weary from a long and hurried journey, he had missed the afternoon sermon, 'whereof being advertised by Mr Alexander he promised not to do so again'. Charles, perhaps reflecting that Henderson was more courteous than Melville once had been, accepted the rebuke with a good grace and regularly attended thereafter. Whether this is capable of a Melvillian interpretation is doubtful, but it is at least clear that Holyrood resumed its severely Scottish countenance. 'One may hear two sermons the Sunday at Court and . . . extempore prayer in the King's presence.' Henderson was always 'at the King's chair in the same manner . . . (as) the bishop of Canterbury (used to) attend'. The church of the Covenant had found its 'archbishop', but the ample revenues of the Chapel Royal bound him to the King in Parliament - and, of course, in the assembly too - rather than the King 'far from us in another kingdom'. The 'worker by contraries' slumbered peacefully and his disciple had been banished to the Court of Session. Divine Correction reigned supreme - or so it seemed [47].

5

A Clerical Church, 1639-51

SAMUEL Rutherford, the theorist of the radical presbyterians, would later, in a deathbed repentance, attribute the defeat of his party to its obsession with power; it had sought to set up a 'state opposite to a state' ([1]). The warning, uttered by Argyll in the closing session of the Glasgow Assembly, had been ignored; at the Restoration, as it had done in 1637, the rest of Scottish society would rise up to dismiss the arrogant claims of an omnicompetent church. And yet theocracy, or at least the threat of something very like it, was built into the Scottish predicament. The ancient feudal structure, in which the centre had so often been too weak to control the periphery, was confronted by a virile church with a new and more coherent organisation at its disposal. John the Commonweil might well have settled for a theocracy - and possibly have regretted it afterwards. The church, whatever its shape and however innocent its intentions, had always been tempted, sometimes almost in spite of itself, to expand into the vacuum left by the weakness of the Crown. But Rutherford and his friends, like the Canterburians before them, were aiming higher than this. They consciously sought to dominate the state, less indeed by supplanting it than by reducing it to a narrowly executive function. The ideology of the new society, its morality and the general outlines of its policy would be determined by the church; the state, purged into passive acquiescence, would survive only to translate policy into action.

It followed inescapably from this that the church must remain entire. Fragmentation, whether schismatic or sectarian, would reduce it to impotence. Thus far at least, the church had successfully resisted the English heresy of Brownism, but the seeds of separatism had been sown long before. Quite apart from the unending argument about episcopacy, now temporarily resolved, there was the fundamental conflict between the conservative constitutionalist and the millenarian zealot. The Melvillian minister lived uneasily with the Lord of Erection - who had, as Rutherford lamented, 'left Him a poor naked Christ, spoiling his servants of the tithes and the kirk rents' ([2]). Indeed the radical tradition itself was a partnership of incompatibles: the *Second Book of Discipline* had envisaged a monolithic church held together by an educated elite; the privy kirk had been a collection of revolutionary cells, each distinct in itself and without any formal link with its neighbour. Rutherford's 'harlot mother' was promiscuous indeed.

All these conflicting elements came together and duly exploded in the assembly held at Aberdeen in July 1640, but they had been rumbling in the undergrowth for some years. Baillie, plausibly enough, traced the explosion back to the experiences of Scottish colonists in Ulster. Deprived of the services of their own ministers, they had been driven to establish conventicles of their own. In 1638 they began to drift back to a Scotland delivered from the Canterburians but still not securely in the hands of its deliverers. They landed in the south-west, a region which was no stranger to the conventicle. Some of them came to Galloway, where a zealous bishop had used his authority to create a local Court of High Commission which, apart from silencing Samuel Rutherford, had stimulated a luxuriant growth of privy kirks. Others may have made for Kyle, the home of the Scottish Lollards, or for Cunningham, recently the breeding ground of the Stewarton 'sickness'. From all these centres, the 'privy meetings', as they had come to be called, spread into central Scotland. In Edinburgh, which had staged the first and most famous of the privy kirks, they were eagerly embraced by a population starved of organised religion by the extrusion of the Canterburian ministers. Now their more orthodox successors were faced with the difficult task of suppressing an abuse which they might previously have condoned. But the conventicle was not, if we are to believe the evidence of its opponents, confined to a capital where religious radicals had always contrived to find an audience. It also appeared in the presbyteries of Stirling (which would stage the most violent conflict), Dunblane, Auchterarder, and Perth. It is reasonable to assume that in Stirling at least the problem was genuinely serious; for here the movement found a leader in the laird of Leckie, a magnate of some substance who was no stranger to Ulster. He appears to have held privy meetings not only in his own parish of Gargunnock - which he incidentally represented as ruling elder in the presbytery - but also in Stirling itself, where he collided with the magistrates, themselves ardent if orthodox Supplicants, and Henry Guthrie, a minister with an almost pathological hatred of sectarianism. But Leckie was, if Guthrie is to be believed, neither typical nor alone. The Aberdeen Assembly was to be scandalised by stories, which were probably exaggerated rather than invented, of 'family exercises' growing into 'frequent and nocturnal meetings' addressed in rotation by 'base and unlearned persons' who expounded the Scriptures as the spirit moved them. It is evident that they bore some resemblance to English sects ([3]).

Guthrie had reported the matter to the Edinburgh Assembly of 1639, but the managers of the assembly had contrived to keep a plainly divisive issue in the background. It was, however, considered privately by the ministers left behind in the capital to lobby the ensuing Parliament. Guthrie was not there, but the conservative case was put by Henderson and Baillie in argument with Dickson and Robert Blair. It is interesting that this conference, apparently without great difficulty, reached a compromise which did not dismiss 'privy meetings' out of hand. Instead it chose to condemn those aspects of the meetings which almost everybody found objectionable. They should not coincide with church services or family exercises; they should not be held at night; they should be exceptional rather than habitual; they should cater for small groups rather than huge multitudes; those attending them should be 'of such quality that they need not be ashamed to meet together'; they should not divide the congregation against itself;

they should not be schismatic; they should not obscure the division of function between the minister and his congregation (⁴).This agreement reflected the collective, rather than the united, wisdom of the revolutionary establishment. There is no reason to doubt that Henderson and Baillie, left to themselves, would simply have published the straightforward condemnation of conventicles which Guthrie wanted. But they could not afford to offend ministers like Rutherford, Dickson or Blair, who had been driven to operate outside the official church and who were understandably reluctant to condemn their own past. Besides, the revolution might yet collapse and, if it did, conventicles would again become relatively respectable.

Henderson and Baillie were establishment figures, but Guthrie was not and, in the summer of 1640, he chose to thrust the issue before a general assembly which might otherwise have been content to write the compromise into the law of the church. He may have realised that the circumstances were unusually favourable. The conservative north, as it was bound to be in any assembly which met beyond the Tay, was more heavily represented than usual and it was not reluctant to show its teeth; ministers and elders alike would respond to Guthrie's prompting eagerly enough. Even more important, the natural leaders of the church, absorbed as they were in preparations for the war, were absent. This was the only early assembly that was attended neither by Argyll nor Henderson. The lid, which had been clamped down so firmly on the assembly of 1639, could easily blow off, especially as the radical ministers, articulate if outnumbered, were there in some strength. It only needed Guthrie to light the fuse.

The tone of the debate was soon established. Guthrie opened the proceedings with a virulent attack on the spectacular orgies, with 'men and women . . . greaping one another filthily' in the night, which were alleged to have occurred in the presbytery of Stirling. Dickson angrily retorted that Guthrie was slandering respectable people gathered together for the 'exercise of religion and piety'. Guthrie went on to parade his formidable array of witnesses with their terrible tales, often heavy with sexual innuendo, of huge field meetings in the countryside and of smaller meetings in Edinburgh, to which none were admitted but those who would 'swear to keep quiet'. A shocked assembly burst into a menacing - and obviously rehearsed - chant: 'Away with them; restrain them'. As the mood became more and more hysterical, Baillie let drop a whisper of sanity so faint that the Clerk failed to record it: 'The confused misorder of a general assembly,' he said, 'was the spoiling of the only remedy for (this) and all other diseases.' But Dickson chose not to hear; disorder and desperation drove him to an indiscretion that merely added fuel to the fire: 'Brethren, I will tell you a secret; we have many friends in England who . . . are not pleased with sundry things . . . in our discipline and now, when we are labouring for an uniformity in England, we should be loath to give offence, as this course certainly will if you condemn this exercise.' There was perhaps more sense in this than in the saying of it, for it only served to spice religious fanaticism with patriotic fervour. The chieftain of the Mackenzies, appearing in the unfamiliar guise of a ruling elder, hotly replied: 'Mr David, if we cannot have their peace . . . we will not buy it so dear, but rather commit ourselves into the hands of God and the sword.' The assembly howled out its joy and cheerfully voted Guthrie's accusations into a committee heavily biased in his favour.

The evidence was examined, and naturally believed, in an atmosphere of relative calm that was soon to be shattered once more. Rutherford, who had simmered in silence too long, suddenly intervened: 'What Scripture does warrant, an Assembly may not discharge; but privy meetings for exercise of religion, Scripture warrants' - and he quoted chapter and verse. Seaforth, perceiving the dangers inherent in a theological debate between Guthrie and Rutherford, hastily told him not to 'bother' the assembly with his 'logic syllogisms' and thus steered the debate into safer - and spicier - channels. At length, as a late northern night fell, the argument receded into a sub-committee of five ministers, including Guthrie, Baillie and Dickson, who were ordered to produce an act by the morning.

It is interesting that Baillie, who was obviously not a Brownist, and Dickson, who had left open the suspicion that he was, agreed on essentials. They believed that the assembly should, in one way or another, enact the compromise of 1639. But Guthrie, whose ideological views were not unlike Baillie's, dismissed this as an inadequate trifle. Limitations, as he had said before, would eventually be 'introductive' of the 'thing limited'; had not caveats brought in the bishops? His version sprang from an alternative approach. The sectaries disguised their conventicles as family exercises and he suggested that an earlier act on the subject, passed in the previous assembly, should be repeated with the addition of a clause specifically confining such exercises to the members of a single family. Dickson, who was perhaps too tired to change his tactics, objected that this would forbid genuine religious discussion among neighbours and it seemed that the wrangling would go on. The solution, which emerged in the cool light of an early dawn, turned out to be almost fatuously simple. Baillie, who was still awake, noticed that Guthrie's act was so badly drafted that it would not stop anything. It might be true that the Brownists had always called their meetings family exercises; but why should they not call them something else and go on holding them? He convinced Dickson that he could safely accept the act and then induced Guthrie to strengthen it with a few of the limitations - to which Dickson could scarcely object. The resulting act was a rather silly hotchpotch, but it served to keep the assembly quiet and that was all that Baillie really wanted. It was passed unanimously as soon as the assembly had re-convened. It was perhaps fitting that nobody should have taken much notice of it. The assembly did not order its publication and this allowed the Clerk - Wariston's servitor - to ignore it entirely. There was perhaps a fairly general agreement that it would be superseded when the opportunity presented itself.

The Assembly of 1641 was a very different body from its predecessor. It was intended for St Andrews and it met in Edinburgh; the north was less well represented. Henderson was its moderator and Argyll was one of his assessors. The agenda was carefully prepared beforehand; debate, at least on the Brownist issue, was ruthlessly restricted; the necessary acts glided through the assembly in a single afternoon and nobody, radical or conservative, presumed to vote against them. Broadly speaking, it was agreed to encourage genuine family exercises, to forbid any form of meeting that might 'breed error, scandal, schisms, neglect of duties and particular callings and such other evils as are the works not of the spirit but of the flesh', and to forbid any novation in doctrine, worship or government that had not first been examined and allowed in a general assembly. This was comprehensive enough, but it did not condemn privy meetings as such. It was very similar to the compromise of 1639 and it was achieved so effortlessly that it must have made the antics of 1640 seem almost unreal - as in a sense they were (⁵).

Rutherford's sectarian syllogism was uttered, probably in some exasperation, in defence of his own past and the friends that might still be useful in the future. It was more or less common ground that conventicles, however undesirable they might be in the abstract, were justifiable in times of persecution; this was a proposition which neither Henderson nor Baillie - and perhaps not even Guthrie himself - would entirely have rejected.But the privy kirk, as Rutherford knew, was an invaluable reservoir of revolutionary energy and it would have been absurd for him to have contrived its destruction. To him, as to Wariston, the revolution was a continuing process and the privy kirks might still find their place in it. It was vital to preserve them, just as it was vital to control them. It is no accident that his celebrated syllogism was perpetrated at the very time when he was, as his letters show, preparing a treatise against such Brownish 'conceits' as the 'independency of single congregations, (and) a church of visible saints' (⁶). Rutherford was ambivalent on the issue, but he was neither a sectary nor, in any deliberate sense, was he contriving a schism. During the thirties he remained in the church until he was driven out of it; at the Restoration, as death and defeat drew near, his advice to his brethren was clear and unequivocal: they should not divide. Rutherford, like Melville before him, sought to use the privy kirks in the service of a clerical church.

The idea of a 'state opposite to a state' had thrust itself into the closing debate of the Aberdeen Assembly when, to Baillie's dismay, the radicals had contrived to reopen the argument about conventicles. An innocent sounding overture, proposing the trial of suspected Brownists by the Commissioners recently appointed to attend the next Parliament, filtered its way anonymously through the Committee of the Bills onto the floor of the assembly. It later transpired that the overture had been made by John MacClelland, a radical minister from Galloway who was known to have favoured privy meetings. It was, in its most obvious aspect, a rather transparent radical manoeuvre to remove the operation of the act from the ordinary courts of the church and to place it in the hands of a central committee, consisting largely of establishment ministers with a vested interest in the pretence that the privy kirk did not exist. Guthrie saw this one coming and mustered his cohorts to defeat it; but the issue had another aspect and Guthrie may have realised this as well. For he also defeated the first attempt to invest this central committee with real power. It was an early, indeed a premature, attempt to create an executive for the church - for the state opposite to a state. This was the Commission of the General Assembly in embryo (⁷).

The first recorded Commission was established by the Assembly of 1641 to lobby the Parliament which met in the same year. It began its work as soon as the Assembly had ended and it went on as long as the Parliament continued. It was busy enough, sitting more than sixty times in just over three months, for the Parliament was greatly concerned with the patrimony of the church; but the Commission's powers were as limited as its purpose. It was essentially a pressure group rather than an executive. It usually respected the sensitivities of a feudal Parliament, which jealously guarded its own prerogative, and the evident wishes of the ruling elders who were still an integral part of the structure of the church ([8]).

The Parliament of 1641 was not unduly concerned about this novel clerical body which continually badgered it about money, and it was at best ordinarily generous in its response. Henderson successfully used his influence to gain the small bishopric of Orkney for the University of Edinburgh, though it was 'spoiled by prior gifts', and the more generous revenues of St Andrews archbishopric and priory for the University there. Elsewhere Aberdeen got its bishopric, but Glasgow had to rest content with Galloway, since its own archbishopric was reserved for the Duke of Lennox as part of the price of his consent to the settlement as a whole. Most of the rest went to uses that Melville would have regarded as profane. A princely income of 4,000 merks from the Chapel Royal went to Henderson, who was already getting £1,200 as one of the ministers of Edinburgh - and some of his comrades plainly regarded this as profane as well. The fate of the mighty abbacy of Arbroath, which Charles had once earmarked for the bishopric of Brechin, was even more revealing. It was granted *in liberam regalitatem* as an endowment for a new earldom ([9]). On 18th November 1641 a 'contented King' left his feudal classes 'content'.

It is arguable that the architects of the settlement of 1641 expected their work to last, and yet its effective life would be short; in a year it would be dying; in a decade it would almost be dead. The flavour of it would linger on to the end of the century and beyond; but it was doomed to fail in its own day. This is not to assert that it was intrinsically unsound. It could reasonably have been maintained that power had been restored to its centre, which was in Edinburgh rather than in Whitehall, and to its appropriate level among a feudal caste that was showing a remarkable capacity to adjust itself to the underlying changes of the period. The new estate of the sub-vassal, or so it might have been argued, was gradually being absorbed - first by the King, then by the Tables and now by a Parliament which only sought to exclude it from the topmost levels of power - into the existing structure. It is true that Wariston and the devotees of the privy kirk might have rejected this, but the limitations of their power had just been painfully exposed. They could prosper only when King Charles reached for an English sword.

The eighth demand presented to the King by the Scottish Commissioners during the negotiations for the Large Treaty in 1640 and 1641 had attempted to place Scotland in the wider context of Britain as a whole, to resolve the difficult triangular relationship between the King and his two kingdoms. One group of proposals, which sought free trade and mutual naturalisation between Scotland and England, belonged to a more peaceful age and, though they were agreed with the King in the Engagement, little more was heard of them; but the rest belonged to their own time. It was asked first and foremost that the King and the Prince should reside periodically in Scotland, that they should keep a number of 'Scottish men of respect' in constant attendance at Court and that they should employ only Protestants there. A further group of proposals stipulated that neither kingdom would make war on the other without the consent of its Parliament and that commissioners should be appointed 'for conserving of the peace in the intervals betwixt Parliaments'. Yet another demanded that neither kingdom should 'engage in war with any foreign nation without the mutual consent of both' and that each should assist the other against 'all foreign invasion'. The Court would become a supra-national institution, composed of individuals from each of the two kingdoms, but itself belonging to neither of them. The King would rule each of his kingdoms separately through its own Parliament. Each would retain its own customs, its own laws and its own institutions; the two governments would each have a free hand in everything except foreign policy and defence. [10]

These proposals, which were the essence of the Eighth Demand, can reasonably be regarded as a logical development from the internal programme of the Supplicants. But another, though also included in it, was more ambiguous. It sought 'unity in religion and uniformity in church government as a special means for preserving of peace betwixt the two kingdoms'. Taken literally, this was harmless enough. It merely expressed the opinion - almost a platitude in an age of religious wars - that diversity of religion was the enemy of peace. But it would become a stupid contradiction if its realisation became a condition of peace, and it is perhaps significant that it was hastily dropped as soon as it met real opposition. In February 1641 the Scottish Commissioners, almost certainly to please the puritan zealots of St Antholin's among whom they were quartered during their stay in London, allowed Henderson to compose a 'little quick paper' proclaiming the constancy of their 'zeal against episcopacy'; it was implied that the Scottish army would remain on the Tyne until the English bishops had fallen. St Antholin's was 'infinitely well pleased'; but elsewhere the reaction was terrible. The King, who had already agreed to abolish episcopacy in Scotland, was 'enraged at it' and only with difficulty dissuaded from branding it as seditious. Almost everybody turned on the Scots, ' many of whom we never doubted did join . . . to malign us and, though they loved not the bishops, yet, for the honour of their nation, they would keep them up rather than we strangers should pull them down'. If the bishops had been in danger, the Scots had saved them for a while; the 'worker by contraries' had gone into reverse. The demand for uniformity was immediately watered down. The Commissioners protested that it would be no less than 'usurpation . . . for one kingdom or church, were it never so mighty . . . to give laws . . . to another free and independent church and kingdom . . . were it never so mean' and that they did not presume to dictate to England, 'the greater kingdom'. But, though they 'loved not to play the bishop in another man's diocese', they could not be 'careless' in that which 'concerned' both kingdoms. They went back to the literal meaning of the original demand, to the meaning which the conservatives had always attached to it. As the Earl of Lothian had written early in the previous November, 'We hope and pray that they may get a reformation like ours . . . but we come not to reform church nor state; we have no such vain thoughts.' But Wariston had been entertaining such thoughts for some time. He had had two separate meetings with members of the English opposition as early as the summer of 1638 and he had been careful to keep them quiet; Baillie, for example, had remained unaware of them. His confidant, David Dickson, had, however ill-advisedly, boasted of them in the Aberdeen Assembly. Wariston and Dickson were both extremists and, in 1641, they still had little support. But there were already two quite distinct attitudes towards the tortured issue of uniformity, just as there were two conflicting views of the nature of Scottish society (11).

During the course of their negotiations, the Commissioners had described the Eighth Demand as the 'chiefest of all (their) desires . . . unto which all the former seven articles' - that is the whole of the internal Scottish settlement - were 'as many preparatives' (12). They saw it as absolutely vital to the interests of Scotland; in a sense their difficulties had arisen from the imperfections of the Union of 1603 and the Eighth Demand was intended to rectify them. It would surely have occurred to a calculating Scotsman that the opportunity was unusually favourable. Scotland, traditionally divided, had just achieved at least the appearance of unity. England, so often united, was about to tear itself apart. It was natural that the Scots should offer their services in mediation and that the Eighth Demand, or as much of it as could be negotiated, should become the price of a settlement. It was no less natural that Hamilton, perhaps the only prominent politician with an interest in all three parties, should have initiated the policy; but it is interesting that he enjoyed the whole-hearted support of Argyll. The correspondence between them, covering the greater part of 1642, overflowed with Argyll's approval: 'I heartily wish you could light on the mid-way, that all matters may be brought to a happy conclusion for his Majesty's honour and contentment of his people which, joined, bring peace but, divided, we can expect little quiet.'

It is fair to say that Argyll was still favouring a policy of neutrality when the correspondence closed in October; but there had been a subtle change in the meantime. In May, the 'Banders' - a coalition between some of the signatories of the Bond of Cumbernauld and the nobles who had supported Charles during the Bishops' Wars - demanded that Scotland should support the King of Scots in his English quarrel. Their motives were mixed, but it is obvious that they were moved by jealousy of Argyll and Hamilton and perhaps more particularly by the rumours of a marriage alliance between them. This was a faction fight which seemed likely to fizzle out for lack of support; but it gave the kirk, which had slowly been receding into the background, its chance to recover. Argyll, who was easily alarmed, resolved to prepare a secure line of retreat. He went in an accommodating frame of mind to the Assembly which met at St Andrews. He resolved to resume as far as he could his old understanding with the leading ministers, some of whom favoured an alliance with their brethren in England and thus with the Long Parliament. In a sense he was hoping to win them over to his own policy of mediation; but he knew that he must make concessions and his next letter to Hamilton, short, muddled and embarrassed as it was, clearly implied that he intended to make them: 'I believe they (the ministers) are very honest men' (13).

Some at least of the ministers intended to discuss patronage and the privy kirk and, although these were successfully buried in committee, Argyll was not able to prevent the renewal of the Commission of the General Assembly.

The Commission was not, as we have seen, unprecedented; but it had previously been of 'small use'. It was now, Baillie rejoiced, likely to become a 'constant judicatory and very profitable'. Its powers were large, for it would exercise the executive, as distinct from the legislative, powers of the general assembly for the period allowed to it; it was indeed 'of so high a strain that to some it was terrible already'. Indeed its powers were as imposing as its purpose. It was given the task of furthering the 'great work in the union of this island in religion and church government'. A committee of ministers and elders, with the imposing organisation of the church at its disposal, was given leave to meddle in the highest affairs of state. We may imagine that Samuel Rutherford allowed himself a smile.

The immediate impact of the Commission was small, since the church was still outwardly committed to the policy of mediation in England. But this was bound to be temporary. The church may or may not have been interested in the Eighth Demand as a whole, but it was vitally concerned with uniformity. It was making a demand which the two Houses of the English Parliament could at least undertake to satisfy and which the King could only refuse. It implied the creation of an alliance between the Scots and the English Parliament and Hamilton was bound to react to it. In September, he persuaded the Conservators of the Peace to invite Henrietta Maria to reside in Scotland. At first glance it may seem odd that an undoubtedly protestant country should have wanted a Queen who was known to be a militant papist. It was presumably confident that powerful advisers, headed by Argyll and Hamilton, would keep her from the paths of temptation; but this was not the point, or at least the only point. Henrietta would shed part of her identity in the act of crossing the Border. She would become the Queen in Parliament and thus a substitute for the King in Parliament who was detained by the necessary affairs of his other kingdom. As the wife of the King, she would preserve the essential link with the Crown and thus with England; as the Queen in Parliament, she would be the ruler of an autonomous Scotland. Her adopted country would be able to steer its own course through the rocks of the English conflict; it could turn aside the King's commands without incurring the taint of treason and it could preserve its independence of Westminster because it need no longer fear the vengeance of a victorious King. It was an imaginative scheme conceived in accordance with the principles of 1641 and it was widely supported at the time; not only Argyll but Wariston, who was also mending his fences, lent his name to it. King Charles, perhaps suspecting blackmail, chose, surely unwisely, to decline it ([14]).

The news of the King's refusal reached Edinburgh at a time when his successes in the field were adding to Scottish fears. After Edgehill and the march on London, the consequent appeal from Westminster was bound to find a sympathetic audience. The danger would pass - and the ardour of the Houses as quickly cool - but its impact was profound. Argyll, spurned by the King and solicited by the Parliament, left Hamilton and attached himself - with a few silent reservations - to the church. Early in January 1643, Pym's agent in Edinburgh urged his master to act: 'The coals now want only blowing from England and this kingdom will be soon on fire.' Hamilton stuck to his original policy, though now with the support of the more amenable of the Banders rather than Argyll. He joined with Traquair to sponsor the Cross Petition, which adhered to the original interpretation of the Eighth Demand. After asking that the Demand as a whole should be 'timeously prosecuted', the petitioners went on to say, 'We cannot but heartily wish that this work of union, so happily begun, may be crowned and strengthened by the unity of church government . . . but . . . noways intending thereby to pass our bounds in . . . setting . . . limits to his Majesty and the two Houses.' It was not, they said, their duty to 'prescribe . . . laws of reformation to our neighbour kingdom'. Hamilton assented to the abstract notion that uniformity would be conducive to peace; but he dismissed as absurd the policy of buying it at the cost of an alliance with the King's English enemies. Union, he claimed, 'could never truly be conceived to be intended to weaken the head whereby it is knit together' ([15]).

Argyll might well have agreed with this but the Commission did not. They told the Council, to whom the Cross Petition had been directed, that no supplication concerning 'unity of religion or trenching upon the Covenant' should be considered, 'unless it came in the direct and ordinary way from the General Assembly or their commissioners' ([16]). Wariston's day was surely dawning and the Cavalier summer of 1643 completed his triumph. Three armies converged inexorably on London. The Borders were threatened by the Earl of Newcastle with an army largely officered by Roman Catholics. At York, where it was based, the Queen, who might have held her Court in Edinburgh, was intriguing with Antrim and a group of Scottish malcontents for a Highland rising backed by papists from Ulster. In July the younger Vane took ship for Leith with instructions to negotiate a 'strict union and league of mutual defence' with the Scots; he was authorised to dangle an alluring half-promise of uniformity before them.

Both the Convention of Estates and the Assembly were in session when he arrived on 7th August, and both hastened to set up committees to negotiate with him. One man, who was shire commissioner for Midlothian as well as Clerk to the Assembly, was common to both committees. At about the same time, this same man also attended a series of private meetings convened to discuss the general strategy to be adopted. They were held in Henderson's chamber and those attending included, as well as the Moderator and the Clerk, the 'prime nobles' and several others of whom Baillie was fortunately one. It was clearly a meeting of the Moderator's Assessors and it strongly suggests that the Assembly, rather than the Estates, was taking the initiative. It is possible that Argyll was present at these meetings; but Baillie, who admired him and always mentioned him when he said or did anything important, does not say that he was there; it is at least clear that he was not playing a leading role. However this may be, it is certain that he was on neither of the two committees and almost as certain that he did nothing of consequence, either in the Assembly or the Convention, from late July onwards.

As the moment of crisis approached, Argyll receded into the shadows ([17]).

The meeting must at least have agreed about one thing. Scotland was, apart from a small army already heavily engaged in Ulster, defenceless in an armed camp. It was inevitable that she should arm herself; but, 'of the way, there was much difference of opinion'. At first, 'all were bent to go as redders and friends of both, without siding altogether with the Parliament'. The policy of mediation from an attitude of neutrality was 'made so plausible' that nearly everybody seemed likely to support it. Indeed it had many advantages. The interests of the northern kingdom, it may well have been argued, could best be served by keeping the English divided; total victory, whoever gained it, would confront Scotland with a united, armed and probably hostile England. The Eighth Demand, whether in its conservative or its radical form, would be lost. It may well have been added that Vane had been a long time coming; he was obviously reluctant to call for Scottish assistance and his promises should be viewed with suspicion. But Wariston 'alone' showed 'the vanity of that motion', and it is not difficult to guess at the points he must have made. The King, or so it seemed, was on the brink of victory; unless the Houses were quickly and effectively supported, he would win. Even if mediation was the ultimate purpose - and many in his audience plainly thought it was - it would still be best to support the weaker party. Besides, the Parliament would pay for the army; could the Scots pay for it themselves? It was a powerful appeal and the solitary Wariston, skilfully pointing his argument to the anxieties of the moment, carried the day. If the church was overtaking the state, Wariston was supplanting Argyll as the leader of both ([18]).

The terms, and indeed the form, of the alliance had still to be decided. It was generally assumed that there would be some reference to uniformity but there agreement ceased. The attitude of the Houses was known to be ambiguous; some of the members were 'for keeping a door open . . . to Independency'; others, and this was perhaps the more important consideration, wanted an Erastian church, dependent in the last resort on Parliament. The Scottish Commissioners, on this as on other points, tended to want binding guarantees of one kind or another and Wariston - and we may surely assume that he was responsible - used this anxiety to carry the revolution one stage further. He boldly countered the English preference for a 'civil league' - which could readily be repudiated if circumstances changed - by demanding a 'religious Covenant' to be sworn by Englishman and Scotsman alike.

The wording of the new Covenant was a matter of some delicacy. There were probably three main versions, all differing from each other on points of substance. The original Scottish draft, which had probably been agreed between the committees from church and state, was essentially a bargaining position. The exact wording can only be inferred, but it almost certainly read substantially as follows: we swear to endeavour ' . . . the preservation of the true Protestant reformed religion in the church of Scotland in doctrine, worship, discipline and government according to the Word of God; (and) the reformation of religion in the Church of England; (and to) bring the Churches of God in both nations to the nearest conjunction and uniformity in religion, confession of faith, form of church government, directory of worship and catechising'. The vital phrase was 'according to the Word of God', which was placed in the clause relating to the Church of Scotland and not repeated anywhere else. Burnet, writing long after the event, stated that Vane insisted on 'reforming according to the Word of God' and that he succeeded in inserting a phrase to this effect in the clause concerning the Church of England. The Scots offset this by adding 'the example of the best reformed churches' to Vane's amendment [19]. The Covenant was ratified in this, its second, version by the Convention and the Assembly on 17th August and was promptly despatched to Westminster for the approval of the English Parliament, which debated it during the first two weeks of September. The Scottish Commissioners found themselves in a bargaining situation weakened by the relief of Gloucester and the impending end of the campaigning season. The Houses were safe for another winter and their resolution stiffened. They insisted on a further change which the Scots were powerless to resist; they struck out 'according to the Word of God' from the clause relating to Scotland and left it in the clause concerning England. A phrase which had originally been included to reinforce Scottish certainties survived only to emphasise English doubts [20].

This at least is the obvious inference from a complex transaction, of which too little evidence has survived. But is it the whole of the truth? For what was the Word of God? In Scotland, it might have been argued, it was enshrined in the *Second Book of Discipline* and the legislation of the Melvillian assemblies of the previous century, now happily laid bare by the annulment of the acts of intervening assemblies which had qualified it. This was the approach which the clerical delegates to the Westminster Assembly would follow. But was this the unequivocal voice of the Church of Scotland? It surely was not. For, although the Glasgow Assembly had borrowed the Melvillian theory of the church's independence of the Crown, it had conspicuously failed, indeed it had not tried, to establish the clerical church implicit in the Book of Discipline; in the Glasgow Assembly, the Word of God had abolished episcopacy in the interests of a church penetrated, at least at the upper levels, by the feudal classes. In England, the Word of God was even more debatable, trapped as it was in a multitude of tracts, as infallible as they were incompatible, so much so indeed that none of them could be taken seriously. For the time being at least, the greater part of political England was committed to the relatively sober proposition that the church, whatever its exact form, would be subordinate to the Long Parliament. To the Houses, though not of course to the kirk, the Westminster Assembly was an entertaining sideshow into which the forces of religious controversy could be diverted until the war had been won. The meaningful forces involved in the debate were the English Parliament on the one hand and the two sets of Commissioners sent from Scotland by the Assembly and the Convention on the other [21].

The Commissioners from the Convention were outwardly committed to the pursuit of uniformity, but their purposes were essentially civil and military. They were appointed to deal with the Long Parliament and to participate in the Committee of Both Kingdoms which would attempt, not always successfully, to direct the several armies gathered to oppose the King. As far as the Scots were concerned, the Committee seemed to mark the partial achievement of an old aspiration which was only distantly related to the ministers' search for uniformity. The Eighth Demand had assumed a supranational Court which would include a strong minority of Scotsmen acceptable to the King in Parliament; defence and foreign policy would be neither English nor Scottish but British. The Committee of Both Kingdoms, though it did not actually use the imposing range of powers which the Scots had claimed for it, was plainly intended to develop in this direction. It might, in Scottish eyes at least, grow into the court of a defeated, chastened and incidentally Covenanted King.

And yet the revolution itself had made this more difficult. A defeated King, or indeed his Court, could scarcely be entrusted with the command of either the English or the Scottish army; victorious Parliaments, though they might be capable of the trust, were the guardians of autonomy rather than the voices of union. A revealing Scottish solution emerged early in 1645 from the stormy prelude to the Treaty of Uxbridge. The two armies would retain their own national identities, but each would be ruled by a supranational committee dominated by the representatives of its own nation but including delegates from the other. It would become very difficult for either kingdom to make war on its neighbour and this was the essential preoccupation of feudal Scotland. But it is easy enough to understand English reluctance. In the 1640s, the significance of armies was largely internal. There was already a Scottish army in the heart of England and its intentions were seen with a suspicion that supranational commissions, nicely balanced though they might be, would never dispel. The Houses were haunted by the spectre, originally raised by the demand for uniformity, of Scottish interference in the internal affairs of England. Their humiliating dependence on a foreign army provided one - and arguably the most important - of the several motives behind the creation of the New Model Army and thus served to change the direction and ultimately the nature of the English revolution. The new army was able to call upon the reserves of English patriotism and to turn them to a revolutionary purpose. In England, the necessities of war and revolution were shifting the balance of power away from a constitutional Parliament towards a radical army; in Scotland a rather similar process was driving a feudal state into the arms of an increasingly revolutionary church.

The ministers who represented the kirk in the Westminster Assembly might well have tolerated the continuance of one kind of Parliament in England and another in Scotland; they would probably have accepted a covenanted King Charles as the titular head of both; but this was not their true purpose. For they went on to imply that all three must depend on a church, initially merely British but ultimately all-embracing, founded on the principles of the *Second Book of Discipline*. On the face of it, this was preposterous. On one reading of the facts, the church established in the Glasgow Assembly had defied Melvillian theory in the interests of a feudal state and, in the late thirties, this had been the reading that had mattered. But Wariston had had the future in mind. The work of the Glasgow Assembly had been as ambiguous as the National Covenant itself had been. It was, as we have seen, capable of another and more radical meaning and the events of the middle forties at least fostered the illusion that this would prevail. Revolutions, once started, seem to acquire a momentum of their own, and now two separate revolutions were busily feeding each other. In the inspired confusion of revolutionary London anything seemed possible, at least while Leven's army held its own. The ministers of the kirk boldly assumed a Melvillian church in Scotland and proposed to extend it to England in the hope that it might eventually be re-exported back to their own country. It was an act of faith like the one which had moved Wariston to challenge the Lords of the Covenant in 1638.

Their defeat was fashioned by Cromwell's army at Naseby. The Scottish army, once indispensable, was now a liability and the truth disclosed itself with an awful clarity. The new Church of England as established by the Long Parliament in 1645 and 1646 was neither Scottish nor Melvillian in its inspiration. Its outward appearance was rather consciously presbyterian and it included a hierarchy of courts that looked very like kirk sessions, presbyteries and synods. But its general assembly could meet only when Parliament chose, while the chain of appeal led not to the assembly but to Parliament itself. In any case, its powers were confined to a limited range of carefully specified sins - and the sin of sectarianism was not one of them. Indeed any controversial case would be referred by the parish concerned directly to a panel of lay commissioners appointed by the Houses. Baillie as always had a phrase for it; it was a 'lame Erastian presbytery' utterly dependent on the whim of the civil power; it would allow a measure of toleration if its masters so decided. It was indeed a logical development from English parliamentary puritanism [22].

The arrival of King Charles in Leven's army briefly interrupted the Scottish decline and secured the removal of the lay commissioners. It is true that they were replaced by a committee of Parliament, but its powers were to last only for three years. This represented an important tactical victory for the ministers, for it allowed Baillie and Gillespie to commend the new church to their comrades in Scotland. The assembly of 1647 duly accepted it as an adequate response to the Covenant, with one rather pointed and obviously significant qualification. The clause in the Confession of Faith dealing with the power of the civil magistrate to convene assemblies was to apply only to kirks 'not settled or constituted in point of government'. It emphatically did not apply to a firmly entrenched church, as the kirk itself was deemed to be, in which assemblies could be called by the 'intrinsical power received from Christ' [23]. It was plainly hoped that the young church of puritan England, once it had outgrown its early weakness, would develop in this direction. But was this really likely? It was obvious enough that the Houses could renew the powers of the committee whenever they wished; indeed they would actually do so in 1648. If England was to have a national church at all, it would inevitably be an erastian church.

Argyll, who personally delivered the assent of political Scotland in June 1646, may have had fewer reservations about this. His famous speech to the Glasgow Assembly had warned it of the dangers of a clerical dictatorship. Since then the chieftain of the Clan Campbell had helped to manage a long series of assemblies and he may still have believed that he could go on doing so. Scottish erastianism might take a different form from its English counterpart, but the result - a church open to the intervention of lay politicians - was much the same. In any case, the demand for uniformity, as it had originally been framed by the Lords of an earlier Covenant, had rested on the assumption that the English church was, at least in the last resort, the business of the English themselves. They had now spoken and Argyll could scarcely object. He even accepted, with every appearance of equanimity, the probability that some independent congregations would function outside the national structure. He rejected a 'lawless liberty in religion', but he deliberately denied the right to 'persecute . . . piety and peaceable men who cannot, through scruple of conscience, come up in all things to the common rule'. He embraced a church which the English zealot, whether presbyterian or independent, was bound to reject, but which the English politician, whether 'Independent' or 'Presbyterian', could accept conscientiously enough (²⁴).

The new church in England was thus supported or at least tolerated by the politicians of both kingdoms, but it was dismissed as inadequate, irrelevant or actively vicious by the radicals to whom they had appealed and on whom they now increasingly depended. Above all it was rejected, together with all the other proposals that came with it, by the King himself. But Charles, after years of fruitless negotiation with his English adversaries, eventually consented to re-open his dialogue with the Scottish magnates. He agreed, in the Engagement concluded with Loudoun, Lanark and Lauderdale at Carisbrooke, to allow the new church to continue for an experimental period of three years, after which its final form would be decided - after yet another consultation with the divines of all respectable shades of opinion - by the Crown in Parliament. But the three noblemen, true as they were to the attitudes of 1641, saw the eighth demand of that year as a single whole and they energetically explored the possibility of a supranational court and here they were fortunate. Charles, discarding his earlier reservations about his freedom to choose his servants, agreed that a third of his entourage would be Scottish 'men of respect'. On top of this, either the King or the Prince would reside in Scotland as his 'occasions' allowed. It was a programme that the magnates could only welcome (²⁵).

But the treaty gave the Engagers what they wanted rather than what they needed. They had told the King that he could expect the loyal support of a united Scotland if he would take the Covenant or agree to enjoin it on all his subjects. Then the alliance that had once come together to defeat him would reform itself to restore him and, in so doing, would purge his kingdoms of the twin vices of sectarianism and malignancy. In Scotland, it would embrace magnate and minister; in England, presbyterians, 'royal' and 'real'. The Covenant, conveniently ambiguous as it was, would mask all differences until an army raised by Scottish magnates had restored King Charles to his English throne. Thereafter - or so it was hoped - he would interpret the Covenant according to the will of those who had put him there. In effect if not in so many words, Charles was asked to take the Covenant and break it later. Only thus, or so it must have been implied, could the peace of two kingdoms torn by civil war be finally renewed. The King's refusal drove the Engagers into a subterfuge even less opaque. As the kirk denounced the

F

proposed invasion as the work of antichrist, the Engagers indignantly protested their virtue. Were not the Houses, threatened as they were by the violence of their own army, in breach of Covenant? Was it not godly to rescue them - to restore them to the innocence of their original intentions? They must invade England in the interests of a once covenanted Parliament and an almost covenanted King ([26]). But these were the words of 1643, when noblemen could still be godly and Parliaments could still be trusted. Now, in 1648, the revolution had moved on. The opposition to the Engagement signalled the simultaneous climax of two revolutions which had hitherto been distinct and would soon diverge again. In both, the substance of power was passing into different hands; in each, the old revolutionary establishment stood aside as if appalled by the confusion it had created.

But the Engagement was also, and perhaps predominantly, the product of purely internal tensions. The elections to the Assembly of 1647 seem to have yielded an unusually large number of future Engagers as ruling elders. They came to the assembly with the evident intention of dividing and ultimately of dominating it. The pretext was neither novel nor inappropriate. One James Simpson, a 'forward pious young man' who was minister of Sprouston, had been courting a 'religious damsel', who was sister-in-law to James Guthrie, the radical minister of the nearby parish of Lauder. They had held 'private meetings and exercises', which had caused 'great offence' to many. It was a familiar story, although this time the conservative forces found a more formidable leader in David Calderwood, who had been young when Melville was ageing and who was now pursuing sectaries with all the energy that he had once directed at the bishops. Calderwood and others - 'honest men opposite to malignants', as Baillie called them - joined with the Engagers to sponsor William Colville as moderator. He stood against Robert Douglas, who had climbed effortlessly enough into the throne left vacant by the death of Henderson. The opposition was formidable indeed, but he, Colville, failed only by the minute margin of four votes; the Engagers were potentially a powerful force in church as well as state ([27]).

This settled, Douglas, whose tongue was as sharp as Henderson's, contrived to divert the main issue into a committee, which duly produced a further version of the usual compromise: '. . . whatsoever have been . . . the fruits of meetings of . . . divers families in times of corruption and trouble, in which case many things are commendable, which otherwise are not tolerable; yet, when God has blessed us with peace and purity of the gospel, such meetings . . . are to be disapproved as tending . . . to the rending . . . of . . . particular congregations and, in progress of time, of the whole kirk'. The necessities of revolutionary unity demanded the discouragement - the word used was mild enough - of conventicles; but the demands of the revolutionary legend were only less insistent and the privy kirk could never be entirely suppressed. And might not the attempt to suppress it be as divisive as the privy kirk itself? The radicals were less numerous than their conservative brethren; but their pulpits were influential and they were solidly entrenched in the revolutionary establishment. In a speech delivered to the Assembly of 1647, Baillie condemned Calderwood, though not actually by name, as a 'cursed soul' whose memory would 'stink to all generations' if he succeeded in dividing the kirk ([28]).

In any event, the course of the opposition to the Engagement provided the privy kirk with a new role. The church revealed itself as a powerful instrument of policy capable, under the direction of the Commission of the General Assembly, of effective concerted action. But the church, united though it almost was, failed in the end. The levy was delayed, but not prevented, and the church was left to lament its weakness. The Engagement, it had said, was sinful and must be opposed. But how could a church, which could not legitimately use the power of the sword, oppose an army? Respectable opinion agreed that it could not. But could Baillie, or even Calderwood, entirely deny the radical remedy? The church could not fight, but the privy kirk could, as it had done in the past and would do again. The Mauchline Rising, abortive though it would almost certainly be, was the logical sequel. In mid-June, some two thousand 'slashing communicants' met on Mauchline Moor. They consisted of 'yeomen' from Clydesdale, of deserters from all over the south-west, and of local farmers from Kyle and Cunningham. There were no magnates among them, but no fewer than 1,200 of them came on horseback. They were men of some substance, but they probably accepted the leadership of the seven ministers who were present and who had certainly organised the meeting. One of these was John Nevay, the most radical member of the Commission, and it is obvious that he was sponsoring a seventeenth century manifestation of the privy kirk.

It is interesting that the local magnates had held an entirely separate meeting of their own at Riccarton two days previously. They seem to have discussed resistance; but, in contrast to the rival gathering at Mauchline, they certainly decided against it. Their reluctance was a reflection of the attitude of Argyll, who had met Eglinton and Cassillis during the course of a tour through Fife and the south-west two weeks earlier and who had now retired to Inveraray in the hope that the storm would pass him by. His attitude to the Engagement had indeed been ambiguous from the beginning. He had been represented by Loudoun in the initial negotiations with the King and, though he was in no way committed to the agreement reached, he was slow to reject it. Indeed the blandishments of the Engagers were intended less to reconcile a kirk that was becoming increasingly irreconcilable than to lure Argyll and his friends away from it and possibly to split the church in the process. Argyll's dilemma was real. He had to choose between his long friendship with Hamilton and all that this implied, and his alliance, cemented in the long years of war and revolution, with the leading ministers of the kirk. His decision to lead the parliamentary opposition to the Engagement was plainly a difficult one and it is obvious that he was not prepared to go any further. He firmly rejected armed resistance and persuaded his colleagues to follow his example. The behaviour of the two Campbell regiments is revealing. One turned north to watch clans - and this was uncontroversial; the other carried the standard of the Marquis of Argyll southwards to Preston and defeat; it was decimated in the service of the Engagers ([29]).

The defeat of Hamilton's army naturally transformed these attitudes. Argyll marched his remaining regiment back to Stirling, where the Castle was held by the Engagers. The privy kirk re-assembled itself in even greater numbers and made for the capital, where it placed itself under the command of David Leslie and the minority of the Committee of Estates which had not supported the Engagement. The Commission of the Kirk re-activated the pulpits and it seemed that the revolutionary establishment was back in the saddle. But this was hardly true. General Munro, whose army from Ulster had formed the rearguard of Hamilton's forces, missed the battle and returned to Scotland with his regiments - all seasoned troops - intact. Moving swiftly, he avoided Edinburgh and made straight for Stirling, where he scattered the Campbells, relieved the Castle and secured his communications with the conservative north. Leslie, who clearly mistrusted his irregulars, hesitated to challenge him and offered negotiations. It is possible that the generals would have agreed among themselves; but the church, and perhaps the humiliated Argyll, wanted a victory which it lacked the resources to win. In the meantime, Cromwell had followed Munro to the Border, where he paused to assess the balance of forces. He was pressed from London to ignore them, apparently on the assumption that they would cancel each other out, leaving the English to settle their own internal arguments free of further Scottish intervention. But this course, rational though it may have seemed from a distance, was rejected by the man on the spot. Cromwell perceived that the Engagers had the armed strength to retrieve Scotland - and thus possibly to invade England again - whenever they wished ([30]). He stayed where he was and let fall the broadest of hints that he would respond to an invitation. As soon as he got it, he hastened to Edinburgh and remained there until the Engagers had surrendered. He then installed the remnant of the Committee of Estates as a provisional government on the understanding that it would finish the Engagers once and for all.

The new puppet government was anxious enough to do his bidding. Argyll was no longer the masterful figure of 1641. He had lost none of his political skill, but the aura of invincibility which once had gathered around him had been dispelled by Montrose; while the Engagers, despite their anxiety to conciliate him, had finally exposed his impotence. The Act of Classes, by excluding the Engagers from political life, left him, if only by default, with the monopoly of power which he had almost achieved from his own resources a decade earlier. He introduced the act with a bitter hatred that surely sprang from a knowledge of his own weakness. It would, he snarled, 'break the malignants' teeth'; he left Wariston to break their jaws.

Wariston and his friends among the ministers must have seen the act rather differently. Argyll was seeking to increase the power of his faction in a feudal state that was plainly in decline; the ministers could rejoice in the decline for its own sake. In its most obvious aspect, the Act of Classes merely excluded the Engagers from a whole series of national and local offices which would henceforth be held by their opponents. The act, perhaps reflecting the embarrassment of those who made it, was so badly drafted that its broader meaning remains doubtful, but one clause made provision for persons excluded from 'their heritable offices', while the list of offices included 'sheriff courts' and 'bailies of regalities'. It is possible that the ministers who whispered into the Clerk's left ear were preparing an assault on heritable jurisdiction as such; it is certain that they damaged the system by demoralising a high proportion of those who operated it. As the state declined, the church could only prosper. The Engagers were to be excluded for a term varying with the gravity of their offence; but this would not be the end of their ordeal. They would then have to satisfy not only the state but the church as well of the 'change of their malignant principles'. The church was given a veto over political appointments. Nearly three months later, the Chancellor of the ancient kingdom of Scotland did penance in St Giles for his sins, long recanted and surely expiated, in the negotiation of the Engagement. It was a symbolic act. A Parliament that had been called to please a foreign general lingered on to become the hangman of the kirk ([31]).

On this level, the victory of the ministers can only be explained by the providential arrival of Oliver Cromwell. But this is merely to say that, in the peculiar circumstances of the late forties, nobody could achieve anything without armed force. The Engagers controlled the Parliament of 1648 from the day that it met; but they could not rule Scotland until they had won over the residue of Leven's old army of the Solemn League; only thus could their levy proceed; only thus could the kirk be frustrated; in a sense, they succeeded only through an ingenious trick perpetrated by General Middleton. In the immediate aftermath of Preston, they, in their turn, were supplanted by the Whiggamores who happened to be able to conjure up an army of irregulars at short notice. But, only a few weeks later, Monro's return to Scotland with a small but disciplined force was enough to restore the balance. The appearance of the New Model in the autumn duly upset it again and installed the kirk in power; its reappearance two years later would leave the kirk in ruins. If it took Cromwell to elevate the ministers, it took Cromwell to knock them down again. The proximate causes were always military; the whole of Britain was locked in a dance of death - and this tells us little about the progress of the revolution in Scotland.

In the summer of 1649, Balfour paused briefly in his narrative to survey the collapse of the carefully ordered society which he had loved - and it is interesting that he did not mention Cromwell at all. The 'chief bellows' of the troubles had been the 'unhappy bishops of both kingdoms', and the 'preachers and ministers' of the revolution had followed their example. They had won the 'conscience of the commonwealth, the rudder which steers the actions, words and thoughts of the rational creature' and now they could use it as they would. The law of the church had been raised above the law of the land; the King's authority had been slighted and now authority itself was questioned; vassals had been seduced and their 'affections' turned against their Lords. The old order was demoralised; its leaders were defeatists wallowing in self-pity. Middleton was later to confess that the Engagers, among whom he had been prominent, had gone into England 'like hypocrites' and had been driven out again 'like thieves'. It was not true, but he thought it was true. A tall story from the long legend of the kirk makes the point convincingly enough. The Duke of Hamilton, on the eve of his departure for England, attended service in his own kirk in the burgh of Hamilton. James

Nasmyth, the second minister and a notorious radical, told him to his face, and in the face of the kirk, that he would never return. Within the year the Duke would be dead and Nasmyth first minister of Hamilton ([32]).

Balfour, in ignoring Cromwell, nonetheless saw the two revolutions as one and it is evident enough that each fed the other. David Dickson had begged the Aberdeen Assembly to avoid an outright condemnation of privy meetings because this could only hinder the pursuit of uniformity; two years later Henderson himself had made the same point. The shape of the debates in the Westminster Assembly had forced Independent and Presbyterian alike into precise definitions and thus into outward disagreement; but, even so, it had not been Independency as such that had been rejected. Rather was it the Erastianism of the Long Parliament and threat of sectarian anarchy if the Parliament should fail. In any event, the stresses of the Engagement sufficed to renew old alignments. The evidence has been obscured by the irrelevant assertion, made long after the event, that the Scots were engaged in a conspiracy to execute Charles I; but it seems clear enough that there was direct contact between the 'rigid party' in Scotland and the 'real presbyterians' of the north of England. A regiment of Lancastrian presbyterians served with distinction under Cromwell at Preston, while their shire committee had been implementing a scorched earth policy which had forced Hamilton's hungry army to disperse in search of food. An outnumbered New Model was able to defeat it piece by piece. It would be too much to assert that the Mauchline Rising had been deliberately staged to delay the Duke's arrival in Carlisle, but it is sufficiently clear that his downfall was engineered by the concerted efforts of two revolutions.

The ministers had one more characteristic in common with the radical Puritans of Cromwell's army. They had, whether consciously or subconsciously, assembled the events of the previous decade into a pattern of success. History was simply one 'step of Reformation' after another. Failure was rare and always temporary; it merely illustrated the truism that the Almighty worked by contraries. History was hurtling towards the Millennium. That this was not true was less important than that the ministers did not know that it was untrue. They surged forward with a confidence that feudal Scotland had long since left behind. They were bound to win; they walked in the sight of God.

The fruits of victory were not slow to appear. In April, the obedient Parliament of 1649 passed 'a most strange act' abolishing the patronage of kirks which had, as Balfour asserted with the licensed over-simplification of the propagandist, 'pertained to laymen since ever Christianity was planted in Scotland'. The act did not pass without incident. The Earl of Buccleuch, the patron of seven kirks in the Borders, left the Parliament protesting that it was 'derogatory of the just rights of the nobility and gentry of the kingdom'. Argyll, who had more patronages than Buccleuch, gave a rather reluctant assent extorted, as Balfour believed, by the fear that the church would desert him if he refused. He may also have reflected that he was in little danger of losing his hold on the church as it had been reformed, perhaps a trifle idiosyncratically, in the frontier province of Argyll. But patronage was more than a local issue; it was a question of principle and one which divided most of the magnates from nearly all of the ministers. The Glasgow Assembly had not required the ministers to subscribe the Books of Discipline because of the 'scruples' of its ruling elders about patronage and the associated problem of the teinds. There was indeed a tacit agreement to avoid both questions as long as the emergency lasted. They were debated in a closed committee of the assembly of 1642 - a year of peace - but neither broke the surface until the Engagers had been defeated. The church of Henderson had been held together by a common determination to avoid fundamentals; but the church of Douglas lived in a different world. In the Parliament of 1649, patronage was abolished on the condition, very deliberately stated, that the ownership of the teinds would not be affected ([33]). But the radical ministers were not impressed and they chose to explore the question on the floor of the assembly which met a few months later. The assembly at once threatened to dissolve into a chaos which it had not known since 1640. Argyll claimed that the ministers already enjoyed a tenth of 'all the rents of the land', although they represented only a hundredth of the inhabitants; they were already wealthy enough; it was 'not good to awake sleeping dogs'. He does not seem to have added that Nasmyth, the minister principally concerned, was rocking the boat, although the Moderator, Robert Douglas, plainly thought he was. But Nasmyth refused to be overawed by words and it was left to 'some lay elders that were barons' to settle the question by reaching for their swords. The demands of the church implied, as they had always implied, a radical revision of the ownership of the church property; but this was not in prospect. The teinds were still secure, although their yield would soon diminish. The Parliament had recently renewed the commission for the augmentation of stipends. It would not, as we shall see, prove ungenerous ([34]).

The abolition of patronage was yet another symbolic act delineating the boundaries between church and state. It was a divisive issue in itself, but it re-activated another no less disruptive. Previously the complex process involved in the admission of a minister to his charge had begun with an agreement between the patron and the minister concerned. Now nobody had the initiative and everybody found a plausible argument. Most of the ministers, it would seem, believed that the 'direction' belonged to the presbytery, the 'election' to the session and the 'consent' to the people. But the consensus was challenged from both directions. Calderwood would have placed the whole process in the hands of the presbytery, with the sole proviso that a majority of the congregation might later dissent. But Rutherford, with the privy kirk in mind, insisted that the right of election itself resided in 'the body of the people'. The resulting act, which bears traces of all these opinions, was complicated to the point of confusion. The initiative would be taken by the presbytery, which also retained its powers of trial and ordination. It would direct a number of candidates to the elders for their approval; but the elders were entitled to add others of their own. The session would then meet, with a minister delegated from the presbytery in the chair, to hold the election. This done, the congregation would be invited to give its consent to the successful candidate. If it did so, the presbytery would then try and, if they found him qualified, admit him. If, on the other hand, the congregation objected, the presbytery was bound to listen to the objection, but entitled to deny it. If, however, a majority of the congregation offered an objection which the presbytery found reasonable, then the presbytery must stage a new election. The act was plainly intended to favour the presbytery - which was incidentally given the right to nominate a minister to a 'malignant' congregation - but the radicals had bored their loopholes in it. According to Baillie, who found the act untidy, the radicals hoped that 'some busy man' in the presbytery would be able, in collusion with 'some leading person in the parish', to get votes in the election for 'any young man' who might 'by desire of the people to the presbytery' be 'put on trials' and, assuming he was found qualified, inevitably elected. Baillie, in common with many ministers, mistrusted the 'people'; they were, he felt, collectively gullible and open to the manipulation of 'busy men' who would soon be called Protesters (³⁵).

Popular election, or even meaningful popular consent, would, as Baillie feared, merely transfer power from a patron to a local bigwig, who might - or might not - be a minister. In the case of a parish of absentee landlords, he might well be a farmer; in an ecclesiastical temporality, he might be a feuar; in a parish dominated by its resident magnates, he might be a baron or even a nobleman. Balfour, here as elsewhere, is obscure, but it seems quite probable that Wariston contrived to persuade a feudal Parliament to abolish patronage with the argument that most of its members would gain by the transaction; barons were many, but patrons were few (³⁶).

The social programme of the new regime was less conspicuous, but its outlines are sharp enough. The Canterburian Parliament of 1633 had, in confirming the Lords of Erection in the possession of their feu duties, reserved the Crown's right to repurchase them, together with the jurisdictions which they represented, at ten times their annual value. This revolutionary process would effectively have abolished the old monastic regalities if it had been completed. In fact it had been interrupted by the revolution and thrown into reverse during the baronial years of the early forties. But the battle was soon to be rejoined. A committee of influential gentlemen, meeting rather mysteriously in the Tailor's Hall in the Cowgate, had lodged an outspoken supplication against the Lords of Erection with the Parliament of 1648; they also appear to have organised petitions against the Engagement and it seems almost certain that they were acting in concert with the Commission. Their supplication, as they must surely have anticipated, was turned aside; but they were back, again with the blessing of the Commission and this time with better hopes of success, in the following year. The ministers' Parliament of 1649, true to the spirit of its Canterburian predecessor, renewed the earlier legislation and extended its scope to include the bishoprics. But it went further than this. The feuars themselves were given the initiative; they could now purchase their own feu duties without waiting for the Crown; they could buy themselves out of the regalities. The ministers were simultaneously exploring the delicate relationship between landlord and tenant. Scotland had long been trampled by marching feet, and boots were expensive; taxation was high and quartering onerous. The burden of both belonged to the heritor; but - or so the ministers alleged - it was too often passed on to the tenant. The remedy was even more interesting than the malady itself. A series of regional committees would examine farmers' grievances and their members, according to the first version, would be named by the presbyteries. In the final version, the vital power of the nomination was entrusted to the Commission itself acting in concert with the shire commissioners of the area concerned. Many of the members thus appointed were reliable barons, but the principle had been established. The welfare of the tenant farmer, like that of the landed vassal, was the business of the church. The ministers would look after their own (³⁷).

The regime of 1649 was using a feudal Parliament to attack feudalism itself. It was a difficult relationship arising out of the peculiar circumstances of the day. Cromwell's defeat of the Engagers had demoralised the greater part of feudal Scotland and it had left the remains at the ministers' disposal. Fundamental decisions were postponed and this suited the gradualists well enough. But the regime did not, and perhaps could not, last. The ministers, delighted with their subservient Parliament, saw the chance of a subservient King - and this brought Cromwell back to torment them. He forced them into choices which they had hesitated to make for themselves. Some went one way and some went another. The monolith was shattered at last.

After his defeat at Dunbar, Leslie had retreated, as the Engagers had done before him, to secure his communications with the conservative north. Stirling became the forward outpost and Perth the capital of a reduced and very different kingdom. The purely secular logic of the situation seemed to demand that the state should repeal the Act of Classes, that the church should forgive the Engagers and that the King, now covenanted and soon to be formally enthroned, should unite them all and drive the invader from his kingdom. *Humanitas* was now covenanted Correction; minister and magnate must recapture the earlier relationships of 1638 and 1641. This was the course that Douglas and the moderates chose to follow, but the zealots were driven to a different conclusion that only the logic of revolution could sustain. The 'worker by contraries', who had once sent Cromwell to reward the faithful, had now sent him back again as a judgment on their faithlessness. The purge, far from being too severe, had not been severe enough. The cause could only be saved if its ruling elite pared itself down to its godliest essence. The revolution had swept away the bishops, Montrose, Huntly and, above all, the hated Engagers who had embraced the cause only to betray it the more thoroughly. The next step was obvious enough. There only remained the Marquis of Argyll and his friends in the Parliament. They must rediscover the pristine innocence of the privy kirk and they must use it to mount a final assault on feudalism itself. Rutherford's sectarian syllogism had been almost irrelevant when it was uttered; it found its relevance now.

The vehicle of revolution was the Westland Army which had been assembled, apparently innocently enough, around the remnants of the western regiments scattered at Dunbar. It was renewed, with the enthusiastic approval of the Committee of Estates and the Commission of the General Assembly, by the committees of its constituent shires. It was supervised, insofar as it was supervised at all, by a 'great committee' not entirely unlike those which had followed the earlier armies of the Covenants. It seemed to differ from its counterpart at Stirling only in its somewhat idiosyncratic refusal - once more countenanced by Committee and Commission alike - to serve under General Leslie. But the Westland Army was less orthodox than its origins. Its shire committees, purged as they had been, included many men of relatively humble origins. In particular, the committee of Clydesdale consisted of a 'few mean persons', and the radical Patrick Gillespie was never far from its deliberations. Similarly, and probably for similar reasons, the committees of Kyle and Cunningham were at the disposal of the ministers who had engineered the Mauchline Rising. The 'great committee' itself may well have had a fairly strong baronial component, but it operated in parallel with a gathering of ministers who called themselves the 'presbytery of the Western Army'. The clerical coterie, which had lured Leslie down from the security of Doon Hill, had formalised itself into a presbytery. It is likely that they exercised discipline within the army; it is certain that they had a moral ascendancy over it. Indeed the Westland Army - like the New Model - was more than a merely military instrument. Its ministers were operating outside the official machinery of the church; its men were drawn from a region famous for its conventicles; it was rather like a gathered church. The 'slashing communicants' rode again (38).

Their commander, Colonel Archibald Strachan, was a sinner who had found repentance in the New Model and respectability as the victor of Carbisdale. He had contrived, under the careful schooling of James Guthrie and Patrick Gillespie, to satisfy the Commission, but he was perhaps a sectary at heart. At first glance, his conduct must have seemed strange. He marched his army off to Dumfries - as far away from General Leslie, the Committee of Estates, the Commission of the Kirk, the great committee and, incidentally, Oliver Cromwell as he could decently take it. Once there, its purpose became obvious enough. Its officers, its gentlemen and its presbytery joined together to issue a manifesto which shattered the monolith beyond hope of repair (39).

The Western Remonstrance rested on the proposition that the King was insincere and that he could not be granted the substance of power until he had given convincing proof of a 'real change' in his principles - and this was a process that could be prolonged to the point of creating a *de facto* republic. It followed inescapably from this that Scottish arms could not be used to restore him to his English throne. The Remonstrance went on to complain that the Estates had used the Engagers to lure the King back to Scotland and that he had been allowed to come with 'malignants' in his entourage. The spirit of the Act of Classes had been violated by the magnates who had passed it. The argument was developed into a sweeping attack on the feudal oligarchy which dominated the Estates. Were they not as self-seeking as the Engagers whom they had excluded? Did they not want the Engagers back again? Had they not 'made their power, places and employments rather a matter of gain and interest to (themselves) than of seeking the good of the cause and the wealth of the people'? How many of them would 'empty themselves' in the service of the revolution? The Remonstrants denied any intention of subverting the 'fundamental government of the kingdom by King and Parliament', still less of adopting 'any levelling way' (40). But this plainly invited qualification. If Argyll and his friends in the Parliament sank into the same swamp that had swallowed the Engagers, who would be left? Would it be Wariston who, if rumour did not lie, had filled himself, or at least his pockets, from the profits of an office conveniently left vacant by the operation of the Act of Classes? Or would it be Strachan, the brewer's boy from Musselburgh? The Parliament of 1652 would surely have been a strange body of men. The Remonstrants wanted a King without power and a Parliament without magnates. All power to the godly of low degree.

The Mauchline Rising and the march of the Westland Army had involved the radical ministers in direct action of a kind that the *Second Book of Discipline* had scarcely envisaged; but it does not follow from this that they wanted direct rule. A purged Parliament would have been left to act out the will of the church. But the Parliament was still unpurged and this could only change the rules. James Guthrie proudly used his pulpit in the strategically vital parish of Stirling to preach defiance and then challenged the right of the Committee of Estates, as distinct from the church itself, to bring him to trial. But Douglas and the Commission, for whom the Parliament was purged enough, conspicuously failed to support him. They claimed that he was guilty of a 'great wronging' of the 'just right' of the state. He was liable to the censure not only of the 'ministry' - the word is incidentally significant - in the 'presbytery', but also of the 'magistrate and the senate'. It was the duty of the Committee to punish any deviation from the policy laid down in the Public Resolutions as the 'antecedent judgment of the kirk'. The Estates were merely adding their 'auxiliatory power for strengthening the church judicatory'. As Rutherford himself had said: 'The King, as nursing father, ought to see that the church's milk be good and wholesome, though it come not out of his own breast.' ([41]) The Commission was asserting the right of the church to determine policy and the duty of the state to enforce it - if necessary, against dissidents within the ministry itself. This was orthodox Melvillian doctrine artfully embellished with a telling quotation from the radical Rutherford. We may imagine that Douglas allowed himself a smile and perhaps the unspoken thought that radical and moderate were not really divided on theological grounds. For the time being|they disagreed about the nature of the state and the composition of its courts - and this was plainly important. One side chose the magnates in the belief, possibly false, that they could still control them. The other rejected them in the belief, probably false, that they were superfluous. The one side treated them with a contempt tempered with caution: they must be pushed, but not too far. The other barely concealed its hostility. In a sense, both parties were seeking the erosion, if not the extinction, of feudal Scotland and, to this extent at least, the differences between them were tactical rather than fundamental.

It is arguable that the ministers were unanimous enough on essentials. They had all taken the Covenants and nearly all had taken them seriously. It was their united belief that the Covenants were the foundation of authority; it was inconceivable to all of them that anyone could hold office in church or state until he had taken both. But both were conveniently ambiguous. The first could be construed as a revolutionary oath or as a bridge between revolution and counter revolution. The second could be understood as yet another manifestation of the vision which

Wariston had shared with Dickson in 1638; in this sense, it was a self-evident truth that would carry the presbytery, or something rather like it, to the ends of the earth. But the moderates, although they had seen the same vision, put a different construction on it. Robert Blair, confronted in 1652 with a blueprint for a Cromwellian union between England and Scotland, likened it - and indeed any other kind of union outside the Covenant - to the 'simple bird embodying with the hawk who would soon eat it up'. He wanted to impose the Covenant on the English because only thus could he save his country from the imperialism of a mighty, if potentially friendly, neighbour. He was reacting to Oliver Cromwell, the ghost of Wentworth and the distant memory of Edward I. It was not too difficult for him to come to terms with the essentially conservative purposes of an aristocracy which was mainly concerned to see a Scottish King restored to his English throne by force of Scottish arms. But there was one condition. The King must take the Covenants and, as far as Scotland was concerned, he must take them sincerely; otherwise the kirk itself was in jeopardy. But England was a different matter, and here suitable gestures would suffice. Four months after Dunbar and eight months before Worcester, the Resolutioners issued a manifesto of their own: 'Let nothing be done through strife or vainglory, but in lowliness of mind. Look not every one upon his own things, but every man upon the things of others, yea, the things of all, the things of God, of the Kirk, of the kingdom and of the King now in Covenant with God and his Kirk and his covenant with the subjects in this kingdom by their mutual oaths passed at his Coronation.' This was a patriotic appeal to a feudal state that must learn, and indeed was learning, to know its place. God came before the church, both came before the kingdom, and all three came before the King. The constitution was now a national Covenant far less ambiguous than the one which had been sworn in 1638. Robert Blair, like the once radical Dickson, became the friend and ally of Robert Baillie who had seen the vision but faintly and mistrusted much that he had seen [42].

6

A State Opposite to a State

IN the wake of Worcester and defeat, Samuel Rutherford, searching as always for the reasons behind God's displeasure, found them in the 'grievous differences of judgments and affections among the Lord's servants'. The kirk, he mused nostalgically, had once been a 'building . . . fitly framed together in love' and he earnestly hoped that the 'breach (would be) made up again that Satan get not advantage therethrough' ([1]). It might fairly have been objected that Rutherford himself had been contentious enough, but this was scarcely the point. The Scottish revolution had matured in a feudal society distorted by the weakness of the Crown. A decentralised environment had almost inevitably provoked a monolithic response; unity had almost become an end in itself; sectarianism and schism were quite simply the instruments of the antichrist. Henderson had devoted most of his revolutionary years to the achievement of the semblance of solidarity with the magnates and the substance of solidarity among the ministers themselves. Douglas had followed his example in more trying circumstances and had not been without success. The differences between Resolutioner and Remonstrant were of long standing; but the final explosion derived less from the argument itself than from the fact that each party had armed force at its disposal. The quarrel was an unfortunate aberration created by external pressures; it was universally lamented and widely condemned; it diminished the strength of the whole; it damaged the mission of the kirk.

This obsession with unity was naturally reflected in a preoccupation with questions of organisation. The kirk was searching for a structure which would centralise power while respecting the parity of pastors. The shape of the original edifice is familiar enough. It consisted of nearly 900 kirk sessions linked to a general assembly through some sixty regional presbyteries and a dozen provincial synods. The kirk session administered a parish and normally met once a week; the presbytery supervised a group of kirk sessions and was still compact enough to meet once or twice a month. The assembly and the synod were relatively remote, meeting once and twice a year respectively. Each element was carefully subordinated to a larger element above it; the membership of each was elected by one or other of the elements beneath it. The church of the first Covenant had the appearance of centralisation, but it was totally inadequate in practice. The assembly could take executive decisions only while it was actually in session - and this was never for long. In practice, the power of decision resided in the Tables - and thus effectively in the representatives of the civil power - and was translated into action by the lower courts of the church - in effect by the kirk session under the oversight of the presbytery. At this level, the church was formidable indeed, for the presbytery was flexible enough to allow frequent meetings and emergency sessions convened at short notice. But the kirk was soft at the centre and the revolution would not wait. The emergence of the Commission of the General Assembly, meeting in Edinburgh whenever it chose, eventually filled the gap and the kirk was suddenly transformed. The Commission, operating through the presbyteries, came to dominate Scottish society. In 1638, the state opposite to a state had been a distant dream; a decade later, it was reality; the godly society had advanced into the middle distance.

At all of these levels, the courts of the kirk included elders who were, in theory at least, equal in status with the ministers. But the elder, though technically an ecclesiastical person, was - or so we shall argue - effectively a layman. A church of formidable political power invited the intrusion of lay politicians; in the very act of separating itself from the civil power, it seemed to open its gates to civilians. It was a strange contradiction and it immediately poses questions of identity. Who were the elders of the kirk? Were they feudal magnates or were they their vassals? Were they rich or were they poor? And, if the church eventually fell to its ministers, who were the ministers who came to control it? Above and beyond all this, did the triumph of the church reflect deeper changes in the nature of Scottish society? The answers can only be discovered in the inner recesses of the kirk.

These vast changes in the chemistry of the kirk were not obviously reflected in the shape of the general assembly which surmounted it. There was no significant alteration in its constitution between 1638 and 1649 beyond the obvious one that it contrived to operate without the King's Commissioner from 1644 onwards. The electoral process improvised by the Tables for the Glasgow Assembly was still operating a decade later. Each participating presbytery continued to be represented by a ruling elder - who incidentally ceased to be described as a baron; each participating burgh continued to send its commissioner; the ratio of ministers to laymen remained more or less constant and no deliberate attempt was made to change it. The assembly, which had been fashioned at Glasgow in 1638, continued to exist, at least to outward appearances, until Cromwell shattered it at Dunbar.

The assemblies of the late forties were thus rather similar in character to those of the late thirties; but there had been a change, small but not without interest, in the quality of their ruling elders. The records of the assemblies do not survive in sufficient quantity to offer a comprehensive picture; there are complete rolls only for the assembly of 1638 and those from 1642 to 1646. In the latter cases, the clerk was often, apparently quite capriciously, content to identify the elders with a christian name and a surname; it is sometimes impossible to be certain of their status. Presbytery records, where they have survived, are usually more useful and the generalisations which follow reflect the ruling elder as he was commissioned by twenty-five of the presbyteries, including several of the vital presbyteries of the south-west, the Lothians and Fife ([2]). If these presbyteries could be regarded as typical, over 90% of the elders present in the early assemblies of 1638 and 1639 were either noblemen, members of Parliament, or lairds with a baronial jurisdiction (^{3}). The assembly of 1640, which was unusual in several respects, showed a dramatic reversal: only some 35% of the elders have definitely been shown to be tenants-in-chief. This exceptionally low proportion can reasonably be attributed to the frenzied preliminaries to the second Bishops' War; Argyll and Montrose and all their more powerful followers were busily engaged elsewhere. A rather similar explanation could plainly be applied to the assembly of 1651, which was almost literally chased across the Tay by Cromwell; in this case only half the elders seem to have been drawn from the feudal classes. During the intervening years, the proportion was usually between two thirds and three quarters. It was considerably smaller than it had been in the late thirties, but it was still substantial nonetheless.

These broad totals conceal almost as much as they reveal. In the heartlands of the Covenant, the fall was less significant. In the four presbyteries of Fife and in the adjacent presbytery of Perth, all the ruling elders known to have been elected from 1638 to 1643 were tenants-in-chief and two thirds of them were noblemen; the proportion of both remained very high up to and including the assembly of 1649. It is interesting that the radical areas of the south-west yielded a rather similar result. If the exceptional assembly of 1640 is disregarded, all the ruling elders known to have been sent up to the assembly from the presbyteries of Ayr, Irvine and Lanark from 1638 to 1651 were tenants-in-chief; and the proportion was almost as high in Stranraer. These figures confirm the impression left by the conspicuously separate meetings held at Riccarton and Mauchline in June 1648. The feudal classes maintained their hold on the official machinery of the church, and extreme radicalism was forced to express itself through the conventicle. The presbyteries of Glasgow - which became a radical stronghold after a conservative beginning - and Dumbarton offer a complete contrast. They included the vast domain, enhanced in 1641 by the acquisition of the lands of the bishopric, of the absentee Duke of Lennox. The Duke, who became an orthodox Cavalier in relation to the English conflict, remained ostentatiously neutral in his attitude to Scotland. He left his vassals to their own devices, and most of them became Covenanters of one kind or another. The leadership of local society fell to its ministers, its feuars and its tenant farmers. The latter often represented both presbyteries in the general assembly and they must surely have been among the yeoman elders who, in 1650, helped Patrick Gillespie to rule the presbytery of Glasgow in the radical interest (^{4}). Here the privy kirk was superfluous.

Glasgow and Dumbarton were perhaps rather special cases. Elsewhere a rather different pattern emerged. In the Lothians, as in Fife, the ruling elder was, except in 1640, normally a magnate; Edinburgh was represented by Balmerino in every recorded year except one; Haddington, which was well supplied, was shared between Yester, the two Lauderdales, the Earl of Angus, and the Laird of Clerkington; although a feuar was elected in 1640 and, more unexpectedly, another in 1647. In the Borders, on the other hand, the enthusiasm of the magnates was less enduring. Jedburgh failed to find a baron from 1641 to 1647, after which the Earl of Lothian - previously a Commissioner for Dalkeith - was elected until 1650; while Peebles was represented by a baron in only half of the assemblies of the period; indeed in the more conservative areas, whether in the Borders or in the North, the indifference of the magnates tended to produce a pattern not unlike that which prevailed in Glasgow, though usually with less radical consequences. It is indeed clear that the Engagers as a group seldom attempted to control the assembly. The Earl of Lanark elected himself for Hamilton in 1645, 1646 and presumably 1647. Crawford-Lindsay - an original supplicant - appeared for Cupar during the same years, while the Lauderdales, father and son, usually represented either Earlston or Haddington from 1642 to 1646. But these were exceptions. Only two prominent Engagers, Southesk and Lour, were elected to the crucial assembly of 1648, and neither took any part in its deliberations (5). If it is fair to assert that the magnates had, through their influence on the Tables, created the church of the period, it would be equally true to claim that most of them lost interest in it. To a remarkable extent, the division in the feudal classes between the Engagers and their opposites was a division between those who continued to attend the assembly as elders and those who did not.

It is perhaps reasonable to ask whether the substance of power, as distinct from its shadow, really resided in a general assembly which met for only a few weeks in the year before sending the majority of its members back to their parishes. It may be granted that the assembly enjoyed the sole right to legislate for the church as a whole and that some of its acts were of the highest importance. But it had executive power only while it was actually in session. The power which had once been wielded by thirteen bishops was dispersed among some sixty presbyteries, each consisting of upwards of a dozen ministers all theoretically equal in status. The presbytery was of a convenient size to oversee the affairs of its constituent parishes; but, at least in the absence of a constant moderator, it did not lend itself to centralisation, and the synod, like the assembly itself, met too seldom to supply the deficiency. Above all, there was no possible substitute for the informal gatherings of bishops, often occasioned by their presence in the capital on civil affairs, which had previously facilitated the unity of the church. The church of the Covenant was potentially as decentralised as the baronial society from which it sprang.

And yet the church of Alexander Henderson had always acted in unison. The Tables, skilfully using the fear of defeat, had imposed unity on church and state alike. The committee of ministers, set up by the assembly to lobby the Parliament of 1639, had assumed, or at least attempted to assume, a co-ordinating role. As we have seen, it successfully negotiated a compromise between radical and conservative on the vital question of privy meetings; but it lacked the power to enforce the settlement which it had fashioned, while an attempt to equip its successor with judicial powers was angrily rejected by the conservative assembly of 1640. The Commission established by the assembly of 1641 was similarly impotent; it was merely the shy embryo of the monster it would subsequently become.

Robert Baillie, in his account of the assembly of 1642, remarked that the committees of earlier years had been 'of small use', but he had no such doubts about the much more sweeping powers granted to the Commission of 1642; it was 'like to become a constant judicatory and very profitable', although, he added prophetically, it was 'of so high a strain that to some it (was) terrible already' ([6]). The outbreak of civil war in England presented the opportunity; from the beginning the prime objective of the commission was the pursuit of uniformity. To this end, it was empowered to meet when and where it chose and to make representations to any official body, English and Scottish alike. But even at this early stage there was a hint of wider powers. It was authorised to strive for 'the continuance of our own peace at home and of the common peace of these islands' as well as the 'keeping of a good correspondence betwixt (their) kirks'.

It is arguable that judicial powers were implied rather than stated; but, if this was so, the assembly of 1643 hastened to supply the deficiency. It authorised the commissioners to 'enjoin' the subscription of the new Covenant 'with all the censures of the kirk' and to 'send their directions to sessions, presbyteries and synods for the execution of their orders thereanent'. The powers of the commission were limited to matters which could be construed as relating to the Covenant; but this was the loosest of constraints and it was finally removed by the assembly of 1648. The Commission was granted 'full powers', to do 'all and everything for the preservation of the established doctrine, discipline, worship and government of this kirk against all who shall endeavour to introduce anything contrary thereunto'. Those who defied its authority were to be 'holden as opposers of the authority of the general assembly' itself. The commission had become an executive entitled to enforce its decisions by all 'lawful means and ecclesiastic ways'. It did not hesitate to use its influence in elections to the general assembly ([7]). It was the vehicle of the state opposite to a state.

The opponents of the commission complained that, unlike the ordinary courts of the church, it lacked the sanction of Parliament; the Engagers would undoubtedly have disbanded it if they had been successful. The commission would presumably have replied that its powers were derivative. Its members took office only when a general assembly dispersed and they laid it down again as soon as it was re-convened. They were accountable for their conduct to the next assembly which was entitled to disown them and everything they had done. The Engagers might perhaps have been forgiven for regarding this as a rather fine distinction, since - or so they might have argued - the assembly and its commission tended to consist of the same people; the right to reject was there, but it was never used. The argument was intricate enough, but one point is clear. The role of the commission can only be understood in terms of its membership.

A hurried glance might suggest that the commission was created in the image of the assembly itself. The ten commissions appointed between 1642-3 and 1651-2 varied in size from 73 to 163, but the ratio of ministers to elders remained remarkably constant at around 3 to 2 - and this was broadly comparable with the ratio as it was in the assembly. But appearances were deceptive. The commission was a large body with a small quorum. In most of the commissions of the period, a meeting of not less than 17 members would have been lawful, assuming that at least 13 were ministers. It is significant that there was no stipulated minimum for elders. Meetings consisting solely of ministers were unusual, but they were not

G

invalid. It is plain enough that the new executive was seen as a small body dominated by ministers ([8]).

Whatever the intentions may have been, the story told by the record, as it survives from 1646-7 onwards, is transparently clear. The average total membership from 1646-7 to 1651-2 was almost exactly 150; the average actual attendance was less than 30. Quarterly meetings were often fairly well attended and there was seldom much difficulty in finding a quorum; but the typical meeting was relatively small. The predominance of ministers was nearly always obvious. Over the whole period, the average meeting was attended by 22 or 23 ministers and half a dozen elders; a theoretical ratio of 3 to 2 became an actual ratio of nearly 4 to 1. In the vital commission of 1647-8, the proportion of ministers was actually a fraction higher still; indeed as many as 35 of the 97 ministers appointed, compared with only 5 of the 59 elders, attended more than a third of the meetings held. The noblemen among the elders were even less active; none of them attended a third of the meetings; only one - Angus - attended more than one in ten.

A rather similar set of conclusions is suggested by the composition of the committees to which so much of the more important work of the commission was delegated. Between February and June 1648, 17 committees were elected to deal with matters bearing directly on the Engagement. A total of 191 appointments included only 42 elders, and of these only 4 were noblemen. All of the nobles served on committees set up in February before the Parliament met - and this may be of some significance. The Parliaments of the period, almost interminable as they must have seemed, imposed such a burden on their leading members that there was little time, or indeed energy, left to serve on a body like the commission which sat even longer. Again the work of the committees, and indeed of the commission itself, was ideological rather than political in character; it called for divines rather than statesmen. The manifestos of the kirk were so obviously the product of the clerical mind that we scarcely need Baillie, or indeed the very full records of the commission, to tell us that they were composed by small committees of ministers. By and large, the Engager Lords chose to oppose the commission from without; while their opposites, including Argyll himself, normally left the ministers to their own devices ([9]).

The leading figures, here somewhat arbitrarily defined as those attending more than a third of the meetings or serving on three or more of the committees, disclose themselves readily enough. This method yields a list of 37 ministers, but only 5 elders, headed by Robert Douglas who, as moderator, attended all 136 sessions of the full commission as well as nearly all of its committees. Douglas can reasonably be regarded as Henderson's successor in the leadership of the kirk, but he belonged to a later generation of revolutionary statesmen. He was a moderate as Henderson had been; he was as conscious as Henderson had always been of an alliance with the magnates. But, at the Restoration, he contemptuously rejected the bishopric that Henderson would surely have wanted to accept. In 1648, he opposed the Engagement as a matter of course - and Henderson would at least have pondered the case for supporting it. Where Henderson might have taken risks, Douglas almost automatically accepted the orthodoxy of the moment. The tide was running rapidly for the radicals and Douglas swam along with it. A rather silent man, he kept his reservations to himself. He five times moderated the assembly and did the job efficiently enough, but this was not his natural habitat. An administrator rather than an orator, he was at his best in smaller meetings of the commission and its committees, where he translated radical rhetoric into practical action. Serene, single-minded, sarcastic and uninspired, he led an increasingly bureaucratic church along routes which it had already chosen for itself.

David Dickson (90 sessions and 11 committees), who combined a radical past with a conservative future, was perhaps his nearest counterpart on the commission. The Engagement found him in transition and he· allowed the majority to resolve his doubts. The role of Douglas and Dickson in the defeat of the Engagers was substantial enough, but the policy itself was the work of bolder men than they. James Guthrie (107 and 11), the scourge of the aristocracy, was radicalism incarnate. Courageous to the point of folly, extroverted and more likeable than martyrs usually are, he would become the natural leader of the Protesters and the natural victim of the resurgent royalism of the sixties. In 1648 he was still overshadowed by George Gillespie, minister of Edinburgh and arguably the greatest preacher of his time. It was appropriate enough that Gillespie should have moderated the assembly of 1648 which finally and officially condemned the Engagement in the eyes of the church. His premature death during the following winter would sanctify the Act of Classes and everything that came with it.

If Guthrie and Gillespie were the leaders of the radicals, Samuel Rutherford was their theoretician. He attended the commission assiduously enough (76 and 7), but his value to his colleagues - and indeed to posterity - was as a thinker rather than as a man of action. Rutherford came to understand the nature of the revolutionary process of which he was a part more profoundly than any of his contemporaries. It is arguable that only he knew where he was going and that only he realised why he had failed. It is impossible to quantify Rutherford, but it is instructive to enumerate his friends. Patrick Gillespie (84 and 2) and John Nevay (86 and 0) were both extreme radicals seeking, as yet without total success, to penetrate the inner recesses of the establishment. The one, in odd contrast to his elder brother, was an instinctive politician who would serve himself as well as he served the movement. The other was a violent insurrectionist who, quite characteristically, led the Mauchline Rising; he had the streak of irresponsibility without which any revolution is lost. Andrew Cant (85 and 7) - who may have been related to Nevay - was another fire eater whose prominence in the commission may have reflected his difficulties in an Aberdeen which was solidly under the control of the Engagers. In all, no fewer than twelve - that is, nearly a third - of the leading ministers can reasonably be regarded as radicals either in terms of what they were saying or doing in 1648 or of the attitudes that they would later adopt. The radicals were only a small minority among the ministry as a whole, but they were heavily over-represented at the top.

The remaining two thirds were all moderates or conservatives of one kind or another. They included one active Engager, William Colville (55 and 1) and would have included another, Andrew Ramsay (28 and 0) if he had been allowed to stay the course. Andrew Fairfoul (66 and 2) and possibly John Adamson (68 and 0) were sympathisers who were cautious enough to avoid serious offence. All four were able and one - the ageing Ramsay - was popular enough to be dangerous; there was a significant reluctance to name any of them to committees. But these were not typical; they merely served to remind their colleagues that the Engagers had been a powerful force in the assembly of the previous year. David Calderwood (69 and 10) was an old Melvillian who had utterly rejected the privy kirk in favour of a clerical autocracy exercised from the presbytery. He had forged a temporary alliance with the Engagers on the basis of a common fear of sectarianism, but this had foundered when the King had refused the Covenant. In 1648, Calderwood, cantankerous and conservative though he was, found a new, no less awkward - and no less temporary - friendship with the radicals. He was revered for his scholarship, which nobody could deny, but often mistrusted for an obstinacy which hardened with the passing years. David Calderwood was a law unto himself and Robert Baillie, who derived his conservatism from different premises, was a more influential figure in practice. Baillie's success in a revolution which he had embraced a trifle half-heartedly was due to a total lack of personal ambition. He was terrified at the prospect, mooted more than once, that he would be asked to moderate the general assembly. Nobody regarded Baillie as a rival and a surprisingly wide range of notables was willing to treat him as a confidant. He was allowed to work patiently in the background, never betraying the confidences so lavishly bestowed upon him - except of course to the faithful Spang and thus eventually to us. As his record (49 and 8) and indeed his letters suggest, he was happier in committee than he was in public debate. Baillie had advanced cautiously into sedition; reared in a tradition of non-resistance, he found the National Covenant, at least in its original form, too rebellious; nurtured in a church of bishops, he had declined to condemn their office as ungodly. He was loyal to his origins, but not so loyal that he might not allow himself to be convinced by men of consequence who instinctively felt that he was worth convincing. But the nature of his conversion must be understood. Baillie exchanged a church protected by the Crown for another protected by the magnates. He was bound to be tempted by the Engagement and to regard the radical opposition to it as a dangerous folly. It merely served to display the physical weakness of a church which had achieved an undoubted moral ascendancy. In a work which was published in 1649, Baillie would boast that the general assembly of the church of Scotland included the greatest magnates in the land. Like his friends, John Smith (75 and 9) and Robert Ramsay (46 and 4), he found it difficult to live in the same revolution as James Guthrie and Samuel Rutherford - and he did not have to endure the agony much longer.

The active elders were a ragbag by comparison and their power was slight. The commission of 1647-8 included only five and this is too few for generalisation. The four commissions appointed from 1646 to 1650 yield fourteen none too famous names, thirteen of them identifiable. There was a complete absence of noblemen;

only five were lairds; only one was a shire commissioner. The remaining eight included three relatively distinguished burgesses of Edinburgh; Sir James Stewart was a merchant and banker who opposed the Engagement and became Lord Provost in 1649; Lawrence Henderson, a merchant prominent in the kirk session and a future Bailie; and Thomas Paterson, a tailor who had represented the burgh in the assembly. The rest were all lawyers and two of them were judges. The largest single group were professional men like the ministers themselves. But this did not matter very much. The active elders of the commission were significant only in their numerical insignificance; the feudal church of 1638 had become the clerical church of the late forties. In some respects the church of 1649 resembled the church of the early and middle thirties more closely than its immediate predecessor.

The Commission of the General Assembly had arisen naturally enough out of the more obvious weaknesses of the Church of the Covenant; it survived to become the instrument of a theocracy. A church with little property and no direct access to the ordinary levers of power contrived to subdue the might of a powerful state. To some extent this extraordinary triumph can be explained in conventional political terms. The conflicting victories of Montrose and Cromwell were used to reduce the state - even the great Marquis of Argyll - to virtual impotence. But this was only part of the truth. Balfour's aphorism of 1649 was distorted by the bitterness of defeat, but his resentment did not entirely obscure his understanding ([10]). As he rightly said, the ministers had come to control the conscience of a kingdom that had lost itself in the confusion of a revolutionary situation. The root causes of the calamity may well have been economic and social in character, but they expressed themselves in the language of salvation. It was a language that only ministers understood. By 1649, the Crown and the magnates had destroyed each other and only the ministers were left. One wonders who they were.

7

The Brethren

ROBERT Pont, Minister of St Cuthbert's, Commissioner of Moray and planter of kirks in Orkney, was one of the pioneers of the Scottish Reformation; he was also a Senator of the College of Justice and Provost of Trinity College in Edinburgh. He contrived to be a parish minister, a judge in a civil court and a titular of teinds at the same time. He skipped from church to state, and incidentally from Melville to King James, with an agility that his successors of the seventeenth century must reluctantly have admired ([1]).

The experience of Andrew Murray, minister of Abdie in Fife from 1622 to 1644, was subtly different. He was the second son of a proprietor and a grandson of the first Viscount Stormont. His expectations had originally been modest and he chose a career in the ministry. He graduated at St Andrews in 1618 and was presented by his grandfather to the living of Abdie four years later. This was perhaps ordinary enough, but his expectations suddenly improved a few years later. The terms of a rather complicated entail gave him part of the inheritance of Scone on the death of his grandfather and a further instalment on the death of his cousin, the second Viscount. In 1641 he was elevated to the peerage as Lord Balvaird in recognition of his services to Hamilton during the opening stages of the Glasgow Assembly. The minister of Abdie found himself in possession of three baronies, including the large barony of Stormont, and the teinds of Blairgowrie, Logierait and Redgorton; he may also have become the patron of his own living. He was a Lord of Parliament, a Lord of Erection and a titular of teinds ([2]).

All this seems to have passed without comment, for the church of the Covenant was a more tolerant body than has sometimes been supposed; but in 1643 he chose to attend the Convention of Estates and immediately aroused the ire of the general assembly. It was argued that he had 'deserted his ministry . . . to voice as a Lord' and he was, in company with another minister who had 'conquished' a lairdship and used it to participate in a shire election, threatened with deposition if he should persist in his defection. The issue was not pressed to a conclusion, since Balvaird resolved it himself by dying in the following year; but the assembly made its point unequivocally enough ([3]).

Andrew Murray was an oddity and indeed an accident; he would hardly have been a minister if he had known that he would eventually become a magnate. But his immediate ancestry, as the younger son of a landowner of modest estate, was less unusual. Alexander Henderson was probably the son of a feuar in Fife and a connection, perhaps fairly remote, of the Hendersons of Fordel. Robert Douglas, who succeeded to his throne, sprang, equally indirectly and incidentally illegitimately, from the Douglases of Lochleven. Robert Baillie's descent took him back through a Glasgow merchant to the Baillies of Carphin, themselves a cadet branch of the Baillies of the ancient house of Lamington ([4]). David Dickson was the son, and less usually the heir, of another, and probably more prosperous, Glasgow merchant who acquired a small estate in the neighbourhood of the burgh. On the other hand, George and Patrick Gillespie were respectively the second and third sons of the only less radical John Gillespie, minister of Kirkcaldy until his death in 1627. Samuel Rutherford, radical intellectual, Professor of Divinity at St Andrews and later Principal of St Mary's, was probably the son of a tenant farmer in the Border parish of Crailing. But, if the theorist of the radicals was the son of a landless peasant, James Guthrie, their leader and martyr, sprang from a family of small proprietors in Angus. The leading ministers of the 1640s, radical and moderate alike, were evidently a mixed bunch. It is reasonable to ask whether they were typical of the ministry as a whole and it is fortunate that the industry of Hew Scott and his continuators has facilitated the search for at least the skeleton of an answer.

Table I

The Origins of the Ministers of the Church of Scotland, 1648

		1	2	3	4	5	6	7
(a)	**South of Tay**							
	Number of ministers	155	37	70	21	(283)	272	555
	%age of all ministers	28	6	13	4	(51)	49	100
	%age of 'known' ministers	55	12	25	7	99		
(b)	**North of Tay**							
	Number of ministers	74	17	42	10	(143)	141	283
	%age of all ministers	26	6	15	3	(50)	50	100
	%age of 'known' ministers	52	12	30	7	101		
(c)	**Scotland**							
	Number of ministers	229	54	112	31	(426)	412	838
	%age of all ministers	27	6	13	4	(51)	49	100
	%age of 'known' ministers	55	12	26	7	100		
(d)	**Scotland, 'Known' Presbyteries only***							
	Number of ministers	155	32	72	17	(276)	162	438
	%age of 'known' ministers	56	12	26	6	100		

N.b. The presbyteries of Perth and Dunkeld, which straddle the Tay, are included with the presbyteries south of the Tay.

*Presbyteries in which more than half of the fathers have been identified.

Column 1 Sons of ministers. *Column 2* Sons of burgesses. *Column 3* Sons of landed proprietors. *Column 4* Sons of other identified fathers. *Column 5* Sons of all identified fathers. *Column 6* Sons of unidentified fathers. *Column 7* All ministers.

Table I attempts, not altogether successfully, to generalise on the basis of a cross-section cut through the whole of the church as it was in 1648. It seeks to divide the 838 ministers, then serving either in parishes or universities, into categories according to the occupation or status of their fathers, insofar as these are known.

The *Fasti* sufficiently discloses the family backgrounds of only 426 ministers - or just over half of the total - and the conclusions which follow are plainly at the mercy of the accidents of survival and indeed of the varying determinations of the numerous researchers concerned. Thus the proportion of ministers of known origin varies widely from presbytery to presbytery, although the general regional spread is remarkably consistent. The proportion of 'known' ministers was about the same in the northern half of Scotland as it was in the south. It is no less fortunate that the proportion of ministers in the main sub-categories remains more or less the same if the enquiry is limited to those presbyteries in which the origins of more than half of the ministers are known (see Table I (d)). These similarities are reassuring; but it is obvious enough that the results have no statistical validity. The conclusions drawn below must be treated with some reserve.

The largest single element among the 'known' ministers of 1648 were the sons of other and earlier ministers. It must surely be significant that all four of the sections in Table I suggest a proportion of from 52% to 57%, or rather more than half, of the sample concerned. It is tempting to suggest that the reformed church was binding itself to the hereditary principle almost as tightly as had the feudal system itself. Indeed this dynastic tendency was not new. The story of the multiplying progeny of John Row, the Reformer, will perhaps stand one more telling. His marriage to the second daughter of Beaton of Balfour was ordinary enough. It produced nine sons and two daughters and this too was not unusual. But the five surviving sons all became parish ministers, while one of the two daughters married Robert Rynd, minister of Longforgan, who was the son of one minister and the father of another. The five sons fathered six more ministers among them and the story did not end there. Altogether, at least seven direct descendants of the Reformer held livings in the church of Scotland at some time during the 1640s. They varied in quality from John, minister of Carnock and the author of a famous history of the church, to James, minister of Muthill and later Monzievaird, who disgraced a distinguished family by perpetrating the 'Pockmanty' sermon and then compromised it through a tactless, if temporary, association with Montrose.

William Row, another grandson, had followed his father in the pulpit of Forgandenny and this, at least in the less fashionable parishes, was almost commonplace. The twenty rural parishes of the presbytery of Perth yielded eight instances in which either father or son held office during the forties and the nineteen rural parishes of the presbytery of Dunkeld a further eight. In Little Dunkeld, the sequence repeated itself a second time: William Glas was succeeded in 1629 by his son, William *secundus*, who was, in his turn, followed in 1647 by a grandson, Thomas. But Little Dunkeld was outdone by St Martins. Thomas Strachan, formerly a conventual brother in the nearby abbey of Scone, was presented to the vicarage of St Martins in 1568. He was succeeded by his son, who was still minister in 1643 when Thomas, son of John and grandson of the first Thomas, was admitted as colleague. The grandson, surviving civil war and restoration alike, went on until his death in 1671, when another grandson Patrick, a regent in the University of St Andrews, was recalled to replace him. The death of Patrick in 1678 was untimely. Thomas, son of the second Thomas and great grandson of the first, was too young and did not succeed his uncle until 1682; he stayed until William of Orange broke the spell. It would almost be true to say that four generations of the same family served the congregation of St Martins from the Reformation to the Revolution.

This dynastic tendency, or at least the appearance of it, was becoming more marked with the passage of time. A recent enquiry, embracing all the ministers officiating in the church from 1616 to 1638, has disclosed the fact that 218, or 17%, of the 1,232 ministers involved were the sons of clerical fathers ([5]), and this compares with 27% of all the ministers involved in the cross-section of 1648. The difference is too substantial to be dismissed as accidental and its reality is confirmed by a survey extending from 1600 to 1659 but confined within the narrower bounds of the Synod of Glasgow and Ayr (see Table II). The ratio of ministers' sons to the sons of known fathers rose from about one in five or six at the beginning of the century to nearly one in two in its middle. Nor is this really surprising. The later years of James VI had witnessed a great expansion of the ministry; by 1620, temporary vacancies apart, almost all the parishes of Lowland Scotland had their ministers ([6]). In the twenties their sons began to replace them; in mid-century, as they died or were deprived, the trickle became a flood. The clerical elite was beginning to perpetuate itself.

Table II
Origins of Ministers in the Synod of Glasgow and Ayr,
1600-59

Admitted to First Parish	Sons of Ministers	Sons of Identified Fathers
1600-19	6	33
1620-39	14	35
1640-59	28	66

The tendency was plainly real and it was obviously important, but its extent should not be exaggerated. The sons of ministers may have represented over half of the ministers of known origin, but this was only a quarter of the ministry as a whole; and the wide variety of backgrounds of the leading ministers virtually denies that it was of universal application. Indeed a quarter of the identified ministers are known to have been the sons of landed proprietors, while a further eighth were of burgess stock. A smaller proportion - only 29 in all - were of known but miscellaneous origin. Nine of these, including Samuel Rutherford and his brother, were the sons of either tenant farmers or countrymen of approximately equal status. A further twelve were drawn from the professional classes; their fathers included three advocates, a writer, two notaries, the commissary of

Hamilton and the sheriff clerk of Banff, as well as three doctors of medicine and the master of the grammar school at Dunfermline.

The exceptional cases are clear enough, but the broader categories are too vaguely defined to be useful. The term 'landed proprietor' could cover everybody from a small feuar to a great Duke; an urban craftsman might have been anyone from a baxter in Burntisland to George Heriot, goldsmith of Edinburgh and the Court of King James; a merchant might have been anybody from a small shopkeeper to Sir William Dick of Braid. Such distinctions are not easily drawn and, particularly among the burgesses, it is often impossible to draw them. The ministers who were sons of landowners include the son - but only the natural son of the Earl of Tullibardine, whose rents in Perthshire were valued at nearly £12,000 per year in 1649 [7]; John Murray, minister of Trinity Gask, was conceived out of wedlock and lived out of context; he was the only nobleman's son in the church in 1648. Andrew Ramsay was the son, but not the heir, of Sir David Ramsay of Balmain, who held a substantial estate *in liberam baroniam* and was shire commissioner for Kincardine in 1609. But Ramsay too was unusual, for there were only six other sons of shire commissioners among the 110 ministers concerned, although 19 more came from families which subsequently produced a county member. Thus William Adair, who became minister of Ayr in 1646 and participated in the Mauchline Rising two years later, was the younger brother of Sir Robert Adair of Kinhilt, commissioner for Wigtownshire from 1639 to 1641 and from 1649 to 1650. The heritable jurisdictions are less easily identified, but it is surely significant that only 20 out of the 112 landed fathers have definitely been shown to have held a barony or a regality. The true figure is almost certainly somewhat larger, but probably not by very much. Only a few of the ministers of the middle seventeenth century were drawn from the feudal classes. Furthermore, only one of the sons of tenants-in-chief was his father's heir. William Fullarton, minister of St Quivox in the presbytery of Ayr, was the eldest surviving son of James Fullarton of that ilk, the commissioner for Ayrshire in 1643-4 and 1648. He would inherit the barony of Corsbie-Fullarton, after the Restoration. But this was an unusual case; the link with the heritable jurisdictions was slender indeed [8].

If the enquiry is extended from the magnates to the landed class as a whole, it appears that only 13 of the 110 ministers were the heirs to their fathers' estates. The rest were, as far as one can tell, younger sons with no expectations of an inheritance, great or small. Only a few of them, as we have seen, were the sons of men of power and it is equally unlikely that many of them were really wealthy. Accurate generalisation is impossible, since the necessary valuation material is not universally available; but a reduction of the scale, from the whole of Scotland to the adjacent shires of Perth and Stirling, sharpens the focus. Only three of the eighteen proprietors on the list - Tullibardine (with lands valued at nearly £12,000 annually), Rollock of Duncrub (£4,000) and Oliphant of Gask (£2,300) - had really large estates. The remainder averaged £370 - a good deal less than the stipend of a typical minister. Furthermore, at least nine of the eighteen proprietors were feuars; only two - Tullibardine and Duncrub - themselves sat in Parliament, although two others had descendants who did so. In any event, none of these designed their heirs for the church. John Murray, as we have seen, was the bastard son of Tullibardine; his namesake, the minister of Strathmiglo in Fife, was the son, but a younger son, of Murray of Ochtertyre; Andrew Rollock, minister of Duns, was the son, but not the heir, of a wealthy laird who was subsequently ennobled. Indeed, only three of the eighteen were certainly heirs, and these to medium rather than large estates.

The ministers who sprang from a landed background were drawn, more or less haphazardly, from the entire range of the landed class; but the virtual absence of noblemen's sons is striking; the relative absence of the sons of shire commissioners, or indeed of magnates of any kind, is only less so. It would plainly be absurd to claim that the 'landed' minister transmitted the values of feudal Scotland to the church; this is at best a half-truth and at worst actively misleading. It might as easily, and as convincingly, be argued that they represented those - the feuar and, in a different way, the younger son - who had most reason to resent them.

The burgess fathers have a rather similar story to tell. Fifty-four, or about 12% of the ministers of known origin, emerged from the burgess communities of the towns of Scotland, nearly all of them from one or other of the royal burghs great or small. Thirty-seven of these are known to have come from one of the large burghs of Edinburgh, Dundee, Aberdeen, Perth, Glasgow or St Andrews. It is perhaps worth making the point that the numbers were small. The burgess community of Edinburgh consisted of rather more than a thousand individuals and it can be inferred that the other five contributed at least a thousand more ([9]). Less than one burgess in fifty sent a son into the ministry. The proportion was higher in St Andrews and, especially, in Glasgow - both university towns with a long ecclesiastical tradition. Indeed it may be significant that the four university towns yielded nearly two thirds of the burgess total.

The burgess fathers included one or two men of consequence. David Aitkenhead, father of the minister of North Berwick, would later become Lord Provost of Edinburgh. The father of John Adamson, Principal of Edinburgh University and an active member of the Commission, was the son of a merchant from Perth who was to become its Provost and its commissioner to Convention and Parliament. William Chalmer, minister of Boyndie in the distant presbytery of Fordyce, was the second son of Alexander Chalmer of Cults, Provost of Aberdeen. Indeed six of the burgess fathers are known to have been magistrates, though one of them was merely Bailie of Newburgh; another was Convener of Trades in Glasgow; yet another was a craft member of the Town Council of Edinburgh. Altogether ten represented their burghs, either in the Convention or in Parliament. It might fairly be estimated that only about one father in four was a member of his own burgh oligarchy. The rest were relatively obscure ([10]).

It is arguable that the ministers of burgess stock emerged from a fairly ordinary urban background. Their fathers are known to have included twenty merchants, two maltmen, a vintner, two sea captains and seventeen craftsmen; these last, in their turn, included a goldsmith, four hammermen of one kind or another, three tailors, three baxters, two litsters, a glazier, a wright, a cooper and a cordiner. It is obvious enough that they represent an accidental selection from the ordinary occupations of a Scottish town of the period.

It is perhaps reasonable to suppose that most of them were prosperous and that few of them were wealthy. Indeed this was evidently true of the nine Edinburgh fathers. Eight of the nine appear in the tax rolls of the burgh, though one only by proxy in the person of his widow. The remaining seven included four merchants, two of them members of the local oligarchy, two tailors and another variously described as a vintner, a tapster or an ale-seller. The two oligarchs made tax payments substantially above the average for the years in which they appeared. The other two merchants paid rather less, and the tailors markedly less, than the average. William Dickson, who kept a tavern and became a burgess rather late in life, paid £2, about one fifth of the average, towards the extent of 1627. William Dick, who was almost his namesake, resembled him in nothing else; he paid £333 - and none of his sons were ministers ([11]). Some of the merchants in the sample were no doubt wealthy enough. John Dickson, merchant in Glasgow, bought the small estate of Busby and passed it on to his son. But the famous David was unusually favoured. Robert Baillie seems to have inherited little or nothing from another Glasgow merchant who probably died young. Robert Blair was the son of John Blair of Windyedge, a merchant in the small port of Irvine, but he was the sixth son and this was an important distinction. Only a small proportion of the ministers of burgess stock are known to have been their fathers' heirs; Blair was more typical than Dickson.

The burgess community of a large burgh embraced a vast range of men. At the apex of the pyramid was the merchant prince who was at once a trader and a financier; he was an important element in the social structure of Edinburgh, but he was rare elsewhere. Beneath him was a large number of merchants engaged in foreign trade and craftsmen who had prospered sufficiently to become employers of labour. Beneath these again was a multitude of shopkeepers and craftsmen, each running a small business of his own. The merchant prince, like the nobleman, seldom sent his son into the church; most of the ministers emerged from the other two layers.

These various calculations relate only to about half of the ministry as it was in 1648. A rigorous search, concentrated on areas - like Dumfriesshire and Galloway - in which the proportion of unidentified fathers seems unduly high, would probably unearth a few more; but it seems unlikely that further research would significantly reduce the gap. The sources have already been minutely searched and sometimes found wanting - and this poses serious problems of analysis. The 'known' ministers represent a substantial proportion of the ministry as a whole, but they are in no sense a genuine random sample from it. The nature of the sample has been governed by the accidents of survival and the varying intensity of research. Above all, it has been biased by the undoubted fact that some ministers are more likely to have been identified than others. It is extremely unlikely that any nobleman's son - or indeed many sons of lairds of substance - remains untraced. If the sons of magnates were only a small fraction of the 'known' ministers, they were an even smaller fraction of the ministry as a whole and the same is probably, though not quite so certainly, true of the wealthier burgesses. Similarly it seems reasonable to assume that very few sons of ministers have escaped the attention of the authors of the *Fasti*. Again, the higher ranks of the legal profession have been studied almost as assiduously as the ministry itself. A few writers' sons may have remained untraced, but it seems improbable that many of the unidentified ministers were descended from lawyers or indeed from any professional group ([12]).

If this is true - and it must surely be very close to the truth - it seems unlikely that the sons of magnates, merchant princes, lawyers and doctors made up more than about 5% of the ministry as it was in 1648. By contrast, the sons of other and earlier ministers accounted for about 30% of the total. In all these categories, the 'known' total is very close to the real total; it is clear that only a very small proportion of the ministers came from a wealthy or a powerful background and that a much larger proportion emerged from the ranks of the ministry itself. But these certainties do not extend to the rest of the 'known' sample. It is evident enough that nearly all of these - about 15% of the ministry as a whole - were the sons of lesser burgesses, lesser landowners or husbandmen. The townsmen among them were mainly the sons of shopkeepers or working craftsmen. The countrymen may have included the sons of some small barons and some gentlemen 'landit', but many of them were the sons of farmers who owned or merely worked their land. It will immediately be obvious that the figure of 15% must be misleading. It relates to families of a kind which were much more numerous and much less likely to have been thoroughly studied; it is certainly too low; indeed it will be argued that nearly all the ministers of 'unknown' origin came from one or other of these categories - and there is some evidence of this.

Some few of the 'unknown' ministers have been partly identified by the editors of the *Fasti* and these cases nearly always suggest a relatively humble origin. Andrew Donaldson, the radical minister of Dalgety, is known to have been born in Perth, though his parentage remains obscure. Robert Edwards, minister of Murroes, was the son of an indweller, again of unknown occupation, in Dundee. It seems quite probable that both belonged to the fringes of the burgess community and reasonably certain that their status was no higher than this. Again Colin Adam, minister of Anstruther Easter and an active member of the Commission of the General Assembly in 1648, is known to have been the brother of a Patrick Adam in Auchleish. Patrick was almost certainly a farmer who had taken over the tenancy of Auchleish on the death of his father; Colin was probably a younger brother who had lived on the farm until he left for St Andrews. William Bell, minister of Dron in the presbytery of Perth, is known to have been born in the same parish. Nothing is known of his father beyond the probability that he was not a heritor; he too was probably a tenant farmer, although it is just possible that he was merely a cottar. James Mercer, minister of Clunie in the lowland part of the presbytery of Dunkeld, is thought to have been of the Clevage family. The laird of Clevage was obviously a proprietor, but the unknown father of James Mercer quite probably was not. As the younger son of a younger son, he was probably a tenant farmer or, just possibly, a feuar. Such examples could be multiplied; it is sufficiently clear that a substantial proportion of the ministry were the sons of farmers.

The case of Alexander Henderson presents a different order of difficulty. The search for his forefathers has been as intensive as it has been prolonged, but it has uncovered only two firm facts - both, unfortunately, relating to his death rather than his birth. He was buried in a vault belonging to the Hendersons of Fordel; in his will, he endowed a school in the farmtoun of Luthrie in the parish of Creich. It has been inferred that he was born into a cadet branch of the family of Fordel and this may well be true. It has also been surmised that he was brought up in Luthrie - and this is not entirely implausible, since no other connection has been established. If this is so - and it may not be - it is possible to go further. The farmtoun of Luthrie in the Lordship of Fife had been subdivided and feued during the first half of the sixteenth century. One of its parts was held at the turn of the century by Seaton of Parbroath, who had a substantial estate in the same parish. In 1601, Seaton sold his portion of Luthrie to David Henderson, the tenant who had previously occupied and presumably worked it. It is evident enough that he could have been the father of Alexander Henderson, who had probably been born in 1583. The estate involved was small, a mere sixteenth of lands that would later be valued for tax purposes at just over £1,000 per year. Alexander Henderson could modestly claim to have bettered himself ([13]).

It is possible to sketch in the career of a typical minister of the 1640s. He was born at about the turn of the century, the son of another minister, the proprietor of a small estate, a tenant farmer or a lesser burgess. The son of the manse was presumably educated by his father; a merchant or craftsman would send his son to the burgh school. The farmer's son may well have been less fortunate. Parish schools were increasing in numbers; but, in the earlier years of the century, they were still relatively rare ([14]). Henderson's bequest must surely have reflected his own early struggles. By one route or another, the typical - if mythical - minister contrived to prepare himself for a university which he entered at the age of sixteen. He graduated Master of Arts four years later and then completed his formal education with a post-graduate course in theology. The ministers were, above all else, educated men; if due allowance is made for the fallibility of seventeenth century registers, at least nine ministers out of ten must have been graduates. But the process of preparation was still far from complete.The minister must now attach himself to a presbytery as an expectant. Here he would attend the exercise - an educative process in itself - supply vacant pulpits, and act as a schoolmaster until such time as a parish could be found for him. The interval between graduation and admission was - to judge from the experience of the ministers of the Synod of Glasgow and Ayr - usually six or seven years, but it is interesting that it was longer during the thirties when the church had ceased to expand. It is reasonable to infer that competition was fiercer at this time than it had previously been. If this was so, the ministers had found another grievance. Our hypothetical minister was thus admitted to his first parish - and fairly often his last - in his late twenties. He would serve it, usually with a dedication which the old order could never hope to match, for rather less than thirty years. He would die, lamenting Cromwell and vainly trying to ignore the schism which had torn his church in two, at the age of fifty-five. He would have spent his working life as the missionary of an intellectual elite in a rural outpost which was at best half literate. It was a lonely life.

The leading ministers of the 1640s were, of course, less isolated, but their origins were strikingly similar. The 'active' group of the Commission of the General Assembly in 1648 consisted, as we have seen, of thirty-seven ministers ([15]), and the origins of twenty-four of these - about two thirds of the whole - are known with some degree of certainty (see Table III).

Table III
The Origins of the 'Active' Group in the Ministry, 1648

		1	2	3	4	5	6	7
(a)	**'Active' Group**							
	number of ministers	11	9	2	2	(24)	13	37
	%age of all ministers	30	24	5	5	(65)	35	100
	%age of 'known' ministers	46	38	8	8	100		
(b)	**All Ministers**							
	number of ministers	229	54	112	31	(426)	412	838
	%age of all ministers	27	6	13	4	(51)	49	100
	%age of 'known' ministers	55	12	26	7	100		

Column 1 Sons of ministers. *Column 2* Sons of burgesses. *Column 3* Sons of landed proprietors. *Column 4* Sons of other identified fathers. *Column 5* Sons of all identified fathers. *Column 6* Sons of unidentified fathers. *Column 7* All ministers.

The sample is small and the conclusions are thus uncertain, but two points stand out. The proportion of sons of landed proprietors was much smaller than it was in the church as a whole; it was indeed only a third as great. By contrast, the ministers of burgess stock were much more prominent. The leading ministers, as distinct from the average minister, were much more likely to have come from an urban background. But these bare figures, relating as they do to broad categories, contrive to obscure the main issue. The two landed proprietors, one of whom was the father of James Guthrie, were almost certainly feuars and fairly small feuars at that; neither was valued at more than £500 per year for tax purposes. The burgess fathers have an only slightly different story to tell. The 'active' ministers included David Dickson and John Adamson, both - as we have seen - the sons of fairly wealthy fathers; but the other seven were at best of local significance. George Hamilton was the son of a bailie - but merely the Bailie of Anstruther Easter. Patrick Schiel and George Gladstanes were the sons of craftsmen in Glasgow and Aberdeen respectively. Bartholomew Fleming, father of James, a minister of Edinburgh, was a merchant in the capital with tax liabilities rather less than average ([16]) and no links with the burgh oligarchy. The remaining two - the fathers of Robert Baillie and James Hamilton - were obscure enough.

Two more of the 'active' ministers - Samuel Rutherford and Mungo Law - were the sons of tenant farmers and it is likely that several of the unidentified, or only partially identified, fathers were of similar status. Colin Adam, as we have seen, was the brother, and presumably the son, of a farmer. James Nasmyth - the radical who so tactlessly pursued the teinds in the Assembly of 1649 - belonged, on exactly the same sort of evidence, in exactly the same category. Zachary Boyd boasted a connection with the family of Pinkhill, but he was probably the son of a farmer or a feuar. Robert Douglas, perpetual moderator of the Commission and the greatest of them all, was the son of a natural son of Douglas of Lochleven. Two more were probably the sons of townsmen outwith the burgess community. Andrew Cant - 'some men are born, if not to raise, yet continually to live in a fire' ([17]) - is said to have been a native of Aberdeen; at least he roasted on his own spit. John Nevay, the wildest of the Whiggamores, was probably his nephew. The ancestry of the rest - seven in all - is totally unknown and likely to remain so. But one point stands out clearly enough: not one of the active ministers was the son of even a minor magnate.

There might in happier circumstances have been one exception; Andrew Ramsay, an ardent Engager who normally appeared regularly, was prevented from attending the later sessions of the Commission. He was the son, though not the heir, of David Ramsay, holder of the Barony of Balmain with lands valued at nearly £2,000 annually and the progenitor of a long line of shire commissioners. It is tempting to jump to the conclusion that the ministers supporting the Engagement were a more aristocratic group than the ministry as a whole. It is indeed true that four of their fathers had large estates worth more than £1,000 per year, but four is not very many out of a total of seventy-eight and a 'known' total of forty-five. It is worth adding that the sixty-seven fathers of Protesters, thirty-six of whom were 'known', included two wealthy proprietors. The seven ministers who directed the Mauchline Rising included four whose origins are known. All four were the sons of landowners, while one of the other three resided, and was presumably brought up, in the household of the Laird of Blair. Three of the four - Matthew Mowatt, Gabriel Maxwell and William Guthrie - were almost certainly the sons of small proprietors, although the last was his father's heir; but the fourth - William Adair - was a younger son of William Adair of Kinhilt, who had large estates in Galloway and Ulster, and was a brother of the shire commissioner for Wigtownshire. Nevay himself could have come from the lower orders of Aberdeen, but most of the rest certainly came from a rural background in the south-west. A rather similar trend is observable among the Protesters as a whole. The 'known' Protesters did not include a single minister of burgess stock. The privy kirk found an echo in the sunless closes of Edinburgh; but it was also, and perhaps pre-eminently, the revenge of the countryside over the town.

But the differences dividing Engagers from Protesters, or either group from the ministry as a whole, or indeed the whole from its active nucleus, are less important than the similarities uniting them all. It is arguable that the ministry as it was in 1648 was drawn from a random sample of Scottish society from the magnate down to the tenant farmer. The sons of magnates or merchant princes were extremely rare - but magnates and merchant princes were themselves extremely rare. The ministers of the period may well have entered the church for a variety of reasons quite unrelated to their social origins. But even if this were so - and it was not entirely so - the main point would still remain. The fathers of the ministers, and especially those of the leading ministers, lived and modestly prospered in a whole series of different settings; but they had no place in the power structure of feudal Scotland. They had only their own obscurity and the fame of their sons in common.

H

8
Poor Naked Christ

JOHN Knox, the first of a long line of famous ministers of Edinburgh, married the daughter of a protestant lord - and lent him money. Alexander Henderson, his successor of the 1640s, lent even larger sums to a series of lords and lairds ranging from the principal heritor of his first parish of Leuchars to the Earl of Rothes. Knox had enjoyed a stipend from the Thirds which was equivalent to rather more than £2,000 in the money of Henderson's time. He earned three or four times as much as the typical minister of either period and indeed much more than any other minister apart from Henderson himself who, if the revenues of the Chapel Royal are included, received more than half as much again. The 'fairest ornament' of the church since 'John Knox of incomparable memory' was also the most expensive. Two mighty men generated two mighty incomes and neither had the time to spend them. Baillie's eulogy of Henderson, delivered in the Assembly of 1647, was surely just:'You know he spent his strength and wore out his days; he breathed his life in the service of God and of this church.' Money came easily to Henderson and he almost negligently left it to earn its keep under the careful management of a nephew who inherited most of it and took it with him into oblivion (¹).

Alexander Henderson, in his emoluments as in himself, was larger than life. At his death, he owed nothing and was owed over £23,000 - and this was exceptional only in its scale (²). The typical minister of the seventeenth century, as we shall see, left behind him a modest stock of 'goods and gear' and a markedly favourable balance of debts. He was relatively wealthy in terms of the life of his own parish and so, as a leader of local society, he was obviously intended to be. In rural Scotland the manse is sometimes larger than the church.

From the first, the new church had necessarily nourished itself from the traditional revenues of the old one and these had contained two main elements. The 'kirk rents' represented the income from the huge estates which had been bestowed upon the church over the centuries; for the most part they had been converted into feu duties expressed in money and fixed until the end of time. The teinds, on the other hand, were a proportion of the agricultural yield of the parish and these again divided themselves into two. The parsonage normally derived from the grain crops of the parish and was usually calculated in kind. The vicarage had originally been drawn from the remaining products of the parish but it had, in total contrast to the parsonage, almost invariably been converted into money. It is important that the real value of the feu duties and the vicarage was gradually reduced by inflation, but that the parsonage normally retained its value.

The *First Book of Discipline* had claimed the teinds and the episcopal temporalities; the *Second* had wanted the monastic temporalities as well. The official attitude of the reformed church asserted that the alienation of church property - that is, the vast endowment of the old church - was sacrilege. In practice, this was a bargaining position. As Samuel Rutherford was later to complain, the church had been 'spoiled' of its 'tithes and kirk rents', leaving it a 'poor naked Christ'; the magnates had plundered the church and they were determined to hang on (³). The early reformers, dependent as they had been on their feudal friends, had inevitably settled for a church that was almost without property. The church of Knox, and indeed of Melville too, had paid its ministers from a centrally collected fund known as the Thirds of Benefices. This was fed from a tax amounting to a third of the annual income from all church property, teind and temporality alike. The yield was divided between the church and a central government which was almost as poor. In 1562, the amount available for church purposes was about £26,000 and this, apart from paying the superintendents, seems to have provided a stipend, usually calculated in money rather than in kind, of about £100 per year for the typical minister (⁴). The ministers of the new church were, and would remain, substantially better off than the vicars and curates of its predecessor; but they were obviously threatened by inflation. By the turn of the century, a fourfold increase in stipends was required to maintain the real values of the 1560s and - to judge from a recent survey of the presbyteries of St Andrews, Paisley and Deer - this was not always achieved. The urban minister, at least in St Andrews and Deer, seems to have maintained and, in some cases, actually to have improved his living standards - and this may well have been typical of towns in general.

But it was probably otherwise in the countryside. There were no country ministers in the Paisley area in 1567 and no useful comparison is possible; but, in five rural parishes in St Andrews, the average stipend increased only two and a half times; while in Deer, where the comparison is less satisfactory, stipends seem barely to have doubled. It seems clear enough that a large number of rural livings had fallen short of the intentions of the early reformers. The Melvillian claim that the ministers were poor merely invited the reply that poverty was relative; but it must have sounded plausible enough to many of the ministers themselves (⁵).

But the first decade of the new century brought the erection of the abbacies into temporal lordships and, with them, a new situation. The Thirds had made no distinction between teind and temporality and there had been no attempt to tamper with the ownership of either. The new system, on the other hand, granted the property permanently to lay Lords of Erection and then burdened the teind element in it with an obligation to pay an adequate stipend to the minister of the parish to which the teinds related. The weakness of the scheme, as seen from the ministers' point of view, resided less in the intentions behind it - for these were not entirely inconsistent with the *First Book of Discipline* - than in the mechanics of its operation. The King in Parliament established a commission charged with the duty of defining a sufficient stipend for each of the parishes concerned and some stipends were substantially augmented; but the resulting stipend exceeded £400 in only 30 out of 133 known cases ([6]). Indeed the actual disposal of the teinds was usually controlled by a tacksman protected by a legally enforceable lease with several years to run.

The ghost of Knox was still uneasy, but his church had found a new champion. King James, as Spottiswood was soon to say, was 'pope now' and he was beginning to support his church effectively. The commissions appointed in 1617 and 1622 were authorised to compel tacksmen – who were usually local heritors collecting teinds on behalf of distant titulars – to pay higher stipends on the understanding that their leases would be prolonged. The situation of the middleman would remain more or less unaltered, but the minister would gain at the expense of the titular. At the same time, the state enacted the principle that stipends should only in exceptional cases be allowed to fall below a stipulated minimum. In 1617, a sufficient stipend was defined as 5 chalders of victual or 500 merks (£333). This was not ungenerous, though it may still have been less in real terms than the typical stipend of the 1560s; but, if this was so, Charles I hastened to redress the balance by increasing the minimum to 8 chalders of victual or 800 merks (£533). The same minimum of 8 chalders was laid down for the Commissions established by the Parliaments of 1641, 1647 and 1649; but the last, a ministers' Parliament if ever there was one, introduced a flexible conversion rate – no doubt justified by the temporary rise in prices of the late forties – of £100 per chalder. In the case of a stipend paid entirely in money, the minimum was now £800 ([7]). But now most augmented stipends included a substantial victual component, while a few arable parishes paid their ministers entirely in grain. The church in the seventeenth century was still haunted by the memory of its inflationary past. A victual stipend seemed an invaluable insurance.

Above and beyond this, a new attitude to church property had emerged. On one reading of the facts, church and state were guilty of a collective act of sacrilege: they had conspired to alienate the teinds. But sacrilege was a big word and ordinary men hesitated to use it. During the controversy over the revocation, it became the monopoly of a handful of Canterburian extremists who were eventually ignored. James Nasmyth tried it again in the Assembly of 1649 and he found a sympathetic audience among the ministers; but sympathy did not extend to support; in the end the demand for the teinds was dismissed as a radical eccentricity ([8]). The church had changed its course or at least its tactics. For the rich victual teinds of the parsonages were property only in a rather special sense. Unlike the temporalities, they did not consist of solid earth; they were merely an entitlement to a part of the fruits of the earth – and there was more than one way of getting this. The church was content to claim an increasing share of the income rather than the property as such. Canterburian and Presbyterian alike were using the power of the state to force stipends up towards the level of the teinds themselves. No need to steal the cow; to milk it would suffice.

It is more difficult to decide how successful they were, since the Register of Decreets, in which the work of their Commissioners was recorded in detail, disappeared in the great fire of 1700. A substitute register, drawn up after 1707 from materials held locally, goes some way to fill the gap, but it includes only cases which happened to come before the Teind Court and it covers only a fraction of the whole picture. Connell, whose monumental work remains the starting point of any study of stipends, used this register, together with the original Sederunt Book, which records in its entirety the work of the Commissioners sitting from 1631 to 1633. But he seems to have been unaware of the considerable collection of miscellaneous seventeenth century papers which survived the holocaust of 1700. These are almost certainly the raw material from which the original Register of Decreets was constructed and, though they are far from complete, they add greatly to our knowledge of the two vital periods from 1634 to 1636 and 1649 to 1650, when most of the seventeenth century augmentations seem to have taken place. They are not, however, comprehensive and the calculations which follow, based as they are on the Sederunt Book, the substitute register and the miscellaneous papers, do not reflect either the total picture or a scientifically selected sample from it. They are based on the accidents of survival and they should be treated with a certain suspicion ([9]).

These calculations relate to the whole of Scotland, apart from the Highlands and the far north, where the surviving evidence is even scantier. They cover the 226 stipends known to have been augmented at some time between 1631 and 1650 and these represent just under a third of the livings in the same area. The proportion of known augmentations varied considerably from presbytery to presbytery. In Edinburgh 12 stipends out of 16 were definitely augmented; in Earlston 7 out of 9; in Paisley 10 out of 15; in Penpont 6 out of 10; in Biggar 8 out of 13; in Haddington 9 out of 16. On the other hand, only 1 living out of 11 is known to have been augmented in Hamilton; only 2 out of 14 in Lanark - which bordered on Biggar. The north as a whole, with about 25% compared with about 35% in the south, seems to have scored rather low. Indeed it seems very likely that the Commissioners were always less energetic to the north of the Tay and that this was especially true in 1649-50 when only 1 stipend in 14 - compared with nearly 1 in 5 in the south - is known to have been increased. Again, the Commissioners of 1649-50 seem deliberately to have concentrated on some of the more remote southern presbyteries which had almost been ignored in the thirties, and the high proportion of known augmentations in Kirkcudbright and Biggar appears to be an example of this. Indeed one of the functions of all the Commissions was quite simply to force up the stipends of poor parishes wherever they happened to be situated. The earlier Commissioners of James VI had been, to judge from the instances recorded by Connell, almost as assiduous in the south-west as they had been in the conservative north.

The surviving evidence suggests that at least 113 livings were augmented between 1631 and 1637 and a further 105 in 1649-50. By contrast, only 19 increases are known to have been granted between 1641 and 1647, despite the fact that Commissioners were empowered by Parliament to act throughout the period. It is easy to understand that little was done in the disturbed years from 1643 to 1646. But 1642 was a year of peace and 1647 a relatively calm interlude in a decade of almost continuous turmoil. The inactivity of the Commissioners during these years surely reflects a reluctance on the part of the Parliament to augment stipends at all. In the thirties the pressure had been applied by the Crown and the Canterburians; in 1649 it would be applied by a presbyterian church with a Parliament in its pocket. In the years between, the balance of forces was rather different; a bishopless church ran in double harness with a feudal Parliament in which the Lord of Erection was a powerful force. By and large, stipends were augmented only when the titular was willing.

The extent of the augmentations is again difficult to determine accurately, since most of the stipends concerned - about two thirds of the known cases - were at least partly paid in victual. This inevitably poses the problem of conversion rates at a time when prices were fluctuating fairly rapidly. It would plainly be desirable to calculate a standard rate which would embrace the whole of the period and the whole of the country as well as the entire range of commodities - mainly bere, oatmeal and wheat - which made up the victual component of a stipend. In fact this is almost impossible, since the surviving sets of fiars' prices are too localised to present a general picture. On the other hand, the rate - of £67 per chalder for all regions and all commodities - used by the Commissioners was at once too low and too crude. The table of rates laid down by the Parliament of 1649 for the land tax was fortunately much more sophisticated; different prices were quoted for each region and each commodity. It is true that the general level of the prices - of approximately £80 per chalder - was still rather low, but - in the absence of a detailed price index they offer the possibility of a more accurate overall picture than any other source. These rates have been used in all the following calculations, in the full knowledge that they slightly understate the value of the victual element in the stipends concerned. Direct comparisons with the incomes enjoyed by other sections of the community - or with the ministers of Knox's day - can thus be made only with caution.

The reservations, imposed on the one hand by the accidents of survival and on the other by the fluctuations of the market, plainly preclude certainty. But it may be possible - from the evidence of the augmentations of 1617, of the teind surveys of 1627 and of subsequent augmentations where these were detailed enough to show the previous stipend - to estimate the situation as it was at the death of James VI. One hundred and twenty four known instances yield an average stipend of just over £360. This suggests that the typical minister was earning more than the minimum stipend (£333) laid down for the Commissioners of 1617 and 1621, though less than the average settlement known to have been imposed by them (£391) ([10]). The contrasts were still vast. Cramond, which may or may not have been augmented, paid about four times as much as Longformacus, a remote hill parish which plainly had not; but well over half of the parishes concerned paid between £300 and £400. It seems unlikely that the ministers of the 1620s were quite as prosperous as their predecessors of the 1560s had been, but James and his bishops had done their best. They had started a process that Canterburian and Presbyterian would combine to complete (see Table I).

The Commissioners of King Charles achieved much more than this. The evidence of 86 cases indicates that the average augmentation of the 1630s awarded a stipend of nearly £550, or rather more than the minimum of £533 stipulated by

Table I
Average levels of stipends known to have been augmented in 1617, 1631-7,
1641-8, 1649-50, (figure in brackets indicates number of known instances)

Area	1617		1631-7		1641-8		1649-50	
Synod of:								
Lothian	576	(2)	581	(17)	604	(4)	633	(24)
Merse-								
Teviotdale	463	(3)	559	(7)	414	(1)	710	(3)
Dumfries	-	(-)	632	(4)	-	(-)	686	(7)
Galloway	347	(10)	567	(2)	580	(1)	724	(5)
Glasgow-								
Ayr	344	(1)	550	(19)	633	(4)	694	(13)
Perth-								
Stirling	359	(5)	523	(11)	568	(2)	736	(10)
Fife	-	(-)	530	(7)	540	(4)	720	(10)
South of								
Tay	388	(21)	558	(67)	578	(16)	685	(72)
Synod of:								
Angus-								
Mearns	514	(2)	554	(13)	583	(1)	642	(4)
Aberdeen	367	(8)	487	(13)	560	(1)	560	(6)
North of								
Tay	396	(10)	521	(26)	571	(2)	593	(10)
Whole of								
Scotland	391	(31)	544	(86)	576	(18)	674	(82)

N.b. It should be emphasised that different parishes are involved in each of the columns of the Table.

the Crown. The awards of the period 1641-7, few though they were, tended to be even higher, but even these dwindled into insignificance compared with the massive stipends - an average of £674 from 82 instances - granted by the Commission of 1649-50. To look at the same question from a different angle, the augmentations of the thirties tended to yield an increase of from 10% to 50% of the original stipend; those of the period 1649-50 tended to produce an increase of from 20% to 60% (see Table II).

One or two regional variations are sufficiently marked to survive the fragility of the evidence. Augmentations in parishes south of the Tay were always more generous than they were in the north, except in 1617 when the reverse was true.

Table II
Percentage increases of stipends granted during the augmentations of
(a) 1631-7 and (b) 1649-50.

	No. of Instances in:	
Extent of Increases (%)	1631-7	1649-50
1 - 10	2	0
11 - 20	11	0
21 - 30	9	6
31 - 40	13	5
41 - 50	9	6
51 - 60	2	5
61 - 70	3	3
71 - 80	3	0
81 - 90	1	1
91 - 100	4	1
100	3	1

The extreme case was the Synod of Aberdeen, which always fared worse than most, and usually than all, of the areas to the south of it. On the other hand, the Synod of Lothian stands out as an area of high stipends in every augmentation except the last when, as we have already suggested, the church, in its hour of triumph, concentrated its attention on its outworks. In Dumfries and Galloway, newly augmented stipends were comfortably above the national average. In the remote upland parishes of the presbytery of Biggar, where the total valuation for land tax purposes ranged from a mere £1,200 to a modest £4,600, the stipends of Glenholm, Kilbucho, Coulter, Skirling and Lamington were augmented to £566, £565, £599, £567 and £679 respectively. Only in the tiny parishes of Dolphinton and Walston, which had been united until 1608, did the stipend remain significantly below the minimum.

There is evidence from Restoration sources that a few livings were not augmented at all, but it seems likely that most were substantially enhanced by one regime or the other and it is certain that a few were increased by both. The stipend of Currie was augmented from £420 to £497 by the bishops and from £497 to £730 by their opposites ([11]); that of Inverkip rose from £416 to £703 in two more or less equal leaps, each of about 30%. In all, eleven livings are known to have been doubly blessed and there is no reason to doubt that others were similarly favoured.

All these calculations refer to stipends known to have been augmented, and these in themselves are at best an indifferent guide to the wider and more elusive question of the general level of ministers' incomes. Fortunately the assessments made for the land tax offer an alternative approach. The shire committee concerned prepared two documents for each of the parishes in its area. The first was a list of heritors showing the annual value of the lands, stock and teind combined, held by each one, less the various allowable deductions. The other was a statement of the total tax liability of each parish, subdivided into money and the various kinds of victual involved, together with an itemised list of the deductions. The minister himself was liable for the tax only in those relatively rare cases where he was also a heritor; but his stipend, which was deductible for tax purposes, was among the items subtracted from the parish total. In many cases, the ministers' stipends were not clearly distinguished from other deductible items; but in one, the meticulously compiled Perthshire roll, the stipend was not merely noted but split into its separate elements of money and victual. If it be true that Perthshire, divided as it is by the Highland Line, is rural Scotland in microcosm, we are fortunate indeed ([12]).

The Perthshire roll was made up in 1649 and thus ignored all, or at least almost all, of the augmentations made in that and the following year, but it should have taken account of all previous augmentations - the more so since there was an obvious incentive to quote the highest figure for any deductible item. Within the limitations imposed by the seventeenth century's contempt for statistical accuracy, the Perthshire figures, comprehensive as they were, represent the situation as it actually was in the forties (see Table III).

The figures are surely revealing enough. The average living was substantially below the minimum laid down by Charles I. To some extent, this can be explained

Table III
Stipends in Perthshire, 1649

Area	Parishes	Average Valued Rent (£)	Average Stipend (£)
Presbytery of Perth	20	5,801	543
Presbytery of Dunkeld	19	4,348	369
Presbytery of Auchterarder	15	5,348	454
Presbytery of Dunblane	12	4,852	411
Highland Parishes	19	4,119	359
Lowland Parishes	47	5,445	475
Total	66	5,110	449

by the inadequate stipends yielded by nearly all the Highland parishes; but this was clearly not the whole story, since the Lowland average was itself below the minimum. Indeed, only the presbytery of Perth, an influential body which had previously enjoyed the powerful backing of the Archbishop of St Andrews, showed a significantly higher average. For one reason or another, the more accessible parishes of the shire tended to pay stipends that were at least adequate. It may well be that the average for the presbytery of Perth - of £543 - was fairly typical of the Lowlands as they were before the augmentations of 1649-50.

However this may have been, there was a substantial variation within the presbytery itself, partly no doubt because some of the stipends had not been augmented. Nine of the twenty stipends were still well below the minimum and it is probably no mere coincidence that these included three of the five livings for which the teinds had been held by a bishop - in which the church as titular stood in direct confrontation with its own parish minister. The bishops' kirks were not specifically excluded from the jurisdiction of the Commission of Charles I - and they were, of course, deliberately brought to the notice of subsequent commissions ([13]) - but the Crown rather ostentatiously declined to encourage the compulsory augmentation of their stipends and very few, either in Perthshire or elsewhere, seem to have been so increased before 1637. This did not, however, exclude the possibility of voluntary agreements in parishes where the teinds were sufficiently valuable to satisfy bishop and minister alike. Thus, in the presbytery of Dunblane only two stipends - those of Kilmadock and Dunblane itself - were above the minimum and both were paid from the bishop's teinds. But it so happened that Dunblane and Kilmadock were also the two wealthiest parishes in the presbytery. The seventeenth century conventionally assumed that the teinds of any given area of land amounted to one fifth of its yield in stock and teind combined, at least in cases where the two were no longer readily distinguishable. It may thus be reasonable to assume that the teinds of Dunblane and Kilmadock were worth, however approximately, a fifth of the valued rent attributed to them for land tax purposes, that is, about £2,000 and about £2,300 respectively. There was plenty here for bishop and minister alike.

Indeed it is evident that, in the last resort, the vital factor was the capacity of the parish rather than the ownership of its teinds or even the preconceived notions of the Commission. In 1649, the average stipends of the ministers of all four of the presbyteries, as well as of those in the Highlands and in the Lowlands, fell, with extraordinary consistency, between an upper limit of 9% and a lower limit of 8% of the valued rent available to pay them. The ministers of the presbytery of Perth were better off than the others, because they served wealthier parishes.

The exceptions remain of some interest. Errol, in the rich though as yet partially undrained Carse of Gowrie, was the wealthiest rural parish in the shire. The valued rent amounted to rather more than £18,000 and the teinds, once the property of the Charterhouse and now of the burgh of Perth, were probably worth about £3,500. They might have supported six or seven ministers adequately enough; they actually paid the best rural stipend - of £912 - in the shire, leaving over £2,500 - less the profits drawn by any tacksmen who may have been involved - to the titular and thus indirectly to the ministers of the burgh of Perth. Once again the church confronted itself. The adjacent parish of St. Madoes was a tiny independent parsonage with a valued rent of only £1,800 - or about one tenth of that of Errol. The minister, who was entitled to the whole of the teinds, received annually no less than £567, nearly one third of the valued rent. This was unusual if not unique, and it is tempting to assume that the Laird of Pitfour, the sole proprietor, was more successful than most in concealing the true value of his rents. Collace, an even smaller parish, was only slightly more typical; its stipend was a mere £350, but this was nonetheless about a quarter of the valued rent and thus substantially more than the presumed value of the teinds. Small parishes naturally tended to pay small stipends, but they plainly did their best.

Errol and Collace were extreme cases; Dunbarney and Scone, though neither could claim to epitomise the whole, were more typical. Dunbarney discloses itself through the records of its titular and patron, formerly the collegiate foundation of St Giles and now the Town Council of Edinburgh. The teind survey of 1627 had declared the teinds of most of the estates of the parish to be a fifth of its rents [14], which were valued in 1649 at £7,206. The parish was relatively prosperous, land having an average value of 18/- per acre compared with 31/- in Errol and about 1/- around the lonely summits of Schiehallion and Ben Lawers; as was usual in an essentially arable parish, stock and teind alike were for the most part calculated in victual, some of it in wheat. The stipend, at first glance a trifle anomalously, was paid in money, perhaps because the tacksmen, having to send the residue of the teinds to Edinburgh, found it more convenient to sell the victual in or near the parish itself. During the twenties, teinds worth about £1,450 yielded a stipend of £380 or rather less than a quarter of the whole. This was augmented in 1635 to £500, which was still to be paid in money. In 1648 a further augmentation, this time entirely in victual, brought the stipend above the minimum to a reasonably generous £592. In the following year yet another augmentation, granted in the very different political climate of 1649, hoisted it yet again to £707 or about half the value of the teinds. The stipend was almost doubled in fifteen years. The diminishing remainder of the teinds, further reduced by the tacksmen's profit to about £500, was administered by the City Fathers in the interests of their own ministers [15].

Scone, slightly smaller with a valued rent of £6,897, and teinds which must have been worth rather less than £1,400, presented a less complicated conflict of interest between the church and the Lord of Erection, the Earl of Annandale, who had succeeded to the substantial inheritance of the abbey. The conflict was resolved by the Commissioners in the thirties with an award which increased the stipend from £480 to £569. The valuation of 1649 records the slightly higher figure of £597 - which probably included an allowance for the Communion elements - and there is no evidence of further augmentation.

David Wemyss, minister of Scone from 1620 to his death in 1684, was locally prominent without being nationally remarkable ([16]), and his stipend of £569, like the man himself, was rather better than average. It is tempting to place him in his own local community. In the valuation of 1649, the Earl of Annandale, Lord of the Regality of Scone and titular of its teinds, confessed to an income, drawn from his proper lands, teinds and feu duties in the parish, of £1,618. His landed vassals - and Scone was naturally a parish of feuars - were collectively worth more than four times as much; but they were thirty-seven in number and it is interesting that they were all poorer, not merely than the Earl of Annandale, but also than David Wemyss. The feuing of the abbey lands during the previous century plainly puts Scone in a special category; but it was not entirely untypical of the shire as a whole. Perthshire had its share of very wealthy men. The Earls of Tullibardine and Perth, whose lands were largely concentrated in the shire, drew rents valued at £12,000 and £13,000 respectively. Two lairds, Hay of Balhousie and Ogilvie of Inchmartin, enjoyed comparable landed incomes of rather over £10,000 and rather under £8,500. All told, nearly a hundred proprietors were worth more than the minister of Scone; but a much larger number - perhaps about a thousand - were worth less. The calculation is imperfect since it is difficult to distinguish a small landed estate from a house and garden belonging to an owner with other interests. It does seem certain, however, that the typical estate yielded rents which were substantially less than the minimum stipend of a minister ([17]).

The testaments present a rather similar picture painted, albeit a trifle haphazardly, across a broader canvas. Testaments were recorded, and thus preserved, by a remarkably wide variety of people extending indeed from noblemen to cottars; unfortunately the act of registration was voluntary and thus, at least among the poor, relatively rare. The Record of Testaments is the essential raw material of social history, but the samples it offers were selected by chance rather than by design. They are statistically interesting without being statistically valid. The figures which follow (see Table IV) are based on a survey of all the testaments recorded in the Commissary Courts of Edinburgh and Glasgow in 1662, when many of the men who were active during the 1640's must have died; but they were not a random sample of the population as a whole or even of those who died in 1662. The results should be treated with some caution.

The average for all testaments suggests a typical inventory of about £530 and a typical total - that is, the inventory together with the balance of debts - of just over £1,400. The comparable figure for ministers only is based on a sample so small that it is useless in itself; the much larger section, based on all the ministers' testaments registered from 1650 to 1659, is probably more illuminating and it is comforting that it gives a rather similar total. The typical minister left moveable

Table IV
Inventories and Totals of Testaments Recorded in Glasgow and Edinburgh
in 1662

	Inventories		Totals		Ratio
	Instances	Ave. (£)	Instances	Ave. (£)	Total/Inventory
All Testaments	449	529	466	1407	2.7 to 1
Ministers, 1662	15	445	15	2684	
					6 or 7 to 1
(Ministers, 1650-59)	(131)	(370)	(150)	(2760)	
Landed Proprietors	45	840	45	3134	3.7 to 1
Other Rural	211	363	217	423	1.3 to 1
All Rural	256	447	262	895	2.0 to 1
Merchants	95	971	102	3194	3.3 to 1
Craftsmen	83	289	87	678	2.3 to 1
All Urban	178	653	189	2035	3.1 to 1

property of about twice the average value, but his inventory was substantially below the average. His income was high, but his temptations were few; he lived only less modestly than the farmers who surrounded him. In consequence the balance of his debts was nearly always favourable. His stipend was often in arrears and he commonly lent money, sometimes at interest, to his congregation. He, alone in his isolated community, accumulated capital regularly. It was natural enough that he should lend it back to the farmers who had produced it.

The other categories in the Table are all open to the objection that they cover too broad a range of disparate individuals. The proprietors include magnates as well as feuars; the countrymen include everybody from a husbandman to a half-hind; the merchants range from shopkeepers to merchant princes; the craftsmen from a village weaver to an Edinburgh goldsmith. The resulting averages are plainly less valuable in consequence, but it is nonetheless striking that none of the totals is much higher than the ministers' total and that most of them are much lower. The minister was a man of some consequence.

These calculations are not without their value; but the passing of the centuries has blurred the image. We know that £12 Scots could be exchanged for £1 sterling, but we know very little about the goods that either pound would have bought. It is perhaps more illuminating to revert, as contemporary Scotsmen so often did, to victual and to stay as close to it as possible. A Cromwellian wage assessment of 1656 [18] defined the annual entitlement of a half-hind as a small house, a kailyard, rather less than two thirds of a chalder of victual and pasture for a single cow or five sheep. It may not be entirely unreasonable to regard this as the equivalent of a living wage as the seventeenth century would have understood the term. If we then proceed, purely as an arithmetical convenience, to translate the victual component back into money at the rates laid down in the Perthshire valuation of 1649, the result is a wage of just under £40 per year, to which must be added the annual produce of one cow. A minister drawing the minimum stipend of eight chalders of victual, or about £580 at the same prices, would receive approximately fifteen times as much as the victual component of a living wage. It is perhaps a mere coincidence that a minister's glebe was originally supposed to yield the equivalent of pasture for 16 cows - that is, sixteen times as much as the grass land available to a half-hind. It is, of course, notorious that some ministers lacked glebes; but it is equally true that the period of the augmentation of stipends also witnessed an attempt to restore the glebes [19]. The exact multiplier must remain a matter for conjecture, but it is surely evident that a rural minister was normally at least ten times as wealthy as the cottars and farm servants who made up the bulk of his congregation.

The ministers in the towns plainly belong in a different category. The *First Book of Discipline* had argued that the minister was entitled to the teinds of his own parish and, in the countryside, the Decreets of the Teind Commissioners were slowly achieving an approximation to this. The Commissioners were also active in burgh parishes like Dunfermline or St Andrews which included a landward area; but they had no competence in an entirely urban parish like Edinburgh. It is arguable that the burgesses of medieval Edinburgh - who were farmers as well as traders - had once paid teinds in the ordinary way and that these were enough to satisfy the modest needs of a small town. But Edinburgh was no longer small. In the middle years of the seventeenth century it was a city of over 20,000 inhabitants [20]; its closes, which had once been fields, were now teeming alleys which seldom saw the sun; along the High Street, its tenements already reached for the sky. Teinds in the ordinary sense of the term had long been supplanted by endowments presented, either individually or collectively, by its inhabitants. These had been enhanced during the 1460s by the erection of St Giles into a collegiate church supported by the substantial teinds of the parish of Dunbarney. The simultaneous erection of Trinity, on the northern fringes of the burgh, brought a further collection of rural teinds including those of Wemyss, Soutra and Kirkurd [21]. These varied endowments, together with the property of the monastic houses in Edinburgh, gradually became available, under the administration of the Magistrates and Council, to the reformed church during the last four decades of the sixteenth century. Broadly speaking, they consisted of two elements. There was no temporality in the ordinary sense, but there was a multitude of small plots of land within the burgh and outside it and many of these had been feued; their value was gradually diminished by inflation. In the seventeenth century, here as elsewhere, it was the teinds which mattered. Most of them were in tack and the increase in their money yield, though certain enough, was inevitably delayed. But, as their yield increased, their burdens grew. Their value was compromised by the local stipends dependent on them; the augmentations of the seventeenth century inevitably tended to confound the ministers of Edinburgh.

These varied revenues, gathered in by the Collector of Kirk Rents, were seldom enough to meet the mounting demands upon them. Edinburgh was at least twenty times as populous as an average parish and this justified an elaborate establishment of ministers. Knox, who was almost sufficient in himself, had eventually been joined by a colleague and an assistant. After his death, Lawson had two colleagues as well as the same assistant, now variously described as a minister or a reader. In the early nineties, Bruce led an establishment of five. At the turn of the century - when the King's men were coming in more rapidly than their Melvillian opposites were going out - the establishment rose temporarily to seven, fell again to six and then rose to eight in the 1620s as the burgh was subdivided into four parishes. Henderson aimed at six parishes and twelve ministers and actually achieved an establishment of ten, which continued through the Cromwellian period and beyond [22].

The fathers of the burgh nearly always wanted ministers of quality and, though they often pleaded their poverty, they were in the last resort willing to pay the price. The ministers in their turn were only occasionally unwilling. They were drawn by the prospect of higher stipends and influential pulpits. Who could resist a congregation that offered everything from a mob to a merchant prince? Knox, Bruce, Henderson and Douglas were men of consequence, and most of their comrades, King's men and Melvillians alike, were only less distinguished - and only less expensive. The burgh was paying Knox £400 a year - at least four times as much as the typical minister - as early as 1560. The Collectors of Thirds, who temporarily assumed the responsibilties of the burgh in 1562, did even better; they paid him a stipend, calculated partly in victual and thus protected from inflation, that would have honoured a superintendent. The burgh resumed the burden soon after the Civil War and thereafter retained it. The stipend of the first minister rose with inflation from £267 to £667, and that of the average minister from £167 to £495, between 1575 and the end of the century. Lawson and Bruce, no doubt because they were only parts of larger establishments, received much less in real terms than Knox had done - though substantially more than most of their contemporaries. But Bruce also had a vast, inflation-proof subvention from the Thirds of Arbroath, acquired while he enjoyed the royal favour and reduced as he lost it. Bruce, like Knox, was exceptional, but his comrades had to wait for the next century; by 1615, all six of the ministers were getting £800. In the 1640s, as we shall see, ten ministers would each be receiving £1,200 per year; in so doing, they would achieve parity not only with each other but with Knox as well [23].

It is obvious enough that the burgh's total expenditure on stipends must have risen much more rapidly. The church of Henderson cost thirty times as much in money terms, and perhaps six or seven times in real terms, as the church of Knox. It is arguable that these sums imposed a lesser strain on the resources of a wealthy city than did a quite ordinary rural stipend on those of a typical country parish. But hypothetical resources did not automatically translate themselves into actual revenue. The kirk rents had survived inflation reasonably well, but they had gradually been eroded by the demands of the country ministers, and it may be doubted if they ever yielded much more than £2-3,000 - and this was obviously inadequate. The Common Good was substantial but largely committed. The medieval sources were drying up; others had to be found.

The reformed church of Scotland was always sensitive about its relationship with the civil power and it had always been open to the argument that it should support itself. In Edinburgh, this could only mean that its deacons should collect its funds from the congregation. These contributions might have been voluntary; they might have been enforced, either by the kirk session or by the bailies acting, in true Melvillian style, as the agents of the kirk. None of these solutions had appealed to the Town Council; they were often solemnly considered but never fully implemented. The final answer disclosed itself during the 1620s as part of a broader agreement which sought to resolve the awkward triangular relationship between Crown, church and burgh. It took the form of a tax, authorised by the Privy Council in 1634 and enforced by the bailies of the burgh; it used the ordinary machinery of taxation and it did not compromise the civil power [24]. But, suggested as it was by the poor money assessment, it broadened the tax base considerably. It would be paid by every householder according to the annual value of the property which he occupied. In a sense, it covered the whole of the population apart from the beggars, the lawyers - who occasionally chose to tax themselves - and the ministers. It was not popular.

The annuity tax was designed to produce £8,000 and thus to increase the total revenue to about £11,000. The Council could now aim to meet the cost of six augmented stipends of £1,200 each, two more at the old rate of £800 each and eight house rents of £133 each, without drawing on its traditional revenues. The Common Good, previously in deficit, was now substantially in surplus - or it would have been if the annuity tax had lived up to expectations. In fact, it yielded nothing until the argument over the exemptions of the lawyers had been resolved in 1637 and, to judge from the experience of subsequent years, very little thereafter [25]. The rabbling of the Canterburians, which reduced the ministers to a total of two, was timely enough. The year 1639 brought three distinguished recruits - Henderson, Douglas and Colville - an entitlement to the pew rents and the unhappy knowledge that they could contribute nothing until the costs of their construction had been repaid. Two years later, the establishment went up from eight ministers to twelve, while the revenues of the bishopric of Orkney, encumbered by a prior gift but worth £6,000 once it had been redeemed, were added to the funds available to pay them [26]. In practice, vacancies continued to keep costs down. There were still only ten ministers in 1644 and, despite a number of changes, the total neither rose nor fell from this level for the rest of the decade. The city was now called upon to find rather over £13,000 per year from revenues which, at least in ideal circumstances, were capable of producing an annual income of about £15,000. But the circumstances were far from ideal. Plague, civil war and high taxation all in their different ways combined to reduce revenue and it is obvious that the annuity tax was the worst sufferer. In June 1646, a commission, representing the Town Council, the kirk sessions and the neighbours, was charged with the duty of finding a 'solid course' to finance the church without recourse to the Common Good. The presence of two members of the College of Justice suggests that the immunities of the lawyers were being questioned; but it seems almost certain that the real trouble was more fundamental. The ordinary householder, and especially the poorer householder, was quite simply refusing to pay the tax. Whatever the reason, the problem was clearly serious. Henderson's stipend was two years in arrears when he died two months later[27].

The defeat of the Engagement left the Town Council, like the Parliament itself, at the mercy of the ministers - and they were merciless enough. In the first place, the annuity tax was altered almost beyond recognition. The rate was increased to produce an estimated income of over £12,000. The special immunities were abolished. Above all, the magistrates were pointedly excluded from any share in its administration. The deacons of the kirk sessions of Edinburgh, who had previously managed the distribution of the poor money, emerged as the Melvillian treasurers of a revolutionary church. The annuity tax was theirs to collect - if they could. At the same time, a new set of augmentation commissioners was preparing, with the enthusiastic support of the Commission of the General Assembly, to descend upon the town's teinds. It was a prospect that the Council, as titulars of at least seven lowland parishes and more in Orkney, could not be expected to relish. Their teinds of Soutra, a small parish, had already gone ([28]).

As the teinds were melting away, the demands on them mounted. The Parliament had already ordained that the proceeds of the annuity tax would be divided among six ministers, each of whom would receive nearly £2,100 including his house rent. Shortly afterwards, the Council conceded the inevitable demand that the remaining ministers should be similarly provided ([29]). A full establishment of twelve ministers, each receiving three or four times the yield of an ordinary rural living, would now have cost about £25,000 - far more than the theoretical yield of the annuity and the teinds combined. The ministers now regarded the Common Good as their own. Cromwell arrived not a moment too soon.

The New Model Army destroyed church and burgh alike, and the yield of the annuity tax, always inadequate, now fell still further. The Council, which had come to terms with the conqueror before the end of 1652, gradually regained the initiative over the church and, in 1654, it exploited its advantage. It brusquely informed the deacons of the kirk that they had neglected their duty and, perhaps a trifle contemptuously, offered the assistance of the 'officers of this burgh' in the collection of the tax. In the following March, the ministers, now hopelessly in arrears, were forced to bargain. They accepted £1,467 for their bygone stipends and house rents and £1,667 for the future. At the same time, they agreed to an establishment of ten instead of twelve and they surrendered their rights in the annuity to the civil power ([30]).

The fortunate survival of an account of 1657 offers a valuable glimpse of the situation as it was soon after the treaty had been concluded ([31]). It shows that the tack duty of the Bishopric of Orkney was still worth about £6,000 per year and that the various tacks of the landward parishes were still bringing in about £2,000. The annuity tax, despite the fact that the bailies could now quarter soldiers from the New Model on reluctant contributors, was still yielding less than £7,000 or considerably less than Charles I had originally expected of it. Total revenue, excluding non-recurring items, was of the order of £15,000 - or about 60% of the demands of the ministers as they had been in 1649. The stipends of the ten ministers officiating in 1657 would have required nearly £17,000. Four of the ten actually received the full amount; the other six got about £1,450 each and a valid legal claim on the remainder. This was not untypical. Stipends had been regularly and fully paid until the augmentation of 1635. Thereafter they had drifted more or less seriously into arrears with the fluctuations of supply and demand. Normality was now returning; the pattern of the future had been set.

The ministers of Edinburgh, despite their recent reverse, were wealthy enough. At the turn of the century, stipends stood at about £500 per year; before the accession of Charles I they had risen to £800 and they were augmented just before the revolution to £1,200; in 1649 they rose, in theory if not in practice, towards £2,000 and eventually settled down at about £1,500, or three times the original level. For the greater part of our period, the ministers of Edinburgh received stipends of £1,200 and house rents of £133 - perhaps twice as much as a rural minister with a manse, glebe and rather more than the minimum stipend. Again the attempt to express this in basic terms is irresistible. The wage assessment of 1656 suggests that it cost 3/- per day, or roughly £55 per year, to feed a casual labourer. The rather earlier valuation for the annuity tax indicates that the occupier of the smallest dwelling house paid a rent of from £5 to £10 a year. This may suggest - for the calculation is dubious enough - that an urban labourer and his wife needed a little over £100 a year to live - perhaps twice as much as a rural cottar. If this is true, a minister in the early forties was worth 12 times as much, and his successor of the late fifties 15 or 16 times as much, as a living wage.

The annuity tax valuation invites a further comparison. In the south-east quarter of Edinburgh there were forty-five houses paying an annual rental of between £110 and £150 per year, or the approximate equivalent of a minister's house rent, and forty-one of the occupiers are identifiable. Twelve of these were merchants, most of them men of some consequence though rather less than merchant princes; and six were vintners, who tended to be prosperous rather than rich. There were only five craftsmen, including three surgeons, one goldsmith and a tailor - all of them from the influential incorporations. But the largest single group - of eighteen - were very close to the ministers themselves. They included at least eleven lawyers - among them a judge and the Town Clerk of Edinburgh - a Regent of Philosophy and a Doctor of Medicine; they might reasonably be described as professional men. The south-east quarter had forty-eight larger houses, two of which paid rents of over £500 per year, and nearly a thousand smaller houses, almost half of which paid rents of less than £20 annually [32]. If the Edinburgh ministers were much less wealthy than Sir William Dick of Braid, merchant, banker, usurer to Charles I and the Parliaments of the 1640s, and Lord Provost in 1638, they were also enormously richer than the multitude of labourers and journeymen who filled their churches.

For the ministers of town and country alike, the first half of the seventeenth century was a triumph which can conveniently be expressed, however imprecisely, in financial terms. It has been shown that, in the areas of Edinburgh, Glasgow and Dunblane, the total value of the average minister's testament tended to increase during the first three decades of the century and that, despite a decline in the thirties, it was higher during the fourth decade than it had been in the first. This research has been extended geographically to embrace the whole of Scotland and chronologically to include the whole of the period up to the Restoration - and the generalisations still survive [33]. A smooth ascent is interrupted only by a sharp decline in the thirties. This rather sudden dip could simply reflect a small and not necessarily representative sample. The testaments of many of the ministers who died in the thirties were not recorded; those who died did not necessarily represent those who lived; they might well have included an unduly high proportion of ministers with stipends still unaugmented. But there is other evidence to suggest that part of the decline may have been real enough. An augmented stipend normally included a substantial victual component and its value almost certainly dropped during the thirties. The fiars for Fife suggest that the price of barley fell from an average of £7.7 per boll during the twenties to £6.8 during the thirties. Prices then recovered slowly during the forties and were very high - always over £10 from 1648 to 1652, after which they gradually returned to their earlier levels. Comparable series are not available for other areas, but prices seem to have followed a similar course in East Lothian and Midlothian ([34]). It is indeed evident that a minister's income depended in part on short-term fluctuations in the price of victual, and it should be emphasised that these were independent of the general price level. The minister had a vested interest, if not in dearth, at least in a poor harvest. By and large, the thirties were a decade of abundance and he suffered. But the emergency was less than a disaster. If the balance of his debts became somewhat less favourable than usual, his stock of goods and gear survived more or less intact; he merely drew in his investments.

It is tempting to find some connection between this decline in the real incomes of the ministers and their involvement in the upheavals of the late thirties. The timing is right and the coincidence remarkable. It would surely be absurd to construct a theory of revolution on grievances so slender, but it is a reasonable inference that the ministers, not for the first time or the last, were somewhat disgruntled about money and that they were, despite the King's augmentations, conditioned to revolt. Be this as it may, it is evident that the ministers were suffering a larger misfortune of which they can scarcely have been fully aware. Ever since the Reformation, their money stipends had been compromised by inflation. The distant voices of Knox and Bruce seemed to extol the virtue of victual - and, when they were heard, inflation stopped.

But, despite his ill fortune, the minister was always one of the more prosperous members of his local community. He did not need more money; indeed he was incapable of spending the money he had; his inventory was always a small proportion of his total wealth. And yet he always wanted more and he was remarkably successful at getting it. He was a member of a professional order which was as contemptuous of individual glory as it was obsessed with its own collective strength. The augmentation of a stipend would benefit the minister himself, but it would also benefit his successors. It would contribute to the wealth - and thus the power - of a young and revolutionary church which had to fight institutions with the weight of the centuries behind them. The church was concerned to buy prestige.

9

The Elder Who Rules

JOHN Calvin maintained that 'courts of judgment' had been established in the church 'from the beginning'. As the founder of a revolutionary church, he naturally drew inspiration and example from a period when Christianity itself had been a new force in a hostile world. Had not Paul left Titus in Crete to 'ordain elders in every city'? A revolutionary church, whether of the first century or the sixteenth, must organise and rule itself. It needed not only pastors who would preach and doctors who would train them, but also elders for its government and deacons to arrange its revenues. Calvin was always careful to deny any intention to subvert the civil power; but he foresaw a system of government erected on separate foundations and capable of standing independently upon them. Ideally the elder would be a bureaucrat totally absorbed in the business of church government and it followed inescapably from this that he would - in an ideal church - be paid. He construed a famous passage in Paul's epistle to Timothy - 'let the elders who rule well be considered worthy of a double honour' - to refer not only to the 'reverence due to them', but also to the 'remuneration to which their ministry entitles them' (¹).

Neither Calvin nor Knox operated in an entirely hostile world and both were willing to work with the civil power when it seemed friendly. Indeed, Knox's first appeal had been to the 'Lords and Barons professing Christ Jesus' and the success of this appeal led to the creation of a church in which the inferior magistrate, and later the Godly Prince, was a powerful force. In these circumstances a clerical bureaucracy was as unnecessary as it was impossible. For much of the patrimony of the church, teind and temporality alike, was already the property of the magistrates, including those whom it was least politic to offend. Knox necessarily settled for a church without property in which the clerical elder could have no place. The *First Book of Discipline* was specific enough: 'We think it not necessary that any public stipend shall be appointed . . . to the elders . . . because they are not so occupied with the affairs of the church, but that reasonably they may attend upon their domestic business.' The elder would be first and foremost a farmer or a rentier, a feuar or a baron, a merchant or a craftsman, who happened to possess a strong moral sense and a sound grasp of protestant doctrine. The eldership, as it originally appeared, was created in the image of society as a whole.

The early reformers seem to have been aware of the dangers inherent in their system. The election of elders was to be an annual event 'lest by long continuance of such offices men presume upon the liberty of the kirk'. If the elder was not to be an indoctrinated bureaucrat, he should be changed as often as possible lest he seize control of the kirk session from its only indoctrinated member, the minister himself.

The electoral process was fundamental and Knox has left an eloquent account of its beginnings in Edinburgh. In the innocent days of the privy kirk, the congregation, then a purely voluntary association, had elected 'some to occupy the supreme place of exhortation and reading, some to be elders and helpers unto them for the oversight of the flock and some to be deacons for the collection of alms to be distributed to the poor'. The intended ascendancy of the exhorter or reader, who would later develop into the professional minister, is noteworthy. As the privy kirk grew into a public kirk, the best of his entourage were selected as the official elders and deacons of a kirk session which now had at least a nominal authority over the entire population of the burgh. These held office for a year and more and were then authorised to nominate double their number as a leet from which their successors would be chosen. The congregation, 'to the end that no man . . . should complain that he was spoiled in his liberty in election', was then granted the opportunity to object and to name substitutes of its own choosing. On the following Sunday, 'the whole communicants (were) then commanded to be present . . . to give their votes as they (would) answer before God, to such as they esteem most able to bear the charge of the kirk with the ministers'. Those gaining the greatest number of votes, 'without respect of persons', were to have 'the first place in the eldership' and 'so proceeding until the number . . . be complete'. And, Knox continued, 'if a poor man exceed a rich man in votes, he precedes him in place' (²).

There is some corroborating evidence that this elaborate system, with its strident insistence on the rights not only of the congregation but of its poorest members, actually operated in Edinburgh. But, if this was so, it seems unlikely that it was ever implemented in its entirety anywhere else. The *First Book of Discipline*, with a striking modesty which may have concealed serious disagreement, left the details to the discretion of the individual kirk session and it has been assumed that this led, either immediately or gradually, to a simplified method of election from which the various intermediate stages were either omitted or reduced to meaningless formalities. The old kirk session, rather after the fashion of a town council, chose its own successor. The congregational trend, where it had existed, tended to merge into the oligarchic. Indeed the Book of Discipline itself had left a loophole; it was always accepted that an elder might be re-elected.

The lay principle, whether congregational or oligarchic, was consciously repudiated by the Melvillians. The *Second Book of Discipline* insisted that the elder was a 'spiritual person' as the minister himself was. He would be ceremonially ordained and thus set irrevocably apart from the community itself. He would be a salaried professional wholly engaged in the government of a church which, far from reflecting society, would seek deliberately to transform it. Melville sought to achieve the ideal church which Calvin and Knox had dismissed as an impractical dream (³).

These notions, irreconcilable as they were, lingered on into the seventeenth century, the one in the actual practice of the church, the other in the minds - or rather the dreams - of the radical presbyterians. For the Melvillian edifice, deprived of the revenues which alone could have lent it substance, had already collapsed. The patrimony of the church, which it was sacrilege to alienate, had already been alienated. By and large, the teinds, which were designed for the ministers, had preserved their value; but the revenues of the temporalities had, as we have seen, been reduced by inflation to a miserable pittance. Even if it had been possible to recover them - and it almost certainly was not - they would not have been worth having. As George Gillespie admitted in 1641, 'the revenues of our church are so small that they cannot spare stipends to ruling elders.' The elder was not a professional administrator for the sufficient reason that there were no funds available to support him. He inevitably remained the amateur, often the devoted amateur, that the early reformers had originally intended him to be. It is interesting that Gillespie, in the very act of recognising this, nonetheless insisted that elders were elected for life. If the facts suggested otherwise, if indeed elders, in some parishes at least, were regularly laying down their office and passing it on to others, they were merely availing themselves of the dispensation, set forth in the *Second Book of Discipline* itself, that allowed them to set aside the office for a spell 'as was among the Levites . . . in serving of the Temple'. The gap between the ideal and the facts was no less disturbing to the latter-day Melvillians than it had been to Melville himself (⁴).

The evidence supports the theory in only two out of a very large number of cases and then only half-heartedly. The kirk session of Kinghorn published a list of elders, long enough to include the whole of the session, on 10th May, 1642. Between the notice and the list itself the session clerk inserted a brief sentence granting 'immunity' for a year 'from the exercise of the office' to three elders, none of whom was named in the list. This plainly implies that the elders concerned had previously been elected for life; but, if this is so, the elders actually named in the list were to hold office only until the next election, which was actually held during the following year. This incident, equivocal as it was, should perhaps be interpreted in the light of another, also dated 1642, in the parish of St Cuthbert's. Here, an unusually large kirk session had been subdivided into smaller groups which had served in rotation. This system, unusual as it was, can fairly be likened to that which had been envisaged, if only as a second best, by the radical George Gillespie. But, if this is granted, the sequel was even more revealing. In February, the presbytery of Edinburgh, a powerful body which normally reflected the views of the church as a whole, brusquely ordered the election of a new session to serve for a single year 'without any intermission and then as many more to be chosen in their stead'. If the parish had flirted with Melville, the presbytery smote it with Knox (⁵).

It was probably no mere coincidence that both of these incidents occurred in 1642, when the general assembly passed an act, incidentally occasioned by the political unreliability of the kirk session of Glasgow, which favoured the traditional system. It stated quite baldly that the old session would elect the new and it clearly implied that the members thus elected would serve for only a limited period before resigning their offices as a body to another session similarly authorised to act for a similarly limited span. But this same act also recognised that practice was far from uniform. It stated that vacancies arising from death or other causes might be filled by the session as they occurred ([6]). Indeed, in the Perthshire parish of Kinnaird and the Ayrshire parish of Dundonald, the practice of electing the whole session at regular intervals had already disappeared before 1638. In Colinton, not far from the southern outskirts of Edinburgh itself, it had disappeared by 1651, the year in which the surviving records begin. In all these three parishes, sessioners were chosen, either individually or in small groups, at irregular intervals. It is obvious that many of them sat for long periods and, in Colinton at least, it is certain that some served until they died. The pattern was plainly somewhat confused; it is worth exploring the surviving evidence more thoroughly ([7]).

To this end, 123 parishes - including the vast majority of those in which a continuous record of five years or more has survived for any part of the period from 1630 to 1660 - have been examined ([8]). In none of these cases has any direct evidence of ordination or election for life been discovered; in only two - the cases of Kinghorn and St Cuthbert's mentioned above - can it be inferred and, even in these instances, the evidence suggests a practice lapsing into disuse; the elder of the mid-seventeenth century was not a 'spiritual person'. On the other hand, the traditional system is known to have persisted in some at least of the towns. In the several parishes of the capital, annual elections were punctiliously held in every recorded year from 1630 to 1660; the tributary burgh of Canongate was only less assiduous. Aberdeen, Elgin, and Burntisland were similarly regular, as was St Andrews until 1647, and this was probably the pattern for the larger towns. In Dunfermline and Culross, both smaller burghs with large and populous landward areas, elections were held at intervals of three or four years. Falkirk, a parish of a rather similar character, held two elections in 1638 and 1640, but was much less regular thereafter.

The countryside, properly so called, presented a more varied picture. The kirk session of Errol elected a complete new session in 1640, 1642, 1643 and 1647; Liberton elected four sessions between 1639 and 1649; Stow eight between 1626 and 1652; Scone four from 1630 to 1639; St Cuthbert's six between 1642 and the Restoration. But these were scarcely typical. Errol, with the rich soils of the Carse of Gowrie and a coastal situation convenient for the shipment of their products, was the wealthiest rural parish in Perthshire and probably the wealthiest anywhere to the north of the Tay. St Cuthbert's, a large arable area with Edinburgh in its belly, was by far the richest rural parish in the whole of Scotland. Liberton was another large arable parish well situated to supply the Edinburgh market. Stow, though pastoral and relatively remote, was vast in area and well within the commercial orbit of the capital; its valued rent was well above average. Scone was smaller than the others, though still above average, and it is interesting that it was, as part of the feued temporality of the abbey, a parish of many proprietors. For this was also true of the other four. The parish of Stow was, with the exception of its northern and southern extremities, a part of the feued temporality of the archbishopric of St Andrews. St Cuthbert's was shared between the feued Burgh Muir of Edinburgh, the partly feued ecclesiastical barony of Broughton, and several civil baronies. Errol was divided between a number of the feuars of the erected Lordship of Coupar, several small civil baronies and the huge, but recently sub-divided, barony of Errol. Liberton, though lacking in church property, was large enough to support several lairds in modest affluence. If the traditional system thrived in towns, it also seemed to flourish in wealthy rural parishes, especially - or so it would appear - where these were divided, as large parishes usually were, among many landowners of one kind or another.

These generalisations rest, more than a trifle insecurely, on the evidence of eleven urban parishes, some of which included landward areas, and five large rural parishes. Thirty-five out of the remaining 107 are known to have elected a full session at some time during the period, but cannot be shown to have done so regularly and, of these, three were new parishes which elected a full session only when they were first formed. Six of the remaining 32 - Dumfries, Dysart, Pittenweem, Kinghorn, Dunblane, and South Queensferry - were small towns, in every case except the last, with a landward area. Two of the others - Dalkeith and Duddingston - were near Edinburgh; two more - Lesmahagow and Kilconquhar - were large parishes sub-divided into many estates. These cases were plainly comparable with those already examined; but the rest, 22 in all, disclose no clear pattern.

Seventy-four out of the total sample of 123 cannot be shown to have elected a full session at any time during the period - in some cases, no doubt, because the surviving record starts late. Three of these - Inveresk, Kilrennie and Anstruther Wester - were small towns; while six more - Tranent, Ceres, Carnbee, Markinch, St Ninians, and Kinfauns - were large in terms of valued rent; but the great majority varied in size from average to small and were at least relatively remote. The parish of Penicuik, with a valued rent rather below the average for Midlothian, may perhaps speak for them all. The surviving record begins in 1654 and continues to the Restoration. In May of 1654, two farmers were added to the session. Just over two years later, the session clerk recorded a list of elders, not because they were newly elected, but - or so we may guess - because he was in danger of forgetting who they were. In December 1657 he noted that the session had been depleted, presumably by death or resignation, and entered the names of four more elders - including Clerk of Penicuik - who had been proposed to fill the gaps. They were duly sworn in, without protest from anybody, a fortnight later. Some of them may have gone on for the rest of their lives, but there was no question of ordination. In a small rural parish the number of potential elders was, as we shall see, strictly limited; under the traditional procedure, with its rigid insistence on the annual election of the whole session, the same men inevitably tended to elect themselves again and again; the election itself degenerated into an empty formality; eventually it lapsed.

There is some evidence that this process was gradually spreading to more populous areas. The kirk session of St Andrews, which could boast a continuous history looking back through the 1560s into the mistier days of the privy kirk, ruled a substantial town surrounded by a rich landward area valued in the seventeenth century at more than £25,000 per year. St Andrews must have been more generously supplied with potential elders than were the vast majority of the parishes of Scotland. But, if this was so, the kirk session of the 1640s was itself a large body, varying slightly in numbers but usually consisting of some fifty members. A complete new session was elected in December 1639 and served for a year, when it was replaced by another. The process was repeated in December 1641 and continued, with only the occasional lapse, into the middle forties. The lists do however indicate that sitting members were fairly often re-elected a second time. Indeed this was much more common than it was in Edinburgh, where a much larger population was ruled, sometimes ineffectively, by a similar number of elders and deacons. The St Andrews election of December 1647 witnessed a significant departure. The session clerk duly noted the election, but recorded only the names of those members who had not served during the previous year. The sequel was almost inevitable; elders began to be added to the session in small groups as vacancies arose. The clerk, like his rustic counterpart in Penicuik, entered a list of the session in 1651, but there is no indication that those named in it had been newly elected. The system, which had tossed aside the strident challenge of Melville, slowly succumbed to irresistible pressures of convenience ([9]).

The great debate concerning the nature of the eldership has fascinated the theologians of later centuries and it is arguable that most of them have misunderstood, and indeed debased, the meaning which the seventeenth century attached to it. For George Gillespie and James Guthrie, Alexander Henderson and Robert Baillie were not arguing about a church in the modern sense, but a powerful organisation which always threatened to become, and occasionally actually became, a 'state opposite to a state'. They always wrote, and often talked, the language of theology, for this they had been trained to do; but they used it to discuss issues which were as meaningful in this world as they would be in the next. Seen in this context, the nature of the eldership was rather more than a debating point. It reached down into the vitals of society. The 'spiritual' elder would have been ordained to a career in a revolutionary organisation, his life would have been dedicated to the forcible imposition of the godly society. The 'lay' elder, on the other hand, was a revolutionary only in a more subtle and less conscious sense. It will be argued that the elders of the church represented the social realities of seventeenth century Scotland more faithfully than did the magnates of a feudal state and, if this was so, then they were revolutionaries whether they wanted to be or not.

The argument over the nature of the eldership has often been confused with another, distinct though closely allied to it, about the meaning of the term 'ruling elder' - and here the seventeenth century itself was partly responsible. The theological literature of the mid-seventeenth century tended to use the term in its modern sense to distinguish the elder who ruled from the elder who preached. But the term also occurs, and indeed constantly recurs, in the records of all the courts of the church, and here its meaning was rather different. The session clerks of the period never described the ordinary members of their sessions as 'ruling elders'. The term was reserved for the commissioner chosen to represent the session in the presbytery or the synod - and, of course, the delegate from the presbytery to the general assembly. The distinction was firmly drawn and, as far as the writer is aware, there were no exceptions.

The term 'ruling elder' came into regular use in Scotland during the summer of 1638, when the Tables were anxious to legitimise the appearance of lay politicians in the coming general assembly ([10]). They drew their precedents from the last two decades of the previous century when - or so they claimed - 'barons and gentlemen' had attended the 'first erecting of presbyteries' and represented presbyteries in the general assembly. They went on to argue that the act of the Dundee Assembly of 1598 had described the lay commissioners from presbyteries to the assembly as 'barons', and then they used act and precedent alike to justify the intervention of magnates in the elections to their own assembly of 1638 - and here they ran into a double difficulty. For the presence of 'lay', as distinct from 'spiritual', elders was offensive to the Melvillians, while the presence of elders of any kind was unfamiliar to conservatives who had entered the ministry since the restoration of episcopacy at the turn of the century. The difficulty was at least partly resolved by insisting that the laymen concerned should be members of their own local sessions - and thus 'ecclesiastical', if scarcely 'spiritual', persons - and by describing them as 'ruling elders'. The term, thus sanctified, persisted until the Restoration, when it inevitably fell into disuse only to reappear after 1690 in the very different climate created by the renunciation of the Covenants. In a church that no longer sought to be a 'state opposite to a state', it quickly reverted to the meaning which the divines, as distinct from the session clerks, had originally given to it.

The act of the Glasgow Assembly 'restoring' the higher courts of the church to their 'constitutions of ministers and elders' did so by reference to their 'powers and jurisdictions according as they are contained in the Book of Policy' ([11]). A process, which had begun with an act of assembly describing commissioners from presbyteries as 'barons' and which had continued through an election characterised by the most blatant forms of baronial intervention, ended with another act of assembly which appealed to the *Second Book of Discipline*. In one sense, this merely reflected the change in the balance of power which had occurred between the middle of 1638 and the beginning of 1639; but it also illustrated the continuing necessity to reconcile the ministers to a process which allowed lay politicians to penetrate the very engine room of the church. The Tables had argued, probably justly, that laymen had once been admitted to presbyteries on special occasions, but they could not reasonably deny that the presbytery had usually been a clerical body. The *Second Book of Discipline*, by insisting that the eldership was a spiritual office as the ministry was, removed some at least of the objections. But it did not, and could not, alter the facts. Barons, whatever they may have called themselves, did attend general assemblies and nearly all the leading ministers accepted them if only because they could not do without them. Their presence at the election meetings of presbyteries was more controversial - but presumably less so than most of the possible alternatives. Irregular attendance for special purposes was resented only because it might lead to regular attendance at ordinary meetings as well. For these had certainly been a clerical preserve since the 1590s and probably since the inception of presbyteries as such. Indeed it was this which had almost split the revolution in the summer of 1638. The act of the Glasgow Assembly, which finally allowed the ruling elder into the secret recesses of the presbytery, promised a real change in the character of the kirk. It poses a vital question: who controlled the presbyteries of the church of the Covenant?

10

Imperious Masters

GILBERT Burnet, looking back perceptively enough from the distant perch of an English bishopric, argued that the ministers, 'glad to have so great a support', had accepted the alliance with the magnates and welcomed them as ruling elders into the higher courts of the kirk. But, he went on, the ministers 'grew weary of such imperious masters' and sought to supplant them. They 'studied to work up the inferior people to much zeal and, as they wrought any up to some measure of heat and knowledge, they brought them into their eldership and so got a majority of hot zealots who depended on them'.

It might be objected that Burnet was a hostile witness peddling second-hand knowledge; but his analysis, over-simplified though it evidently was, is substantially supported by contemporary sources. In 1641 the radical George Gillespie complained of the election of 'disguised and histrionical men puffed up with titles' as ruling elders; while James Guthrie, Protester and martyr, enlarged on the same theme a decade later. The 'Lord's design upon Scotland', he declaimed, had long been to 'purge his house', to 'have his ordinances pure' and to 'have his people and his officers also pure'. But aspiration had outstripped achievement. The kirk had 'boasted of reformation of the ordinances without seeking really to reform church officers'. There was a 'generation of ignorant, slothful, earthly minded men who (bore) the name of elders'. The office had been bestowed on 'those of the richer and higher sort . . . (because) their secular power . . . (seemed) the best means to promote the kingdom of Jesus Christ', while men of 'christian and godly carriage' were passed over because of their 'mean condition in this world'. Better, he concluded severely, that they be 'of lower degree if godly than of higher degree if otherwise'. Guthrie came very close to the assertion that wealth and power were evil in themselves.

But it is interesting that Robert Baillie - who loved a Lord - could assert the reverse. Writing in controversy with an anglican divine who asserted that presbyterians were exactly as Guthrie wanted them to be, he claimed that the higher courts of the church were the preserve of the mighty. The elders attending presbytery and synod included 'the most qualified noblemen, gentlemen and burgesses' that the area could 'afford'. Above all, he boasted, the general assembly attracted as many 'burgesses and more gentlemen from every shire than come to any Parliament' as well as the 'prime nobility'. It is, of course, easy enough to reconcile Baillie's boast with Guthrie's complaint; the one described the church of the Covenant as it was - or at least as it once had been; the other yearned for a godlier church of lower degree - and we have already found some evidence that he was not entirely unsuccessful. It will be remembered that Patrick Gillespie was using 'yeomen elders' to control the presbytery of Glasgow during the early fifties.

Alexander Henderson - who used Lords without loving them - lived in a real world where magnates mattered and his remedy for aristocratic interference was necessarily more evasive. He accepted that the barons had their place in the general assembly, probably finding some comfort in the knowledge that it met only briefly and that its executive impact was small; it legislated for the church without ruling it. Similarly he accepted that they should attend presbytery meetings if there were matters 'of great weight to be handled' - and these would include the election of commissioners to the assembly. But he obviously did not want them to come too often. He observed that ministers were compelled to attend the presbytery and then added, perhaps a trifle ironically, that the elder was 'not so strictly tied'. Indeed it had been suspected from the first that the ministers would not encourage ruling elders to come to the ordinary meetings of presbyteries. It is at least arguable that the presbytery remained to all intents and purposes a clerical body - and this is an argument that only the presbytery clerks of the period, or rather those who were industrious enough to record attendances, can resolve ([1]).

The story really began as early as May 1638, when the first rumours of a general assembly began to drift northwards from the court of King Charles. In Kilconquhar, and presumably at least in some of the other parishes in the vital presbytery of St Andrews, the kirk session, significantly augmented to include the heritors of the parish, drew up a rota, consisting solely of proprietors, to attend the 'weekly meetings' of the presbytery according, they added in a phrase that would have seemed eccentric only a few months earlier, to the 'ancient and laudable custom before observed in this kirk of Scotland'. The precise meaning of this episode is debatable. It was obviously occasioned by the possibility of a general assembly and, to this extent, it merely anticipated the election meetings that would be held all over Scotland during the following autumn. On the other hand, it plainly foreshadowed the attendance of laymen at all the sessions of the presbytery, at least until commissioners had been elected to the assembly. It is easy enough to understand the complaint that came from the Ministers' Table in the following August; in St Andrews at least, the electoral system designed for the new assembly actually did bring the ruling elder into the ordinary meetings of the presbytery ([2]).

But St Andrews was hardly typical. Elders began to attend the ordinary meetings of the presbytery of Perth during the following January - that is, immediately after the Glasgow Assembly had formally authorised their coming - and its example was followed by a number of other southern presbyteries. Others were notably less enthusiastic; indeed the important presbyteries of Haddington and Dalkeith waited until the following autumn. In the presbytery of Ellon, elders attended the election meeting of 1639 without coming to the ordinary meetings before and after it - and this was almost certainly true of the north as a whole. The impression remains that the ministers, or at least those outside the heartlands of the Covenant, sought to keep the presbytery as a clerical preserve as long as possible and that the laymen, election meetings obviously excepted, did not hasten to intrude (^{3}).

A succession of clerks to the presbytery of Haddington, unlike many of their colleagues elsewhere, recorded attendances and thus revealed the naked truth. On 8th July, when the elections to the assembly of 1639 were held, all of the fifteen parishes of the presbytery were represented by ruling elders; but this was no ordinary meeting and no further laymen seem to have attended until the middle of October, when two successive sessions were each visited, perhaps to the surprise of some of the ministers present, by a modest total of six elders. It was eventually decided to invite each minister to bring an elder to a third meeting, to be held on the 13th November, which would lay down a 'constant course' for their 'keeping of the presbyterial meetings' in the future. The two intervening sessions were kept by only four and six elders respectively, but the long-awaited gathering of the 13th was greeted by an improved attendance of twelve. This substantially augmented gathering finally passed an act which must surely have seemed an anti-climax: no formal procedure was laid down; everything was left to the 'care and diligence' of local ministers and their kirk sessions; every allowance would be made for the difficulties of distant kirks in winter time. This long, and surely dilatory, sequence can only suggest indifference or hostility - and indeed the impact of the act was less than impressive; the next twelve meetings attracted an average attendance of seven or eight elders, or about half the potential total.

The passage of time brought no improvement. The first ten meetings of the following year yielded a similar average but, after the middle of the year, attendances fell markedly. Indeed the average for the whole of 1640 was only four and the trend continued for the rest of the decade. On 3rd July 1644 the presbytery passed an act, for which there was an evident justification, ordering ruling elders to 'keep better the meetings of the presbytery'. The resulting improvement was modest rather than spectacular; the average went up from a little under one to rather over two and the figure for the year as a whole was only three. But the decline was still to continue; in 1649, when the ministers were supreme, a typical session of the presbytery of Haddington was attended by only one or two elders. The figures speak eloquently for themselves (^{4}).

It might reasonably be objected that the clerical tradition was particularly strong in Haddington and it was certainly reinforced by the arrival of David Calderwood, who became minister of Pencaitland in 1641. But a cross-section, necessarily accidental rather than representative, through the church as it was in the late 1640s and the early 1650s may suggest that Haddington was not entirely untypical. In Perth (with an average attendance of 2 ruling elders from an effective total of 19 parishes) and in Dalkeith (2 out of 16) attendance was about as bad. In Linlithgow (4 out of 13) it was better but still low enough. The peripheral presbytery of Dumbarton (3 out of 14) was probably, to judge from the scattered evidence of clerks who seldom bothered with *sederunts*, better than most of those from north of Tay or south of Lammermuir. The traditional strongholds of the Covenant - if Dunfermline (4 out of 11) and Ayr (7 out of 21) can be regarded as typical - recorded averages of about a third of the potential total; their ruling elders attended more regularly than those of the country as a whole, but not strikingly so. In a sense, the widespread habit of noting an elder's presence and a minister's absence tells its own story. The minister usually came; the elder usually stayed away. Unlike the elder, the minister nearly always had to account for his absence. Ministers did not always attend meetings; they might be too ill, too old or too distant; they might be engaged on the official business of their church; but, for the most part, they came. The evidence of the sederunts strongly suggests that the presbytery, like the Commission, was becoming an essentially clerical institution (⁵).

All this might have been true without denying the accuracy of Burnet's analysis or the justice of Guthrie's complaint. Election meetings were usually well attended and it is obvious enough that the earlier general assemblies of the period were shaped by barons who called themselves ruling elders. It may be true that ruling elders did not attend presbyteries as regularly as ministers did; but 'disguised and histrionical men', whether or not they were actually 'puffed up with titles', might have dominated the ordinary meetings of presbyteries without coming in great numbers. The arithmetic of attendance is instructive rather than decisive; in a sense, quality was more important than quantity.

The presbytery of Perth comprised nineteen rural parishes, ranging in wealth from Errol (valued at £17,000 in 1649) to Collace (£980), and in structure from Abernethie (with 46 proprietors) or Scone (with 38) to Aberdalgie (with 2) or the tiny St Madoes (with 1), besides the largely urban parish of Perth itself. On 26th September 1638, all of the nineteen had sent ruling elders to the presbytery to elect a commissioner to the Glasgow Assembly. This had been an exceptional occasion; but, shortly after the assembly had closed, a slightly smaller but otherwise strikingly similar group was sworn in to attend the ordinary meetings of the presbytery. At the first session of the reconstituted synod of Perth and Stirling, held at Perth in the following April, the same nineteen parishes were represented by eighteen ruling elders - an impressive attendance lacking only an elder from St Madoes - and again most of the names were familiar. It was obvious enough that the laymen who had sent the Earl of Wemyss to the Glasgow Assembly intended to control the presbytery and, no doubt in partnership with their colleagues from surrounding areas, the synod as well.

The synod list is perhaps the most useful of the three, since it alone can be compared with similar lists for later years. The eighteen elders included thirteen landed proprietors, a miller and four others who were probably tenant farmers. Five of the proprietors held the largest estates in their parishes, two more the second largest and another - from a parish of several substantial estates - the third; the least of them - Andrew Grant of Balhaghills, ruling elder of Kinnoul - was the sixth proprietor (valued at £299) of a parish subdivided into one large and seventeen other estates. One of the thirteen, Viscount Stormont, was a Lord of Erection; two others represented Perthshire in the earlier Parliaments of the period; another had recently inherited the substantial possessions of a former shire commissioner. The group, which represented the parishes of the presbytery of Perth in the April synod, closely resembled that which had sent the Earl of Wemyss to the Glasgow

Assembly. They were dominated by a group of reasonably wealthy magnates. The average annual valued rent of the proprietors among them was nearly £900, greatly above the average for the presbytery as a whole.

The spring synod of 1639 illustrates aptly enough the original intentions of the three feudal Tables as well as the fears of the clerical fourth. But achievement only rarely matched up to aspiration. Even in 1639, the more distant parishes of the synod were unrepresented. Hardly any ruling elders came from rural Perthshire to subsequent synods held in Stirling. Not until the autumn synod of 1643 were the parishes, which had hopefully sent so many ruling elders in 1639, again represented comprehensively enough to permit a valid comparison. The contrast was dramatic enough. It is true that ten out of the fourteen elders present were proprietors, but their average valued rent was only just over £350, or less than 40% of the figure for 1639. None of the proprietors concerned was the wealthiest of his parish; none had a valued rent of more than £1,000; none was a member of Parliament; one or two held small baronies, but not one could reasonably be described as a great magnate. Scone, once represented by a Lord of Erection, now had a feuar with a valued rent of £258 as its ruling elder.

In the synods of 1649-51, Scone, as though anxious to mirror the times, was represented by one David Mitchell, who did not appear in an exactly contemporary valuation roll at all. A parish with thirty-eight proprietors elected a landless peasant as its ruling elder. Indeed, in 1649, only five of the nine elders were landowners and their average valued rent had fallen once more from £356 to £317. Only one of them - Andrew Lundie, feuar of Provost Mains (£697) in Abernethy - was the richest in his parish. None of them were men of any consequence.

The impressions conveyed by the records of the synod were substantially confirmed by the clerk of the presbytery, who belatedly began to record attendances towards the end of 1649. In 1650, 37 meetings yielded a total attendance of only 43 shared among 9 elders. Of these 9, only 3 were proprietors and they accounted for a mere fifth of the total attendance. Balmanno was a laird with a valued rent of rather less than £1,000, but he came only once; the other two were feuars. James Guthrie, who incidentally became minister of Stirling in 1650, could scarcely complain of this.

The identification of elders in Fife is more hazardous in the absence of contemporary valuation material; but the background of the ruling elders, sent from the parishes of the presbytery of Cupar to the Synod of Fife, suggests similar, if more crudely based, conclusions. By and large the elders of Cupar were more assiduous than those of Perth, and a typical synod meeting attracted representatives from about three quarters of the parishes. In the eight synods held during the years 1639-42, almost half of the elders attending were designated as proprietors in the rolls of the synod. During the years 1643-46, the proportion was almost exactly a third; in 1647-50, it was rather less than a third and was probably tending to fall. A full complement of nineteen ruling elders was nominated in the spring of 1650 to attend the last synod of the period to be held in normal circumstances. A meticulous clerk - who was incidentally David Dalgleish, minister of Cupar - noted them all, including the ten who did not actually come.

Only three were lairds. It is just possible that one or two of the others were small proprietors, but it is surely evident enough that the typical ruling elder of Cupar in 1650 was a tenant farmer ([6]).

The presbyteries again reflected the synod. In Dunfermline and Cupar alike, only about a third of the elders nominated to the presbytery were designated as proprietors; in Dunfermline from 1647 to 1649, proprietors accounted for only just over 30% of the total attendances and most of the rest were tenant farmers. The proportion of proprietors attending the presbyteries of Fife was substantially higher than it was in the Lothians. In Haddington in 1649, the equivalent figure was 20%. In Linlithgow, it was probably only 10%; in Dalkeith it was lower still; indeed the Earl of Lothian was elected to the Assembly of 1649 by a meeting which he did not attend and which seems to have been totally innocent of landed wealth. The western presbytery of Ayr in 1649 had been attended by an average of rather more than seven elders and, of these, only two were proprietors. The ministers of Ayr included five of the six contrivers of the Mauchline Rising; they vied with Irvine and Glasgow for the distinction of being the most radical presbytery in Scotland; it is plainly arguable that the radicals of Ayr, like Patrick Gillespie in Glasgow, were using 'yeomen elders' to control the presbytery. But, if this was so, the figures for Ayr were not very different from those in Fife and the Lothians. Almost everywhere, the proportion of proprietors was about a third or less - and sometimes quite a lot less ([7]).

The three Clydeside presbyteries of Dumbarton, Paisley and Glasgow were all exceptional in one way or another. In Dumbarton, where attendance was well up to average, the proportion of proprietors was (at almost 50% in 1649) unusually high; in Paisley, where attendance was well above average, the proportion of proprietors was (at 67% in 1649) quite extraordinarily high - about double the figure for Fife and perhaps four times the figure for the Lothians; in Glasgow - or so Baillie tells us - elders, albeit under the guidance of a minister, played a significant part in the control of the presbytery ([8]).

The proprietor-elders of Dumbarton and Paisley had at least one thing in common. Most of those from Dumbarton held land in the huge regality of Lennox; they were the dependents of a distant Duke who had quite explicitly left them to their own political devices and effectively abandoned his jurisdictions in the process. Most of their comrades from Paisley came from the large barony of Renfrew - part of the abandoned patrimony of the heir to the throne - or the ecclesiastical regality of Paisley which was held by the papist Abercorn. Some of them may have held a devolved jurisdiction of a minor kind, but hardly any of them were barons in the ordinary sense. In Dumbarton and Paisley alike, the pattern of jurisdiction had become indistinct and this was also true of part of the presbytery of Glasgow. It may be guessed that most of the 'yeomen elders' represented the nearer parishes of the presbytery and these roughly coincided with the barony of Glasgow, the centrepiece of the bishop's temporality. The typical husbandman of the barony was a rentaller who had become a feuar in the latter half of the sixteenth century. Patrick Gillespie's 'yeomen elders' had a long tradition of ownership or near-ownership behind them - and now the bishop had gone, to be replaced by the distant duke who did not care. In the barony of Glasgow, as in the Lennox and in the barony of Renfrew, the feudal system, as it had previously been understood, was breaking down. The reality of local power now resided in the shire committees and, to some extent at least, in the church. The magnate was slowly fading away and his vassals, organised by a minister who was the son of another minister, were taking his place ([9]).

In September 1641, the minister of Fintry in the presbytery of Dumbarton canvassed his kirk session in the vain hope of finding a ruling elder for the autumn synod in Glasgow. The elders replied that they were 'ignorant' men unfit for 'such a business' and that there was no 'gentleman' in the parish 'but one who (was) employed abroad in his own and friend's affairs'. The meetings of presbyteries and synods were gatherings of educated and articulate men who might be overawed by magnates but were unlikely to be impressed by landless peasants - or even by rentallers who had become feuars. An elder with little land or learning was merely a pawn, as Patrick Gillespie, the most adept of manipulators, was to discover to his own manifest advantage. The gentlemen vassals of the Lennox may have been rather more formidable and they were, as the elders of Fintry seem to have thought, educated men capable of holding their own with the ministers. Indeed Masters of Arts were occasionally elected as ruling elders throughout lowland Scotland, but the practice was significantly uncommon. Our cross-section through the presbyteries suggests that, with only one exception, elders designated as Masters of Arts nowhere accounted for more than about 6% of a total attendance that was almost universally low enough. The exception was the ill-attended presbytery of Perth, where Mr George Oliphant appeared at nearly half of the meetings held in 1650 to produce an average as impressive as it was insignificant. In the latter years of the church of the Covenant, the educated elder was almost as rare as the magnate. The minister was supreme ([10]).

The ruling elder had originally been conceived by the Tables, on the basis of precedents from the last two decades of the previous century, with the deliberate intention of intruding powerful laymen into the church. The immediate purpose had been to influence the elections to the general assembly; but, to the ministers, there had always been another - and more sinister - intention to invade the presbyteries and synods as such and thus to take over the church in its entirety. The records for these early years are seldom entirely satisfactory, but they at least suggest that this was no idle threat. Indeed the times were uniquely favourable to the idea of lay penetration. The church was destined to play a crucial role in the organisation of an insurrection, if only because the machinery of the state was not available. The assemblies of 1638 and 1639 dressed a rebellion in the robes of respectability and, arguably at least, of legality; the civil presbytery and the civil parish, both closely allied to their ecclesiastical counterparts, became the regional and local agencies of a revolutionary organisation with aims that were only partly ecclesiastical. In these circumstances, the penetration of the presbyteries, as of the general assembly, was natural to the point of being inevitable. But this was a passing phase. The asserted legality of the Parliament of 1640 and the undeniable legality of its immediate successor provided the insurrection - which was thus

K

insurrectionary no longer - with a purely civil centre. The civil presbyteries drifted away from the church and transformed themselves into regional committees responsible to Parliament rather than to the Tables. Lay participation in the church lost its attraction as well as its justification at a time when the chief participants were increasingly preoccupied elsewhere. The attendance of ruling elders at the ordinary meetings of presbyteries and synods fell away and, at the same time, the very character of the office began to change. The magnate receded into the background; the tenant farmer and the bonnet laird advanced to take his place. The ruling elder came to represent the social classes from which so many of the ministers themselves had sprung. The castle gave way to the cowshed. A church which had once acted as the agent of a feudal reaction against the Canterburian bureaucracy was now poised to attack the feudal system itself. But it did not wholeheartedly attack it. The mainstream of revolutionary opinion, as represented first by Henderson and later by Douglas, always accepted the necessity of an alliance with the barons at a national level; they granted a substantial measure of legislative power to the magnates in the full knowledge that this involved concessions on divisive issues like patronage and the ownership of church property. But, this apart, the general assembly was relatively harmless since it met so briefly that it could have little executive impact. Its will, nominally supreme, would be interpreted by its Commission acting in collusion with the presbyteries - and the magnate was being eased out of both. The ruling elder was not so 'strictly tied'.

These attitudes were perhaps orthodox enough. Melvillian theory - or at least one reading of it - had envisaged a professional church acting as a policy-making body and a subordinate state translating theory into practice. The moderates wanted a hangman who would be powerful enough to quell opposition - and they did not want him in the church itself. The radical did not entirely reject this. He naturally viewed the 'disguised and histrionical men' with the deepest suspicion and he obviously shared the moderate's anxiety to get them out of the internal machinery of the kirk. But he went at least one step further than this. He did not want a feudal hangman and he was doubtful about magnates in the general assembly. The radical attitude to the patrician elder was consequently less inhibited. Henderson had seen him as an unwelcome intruder; Guthrie condemned him as evil in himself - and invited the 'godly' of 'low degree' to take his place. The radical ministers came to regard the ruling elder, an 'imperious master' no longer, as a kindred spirit or at least as a useful servant of the grand design. These differences should not perhaps be exaggerated. Henderson and Guthrie were both seeking a church that would be essentially clerical in character and they succeeded because the circumstances were favourable; the magnate, preoccupied elsewhere, was, perhaps mistakenly, losing interest in the church. Moderate and radical alike, denied the professional eldership that had been promised in the *Second Book of Discipline*, found consolation in an amateur eldership composed of men who, ill-educated and insignificant as they often were, would be obedient to the ideological authority of the ministry. The elder who ruled well was now well ruled.

11

The Wisest of the Flock

DAVID Calderwood claimed that the kirk session had 'no divine right in particular' and that it was only 'a committee from the presbytery' (¹). His opinion was widely regarded as eccentric, but the fears underlying it - that power to the parish meant power to the privy kirk - were as widely shared. The Reformation had been engineered by a series of revolutionary cells which eventually developed into kirk sessions, each consisting of a number of elders taken over from the privy kirk and a professional minister imposed from without. The appearance of the presbytery, which normally consisted solely of ministers, only served to emphasise the tension between the two conflicting elements. The minister, whether he considered himself a Melvillian or not, introduced the Melvillian concept of the professional churchman into a kirk session usually consisting of upwards of a dozen part-time amateurs. It is arguable that the minister was normally the most powerful, as he was invariably the most articulate, of the two elements; but the elders collectively represented a formidable aggregation of local power. It is vital to know who they were.

Robert Baillie described the ruling elders of the higher courts in terms of their social class; but he was content to describe the ordinary sessioner in more or less conventional terms as the 'most wise', the most 'pious' and the most 'learned' of the flock. It was implied that he might come from any social class that might be represented in his parish. He might in practice tend to be drawn from the leaders of his local community; but, in theory at least, he might be anybody with a strong moral sense and a sound grasp of Protestant doctrine. He would, as the early reformers had intended, reflect the society in which he lived (²).

The parish of Liberton in the presbytery of Edinburgh illustrates Baillie's argument well enough. It was relatively flat and low-lying; its rainfall was light and its rich acres were well suited to arable cultivation. It was conveniently situated to supply the necessities of a hungry city and it was, by the standards of the seventeenth century, intensively tilled and densely inhabited. Liberton was unusually wealthy, with land valued at an average of £3 per acre compared with only 5/- in the upland parish of Heriot in the same shire. The pattern of land ownership was fairly simple. There was little church land and, though there had been some feuing, there had been nothing comparable with the upheavals which had tortured the temporalities. Rents had, as was usual in arable areas, traditionally been collected in kind and had resisted the inroads of inflation. For one reason or another, the lairds of Liberton were affluent enough. They included some - like Wauchope of Niddrie, Preston of Craigmillar or Somerville of Drum - of ancient lineage, and others - like Winraham of Liberton, advocate and judge - who were newcomers. In both cases the estate, as well as the jurisdiction that came with it, had been preserved more or less intact. Liberton was essentially a parish of prosperous proprietors dispensing local justice in baronies which had been erected in the Middle Ages. The feudal system was surely flexible enough.

The membership of the kirk session was, at least at first glance, a trifle odd. Four full sessions, each with rather over twenty members, were elected between 1639 and 1649. Not one of the elders so appointed was a baron; not one was a substantial proprietor; there is no positive evidence that any of them owned any land at all. One wonders who they were. In part of the parish at least - that part which corresponded with the barony of Craigmillar - the facts are clear enough. Six elders - James Jack, Edward Peacock, Walter Stoddart, William Shillila, John Peacock, and Michael Paton - were involved in the four elections of the period and they were between them appointed thirteen times. The testament of Robert Preston of Craigmillar shows that the first four, representing a total of ten appointments, were all paying rent directly to him in 1639. In addition, John Peacock was probably related to Edward and may well have been a later tenant. However this may be, it is reasonably clear that the elders of Craigmillar were, to all intents and purposes, the tenants of the barony of Craigmillar. It may be added that two of them, to judge from the rents they paid, were men of some substance. The other two, who incidentally served less often, were smaller men. It seems quite likely that the typical elder of Liberton was a husbandman ([3]).

However this may be, it would seem that a parish of prosperous proprietors had a kirk session without any proprietors at all. But this, if true, was less than the whole of the truth. The ordinary affairs of the session may have been conducted by a rather miscellaneous collection of farmer elders stiffened by a professional minister with a powerful presbytery at his back, but the session fairly often joined forces with the heritors when anything unusual occurred. The session thus augmented framed regulations for dealing with the plagues which so often infested the nearby capital; it settled an argument with a proprietor about a seat in the church; it forbade the sale of drink on the sabbath; at least in the earlier years of the period, it elected ruling elders. It is evident that the membership of the session varied with the demands made upon it. Indeed a laird was suddenly - and unfortunately for reasons unspecified - added to the session in April 1640 and another was added in May of the following year; neither had been elected in 1639; neither would be elected in 1642 ([4]). They were obviously temporary additions to an organisation which normally functioned without them. In a sense, it might be argued that the session was not sufficient in itself; it required the occasional support of the landed class. But it is equally true that the proprietors, once they had disdained full membership of the session, could only, at least in theory, appear as its invited guests. The civil parish was still in its infancy; it could grow only slowly in an area of thriving baronies; it naturally grafted itself on to its ecclesiastical counterpart. The initiative remained with the session and above all with its minister. Liberton's petition against the Engagement was signed by all the heritors who could be induced to put their hands to it - but it was born in the kirk session.

The parish of Stow presents a contrast. Where Liberton was flat and low-lying, Stow was a parish of valleys sharply etched into the high Lammermuir plateau. Where the one was mainly arable, the other was largely pastoral. The one was compact and densely peopled, the other large and sparsely inhabited. The one was a parish of civil baronies, the other roughly coincided with a large ecclesiastical regality which formed part of the temporality of the bishopric of St Andrews. Indeed Stow conveniently epitomises the stresses and strains which had tormented the temporalities during the previous hundred years. The whole of the Lordship of Stow had been feued in the 1540s and its revenues were now almost valueless - less than £500 from lands valued at nearly £10,000 in 1649. By contrast, the feuars had waxed fat on the profits of the price revolution. The largest of them, Lord Borthwick, with lands valued at about £3,000 in 1667, was, as the archbishop had been, an absentee. The next two, Pringle of Torsonce (£1,600) and Borthwick of Crookston (£550), resided in the parish and farmed their lands through tenants. The remainder (all less than £500) were, at least in most cases, working farmers ([5]).

The regality jurisdiction which attached to the Lordship of Stow resided nominally in the bishop, but effectively in an hereditary bailie, who was also an absentee dispensing a remote justice through a salaried official. The local proprietors, modestly prosperous though they were, could not in the nature of things share either in the local civil administration or in the election of members of Parliament. Their power was not commensurate with their substance. The story of Stow was distorted by the problems presented by the absentee landlord and the absentee magistrate. It is at least arguable that the kirk session, which necessarily consisted of local residents, provided at least a partial answer to them.

In Stow, as in Liberton and indeed in most large parishes, the parish was divided into quarters which respected property boundaries without surrendering to them. The whole parish, with some few reservations about its more distant outposts, was represented on the session; it was difficult for one part of the parish to dominate the rest. But, if this was true, there was a definite tendency for each part to be represented by one of the heritors in it. Thus the northern tip was nearly always represented by - among others - Borthwick of Crookston (£550) or his son. Pringle of Cortleferry (£320), Pringle of Muirhouse (£263) and, until 1640, the major resident, Pringle of Torsonce (£1,600), were only less regular. In total, about a quarter of the appointments to the session were accounted for by proprietors or, to look at the question the other way round, all the resident proprietors were appointed at one time or another.

Most of the remainder of the parish was owned by the absentee Lord Borthwick who, though prominent at heritors' meetings, was not eligible for the session as such. An area which included upwards of a dozen farms, as well as the small village settlement near the parish church, was necessarily represented by landless men. The same applied to the small, isolated estate of Princadoes, also held by an absentee, and to the outworks of the scattered estate of Torsonce.

It is difficult to be certain of the exact status of many of these men. The session minutes themselves tell us only their names and where they lived and worked; they are precise only where the residence concerned was a mill, and this offers us the fact that about one tenth of the sessioners were millers. A further group represented the small settlement near the church and this, at the end of the century at least, consisted predominantly of village craftsmen. It seems quite likely that rather less than one tenth of the session were craftsmen of one kind or another - with a probable predominance of weavers and tailors.

This still leaves over half of the elders unclassified, and a testament - that of Thomas Allan in Muirhouse - furnishes at least a clue to their identity. It shows that he paid rent directly to a proprietor - as did most of the elders of Craigmillar in Liberton - and that he employed several farm servants. His goods and gear were valued at the substantial sum of £790; about three quarters of this was made up by farm animals and most of the rest consisted of grain; 'plenishings' were trivial. He was the tenant of a fairly large sheep farm of a kind not uncommon in upland areas. He lived frugally but was far from poor. Indeed his wealth was comparable with that of a small proprietor like Pringle of Cortleferry who left a strikingly similar testament (⁶). It may be that these two men were fairly typical. Most of the elders, whether feuars or tenants, were probably working farmers; but the proprietors of Stow, great and small, were more conspicuous than the lairds of Liberton.

In Penicuik, the uncertainties of Liberton and Stow disappear altogether; a Cromwellian assessment, relating to a tax paid by husbandmen and craftsmen as well as proprietors, reveals the session in its entirety. The original medieval parish of Penicuik comprised a short stretch of the South Esk valley descending from the Peeblesshire border to a point slightly below the present centre of Penicuik. The river had cut a deep trench through the glacial deposits overlying most of the valley floor. The soils were light in patches and easily drained either into the river itself or into tributaries similarly entrenched, and this partially offset the effects of a rainfall rather high for arable cultivation. The tax survey laconically described the typical farm as 'half corn half grass'. But the original parish had recently been united with two others too poor to sustain ministers of their own. Mount Lothian stretched south-eastwards and gently upwards towards the distant slopes of the Moorfoot Hills; apart from the pastoral settlement of Mount Lothian near its eastern extremity and the small farmtoun of Mosshouses, it was mossy, ill-drained and almost uninhabited. By contrast, St Catherine le Hopes, straddling the Pentlands as it did, was a parish of steep slopes and high rainfall. A string of pastoral farms lined the deep valley of Logan Burn which bisected the parish; while another group, again mainly pastoral, clustered about Bavelaw Castle at the foot of the north-western slopes. The old medieval parish of Penicuik was a series of conventional farmtouns, interspersed by single, unified farms; St Catherine's was essentially a sheep run sending wool to the Edinburgh market; Mount Lothian, for the most part beyond the reach of seventeenth century farming technique, was largely a waste land. The clerk of the presbytery of Dalkeith, writing in 1648, described the united parish as 'exceeding spacious and vast, being six miles long and four miles broad and about fourteen miles in circuit'. In winter, he went on, 'a part of the people are witholden from the church by high and inaccessible mountains, another part by many waters, whereof two are oft impassable either to foot or horse'.

The mixed farms of the old parish were divided between the civil barony of Penicuik (valued at £1,575 in 1670) and the much smaller estates of Newhall (£176) and Spittal (£300), once indeed a hospital and now a feued outlier of the temporality of Holyrood. All three were held by residents - Clerk of Penicuik, Dr Alexander Penicuik and Oswald of Spittal respectively - over the period for which the kirk session record survives. The sheep farms of Logan Burn (£850) pertained to the absentee Sinclair of Rosslyn, but the small barony of Bavelaw (£244) was owned by the at least occasionally resident Mr Lawrence Scott, who may have been an Edinburgh advocate. Mosshouses (£226) was held by an absentee, but Mount Lothian (£244) may have been occupied by its proprietor, James Logan. There were four or five resident landowners of whom one, Clerk of Penicuik, was a man of consequence.

The parish as a whole had between 300 and 400 communicants and thus a total population of about 500 (see Table I).

Table I ([7])

	Barony of Penicuik	Town of Penicuik	Rest of Parish	Whole Parish
Adult Population	(180)	(70)	(170)	(350)
Adult Males	(90)	(35)	(85)	(175)
Resident Proprietors	1	0	4	5
Tenant Farmers	26	11	24	50
Millers	1	0	0	1
Craftsmen*	7	6	0	7
Mealmakers	1	1	0	1
Innkeepers	3	1	0	3
Drovers	1	0	0	1
Others**	(50)	(16)	(57)	(107)

N.b. The town of Penicuik, in which the kirklands have been included, formed part of the barony of Penicuik. Approximations have been put in brackets.

* 4 weavers, 1 tailor, 1 smith, 1 cooper.

** mainly farm servants and cottars.

The figures in Table I imply an adult male population of about 175. Fifty of these were tenant farmers in the sense that they paid a rent - incidentally calculated in money rather than kind - direct to a proprietor; and one other, described as the 'goodman of the mill of Penicuik', fell into the same general category. The tenants of the barony paid rents ranging widely from £33 to £546 per year. Nearly all the smaller tenants were clustered in the farmtoun of Penicuik, lying between the church and the newly erected mansion of the baron. The larger tenants occupied the rest of the lands between the river and the nearer slopes of the Pentlands. The largest of all was John Simpson (who paid £546 annually), bailie of the baron court and husbandman of the whole of Brunston - which had once been an independent barony - a third of Walston and the recently developed farm of Auchencorth on the opposite side of the river; his son - also John - was the sole tenant of Braidwood (£200). Two others - David Dryburgh and John Ramsay (£333) - had large consolidated farms. The miller - James Lowrie - paid £267 for the mill itself and the farm that came with it. The average rent in the barony was £136; the pastoral farms of the parish periphery seem, on evidence rather less certain, to have paid rents of from £100 to £267, with an average of about £150. One of the larger tenants died possessed of the substantial flock of 800 sheep. The craftsmen, the innkeepers, the drover and the mealmaker all belonged in the lower tiers of the parish hierarchy. They were probably approximately equal in status to the smaller tenants of the town of Penicuik - that is, those who farmed a sixteenth of the whole for an annual payment of £33. They were probably little more than cottars.

The elders of the parish can be identified fairly readily from 1654 when the surviving record begins. There is no evidence that a full election of the whole session was ever held; but three groups of new elders - numbering two, three and three - were added in May 1654, June 1655, and December 1657; on the last occasion, the clerk entered a complete list of the session in the minutes. These various lists yield a total of sixteen elders, of whom fifteen were in office at the end of 1657. The exception was perhaps revealing enough. It is reasonably clear that one of the elders then added - George Tait in Penicuik - was the son of Henry Tait in Penicuik and his successor, not only on the kirk session, but also in the tenancy of one eighth of the town of Penicuik. It is possible to believe that the hereditary principle sometimes filtered down through the landed classes into the tenantry and thence into the eldership ([8]).

One of the names added in 1657 identifies itself. Sir John Clerk of Penicuik, born in Montrose, had emigrated to France to become a merchant in Paris. He had made a substantial fortune by importing continental works of art into Scotland and had become a merchant burgess of Edinburgh in 1646. In 1654 he bought the estate of Penicuik and seems to have resided on it regularly thereafter. At the other extreme, Thomas Morton, who must already have been on the session in 1654, can only have been the weaver in the town of Penicuik mentioned in the Assessment of 1656. But these were the extremities of the session and the remaining fourteen - 85% of the whole - were more of a piece. Every one of these - and there were no exceptions at all - was assessed as a tenant farmer in 1656. But, if this was so, they were scarcely typical tenants. Seven of the farmer-elders were tenants of Sir John Clerk and they paid an average rent of £248 per year, compared with an average of £136 for the estate as a whole. The town of Penicuik had nine tenants, one farming a quarter, four an eighth and four more a sixteenth. The two elders drawn from the same area between them farmed the quarter and one of the eighths. In the valley of Logan Burn, there were four tenants, two paying £267 and two £100 per year. The first two were elders; the other two were not. It is impossible to be certain about the wealth of the other four; but it is clear enough that the typical elder was a tenant, and the tenant of a large farm rather than a small one.

The session minutes of Penicuik do not disclose attendances and it is thus difficult to distinguish between active and nominal members. They do, however, record a rota of nine elders charged with the duty of patrolling the town of Penicuik on the sabbath. The list does not include either Sir John Clerk or the village weaver; it consisted solely of tenant farmers - and substantial tenants at that. The weaver no doubt lacked the required authority, but this obviously did not apply to the laird. Sir John was not elected to the session until the end of 1657, that is, more than three years after he had acquired the estate. In July of the following year, he attended a meeting, consisting of sessioners and heritors, called to arrange a stipend for the schoolmaster - and he attended as a heritor rather than an elder. He was obviously not an active elder and his relationship with the session seems to have resembled that of the lairds of Liberton during the previous decade. However this may be, it is certain that the other resident proprietors had no connection with the session at all - though Scott of Bavelaw and Penicuik of Newhall had acted as ruling elders during the forties. It may be added that the ruling elders of the fifties were almost always tenants; it is scarcely surprising that John Simpson senior was among them ([9]).

Falkirk, valued at nearly £30,000 in 1649, was five times as wealthy as Penicuik. The parish fell naturally into two unequal and somewhat dissimilar parts - the rich, though as yet only partly drained, carselands along the southern shore of the Firth of Forth and the interior sloping gently upwards towards the poorer soils of Slammannan Muir.

The coastal fringe, together with a narrow strip projecting inland and roughly corresponding with the modern parish of Polmont, had pertained to the Abbey of Holyrood and was now divided between the Earl of Roxburghe, the Marquis of Hamilton, and Sir Thomas Hope of Kerse. Kerse had not been feued, but the remainder wore the patchwork clothes of a typical temporality. The other part, larger but generally less productive, was essentially Livingston country. It included the large estate of Bantaskyne (£1,200) and the smaller estates of the lesser Livingston lairds, but it was mainly occupied by the larger barony - soon to become a regality - of Callendar (£4,700), anciently held by the Earls of Livingston and now, since 1634, by Lord Almond, a cousin rich from the booty of the Thirty Years War. Falkirk itself stood between the two parts; it was the natural focus of a large rural area and it had been a burgh of barony since 1600. The parish as a whole may have had a population of about 2,000 in the 1640s and a substantial proportion of these must have lived in the burgh.

The kirk session, as it was elected in 1638 and again in 1640, reflected all these elements (see Table II). The three resident magnates - Almond, Kerse, and Bantaskyne - were elected in 1638 and two of them were re-elected in 1640; one of the lesser Livingstons was included in each list; Almond's bailies figured prominently in both. The feued lands of the Polmont quarter were, in 1638 and 1640 alike, represented by three feuars and two tenants. By contrast, Kerse and Callendar were represented each by its Lord and a cluster of tenants. The burgh members, who included deacons as well as elders, were four merchants - who were plainly not merchant princes - three craftsmen - two of them smiths - the tenant of the local *carbonarium* - who must have been a coalminer or a charcoal burner - a notary, and two men described as portioners - who were presumably feuars of land within the area of the burgh.

Mr John Dishington, clerk to the session of Falkirk, was perhaps more conscientious than most of his kind. Like the clerks of Cramond and St Cuthbert's, he recorded attendances at session meetings. In so doing, he disclosed

Table II ([10])
Falkirk kirk session analysed (a) by status and (b) by area

| | 1638-39 | | 1640-41 | |
	Elders	Active Elders	Elders	Active Elders
Magnates	3	0	2	0
Other Proprietors	2	0	3	1
Bailies	4	1	4	1
Tenants	10	0	11	1
Burgh Members	13	5	10	6
Unidentified	1	0	0	0
Total	33	6	30	9
Polmont	6	1	6	1
Kerse	2	0	2	0
Callendar	7	0	7	1
Burgh	14	5	11	7
Other	4	0	4	0

N.b. (i) For the purpose of this table deacons are included as if they were elders.
N.b. (ii) The 'Active' elders are those who attended more than a third of the meetings held from September 1638 to December 1639 and those who attended more than half the meetings held from December 1640 to December 1641. The session was better attended during the latter period.

the interesting fact that six of the elders elected in 1638 - all tenants from the more distant farms of the parish - did not attend any of the forty-five meetings held from September 1638 to December 1639. Indeed only six of the thirty-three elders attended more than a third of the meetings. The succeeding session of 1640 was rather better attended; but, even so, only nine of its thirty members came to more than half of the meetings. Nor was the active group thus defined a mere random sample from the session as a whole. Five of the six active members of the session of 1638 came from the burgh and the other was a bailie of the baron court which sat in the burgh. The active group of 1640 was similarly composed; seven of the nine represented the burgh; one was a bailie; the odd man out was a feuar from the Polmont quarter with an estate valued at £500 annually. In some respects, notably in the reluctance of the tenants and most of the feuars, Falkirk was far from typical; but the evident determination of the burgh members may well have been reflected in larger burghs with substantial landward areas.

No less significant was the inactivity of the magnates. Both of the Falkirk lists were headed by Lord Almond, both included Bantaskyne; the first included Kerse. But they actually attended only 17 meetings between them out of a possible combined attendance of 264. Their direct interest in the kirk session was almost confined to the election of ruling elders. The story of St Cuthbert's was significantly similar. The outer fringes of an even wealthier parish, largely taken up by the craft suburbs of Edinburgh and the feued lands of Holyrood and the Burgh Muir, were occupied by the substantial civil baronies of Dean, Inverleith and Braid. Unfortunately the clerk recorded names as assiduously as he ignored the designations which alone could have given them meaning. But the magnates are still identifiable, in one interesting case by his absence. The great Sir William Dick, who took his designation from the barony of Braid, was not a member of any of the six sessions elected from 1642 to 1655. Nisbet of Dean and Touris of Inverleith, both of whom were elected in 1642, seldom attended. From the election of 1642 to that of 1646, the average sessioner, using the word to embrace deacons as well as elders, attended 23% of the meetings held during those years; but Dean and Inverleith could boast a combined attendance of only 13% ([11]).

The session minutes of Cramond, which survive from 1651 onwards, are much more useful; designations were included; attendances were recorded. It emerges that the average sessioner attended almost exactly 50 per cent of the meetings - and this was much better than the equivalent figures for St Cuthbert's and Falkirk. Cramond was a more compact parish than either of the other two - which might account for the better attendances - and it was purely rural in character - and there was thus no conflict between urban and rural elements. On the other hand, it was, like St Cuthbert's, within the commercial orbit of Edinburgh; it was a relatively wealthy parish, valued at nearly £12,000 in 1649. The pattern of land tenure was varied enough. Nether Cramond was a distant outpost of the temporality of Dunkeld; it had been feued as a single large estate (valued at £1,200 in 1680) during the previous century and was now held by Inglis of Cramond, who came from Edinburgh burgess stock. Grottall and Craigcrook had been prebends of St Giles and had also subsequently been feued. The former was now owned by Sir John Smith, a merchant and ex-Lord Provost of Edinburgh living in rural retirement. Cramond Regis, though its prehistory is more obscure, had probably been a royal estate and was now held freehold, but in most cases without a baronial jurisdiction, by a number of relatively small proprietors. One of these was Sir John Smith; another was his son Mr Robert; yet another was Howieson of Braehead (£220); it is not entirely clear that Young of Leny, an Edinburgh lawyer and farmer of the Customs, belonged in this group, but he too had no baronial jurisdiction. All these men - Inglis of Cramond, Smith of Grottall, Mr Robert Smith, Howieson of Braehead and Young of Leny - can, despite the Edinburgh connections of nearly all of them, reasonably be regarded as resident proprietors and all of them were included in the lists of elders. Some of them acted as bailies for other and more remote superiors, but not one could claim an heritable jurisdiction of his own - and this served to distinguish them from the other five proprietors in the lists. Balmerino, Hope of Craighall, Houston of Houston, Hamilton of Muirhouse, and Hamilton of Little Preston can all properly be described as magnates, great or small. They all held baronies either in Cramond or elsewhere. The remainder of the session, some of them elders and some of them deacons, were all either tenant farmers or men of equal or lower status.

The kirk session of Cramond thus divided itself into three distinct parts - the magnates, the proprietors without baronial jurisdiction and the tenants; it is of the highest significance that the intensity of their interest in the kirk session was dramatically different (see Table III).

The typical tenant, whether elder or deacon, attended the remarkably high proportion of three-quarters of the meetings; the lesser proprietors attended more than half of the meetings; the magnates, it is almost true to say, did not come at all. To all intents and purposes, the kirk session of Cramond, like that of Liberton, was outside the feudal system. A minute examination of the histories of the families concerned might explain this away in terms of illness, death, youth or absence; but

Table III [12]
Attendances at Meetings of Kirk Session of Cramond,
1652-57, by various groups of sessioners

Group	Potential Attendance	Actual Attendance	Percentage Attendance
Magnates	1,488	36	2
Other Proprietors	1,042	575	55
Tenant Elders	1,054	810	77
Tenant Deacons	1,564	1,165	74
All Proprietors	2,530	611	24
All Tenants	2,618	1,975	75
Whole Session	5,148	2,586	50

the record of Balmerino is possibly revealing. He did not attend at all from November 1652 to June 1656; but, from June 1656 to the end of 1657, he attended no less than twenty-eight times. Was it a coincidence - and it may well have been - that the heritable jurisdictions were abolished at about the time of his conversion?

The odd, and rather elusive, relationship between the magnates and their kirk sessions was, however unintentionally, epitomised by the session clerk of Scone. He normally described his masters as the minister and session and, in doing so, he was referring to a body which, as one would expect in an ecclesiastical temporality, consisted of feuars and tenants in more or less equal proportions. But, on a few rather special occasions, he made an exception. The minister was preceded by the Lord of Erection of the ancient abbey of Scone. It should perhaps be emphasised that Viscount Stormont was, unlike the lairds of Liberton, a duly elected elder. But it is equally clear that he was no ordinary elder; he was named and they - the vassal elders - were not; he preceded the minister and they came after him. It was a relationship that the *Second Book of Discipline* had not envisaged - but he did not often come [13].

It would seem, from the evidence furnished by some fifty parishes, that rather less than a quarter of the sessioners of rural Scotland were landed proprietors and that most of the rest were tenant farmers. The calculation is unsatisfactory in more ways than one. The lesser feuars are often difficult to distinguish from tenant farmers - perhaps because the seventeenth century was not greatly concerned to make the distinction. The parishes concerned were not necessarily typical; indeed they tended to be larger and wealthier than average. Above all, individual parishes differed considerably. In a parish situated in an ecclesiastical temporality where the superior was an absentee, the kirk session became a vital organ of local government and the landed vassal was prominent in its deliberations. The Tweeddale parish of Lyne displayed an opposite tendency; the sole proprietor was an absentee and the kirk session necessarily consisted of his tenants - and several other remote hill parishes conformed to a similar model [14]. But in many parishes the typical estate was an unfeued civil barony held by a resident proprietor, and here the normal machinery of government was still fully effective. In a parish of this type, the baron was often a member, but usually only a nominal member, of a kirk session which was again abandoned to the tenantry. By and large, the lairds held aloof; they already had power to spare - or at least they thought they had. The typical elder was either a small landowner, whether feuar or freeholder, or a tenant;

he was often a working farmer. He emerged from the same background as did Alexander Henderson and so many of his comrades.

John Calvin, discussing the intricate relationship between church and state, observed that the one was entirely independent of the other and then went on to add, perhaps a trifle disingenuously, that the church could help the magistrate to ensure that 'not so many may sin'. The functions of the two jurisdictions should be 'so joined that each served to help, not hinder, the other' ([15]). This was the ideal which Knox and his comrades sought to implement in the complex environment of Reformation Scotland. The throne was bound to seem untrustworthy at least as long as Mary occupied it. A powerful faction among the magnates supported the reformed church; but another, only less formidable, would long continue to oppose it. The new church was bound to have its reservations about the inferior magistrate in the countryside; but it had no such reservations about most of the towns, where something very like the ideal relationship envisaged by Calvin developed early and took root. Had not the burgh of Edinburgh offered a princely stipend to Knox long before the ministry as a whole had any proper provision at all? And did they not actually pay it?

The church of Scotland had always had a special affection for the burghs and this was reflected in the special treatment accorded to them during the prelude to the Glasgow Assembly of 1638. The lay commissioners sent up from the presbyteries to the assembly were very like the 'barons' envisaged in the act of assembly of 1598; but the Tables, probably as a concession to the objections of the radical ministers, allowed them to be described, in ecclesiastical rather than civil terms, as elders or ruling elders. But the representatives of the towns were always regarded as the commissioners of the burghs which had - admittedly with the formal consent of their kirk sessions - elected them. The burgh commissioners in the Glasgow Assembly were sent there by the civil power and the clerk did not describe them as elders. John, Lord of Balmerino, who represented the presbytery of Edinburgh, was called an 'elder'; James Cochrane, the senior representative of the burgh, was merely described as 'Dean of Guild in Edinburgh' ([16]). There was no urban parallel to the bitter clerical reaction against baronial intrusion into the church. Indeed the Assembly of 1640 passed an act which, though rather obscurely worded, plainly indicated that the bailies of burghs were expected to be members of their kirk sessions. It was the common opinion of the Court of High Commission, of the archbishop of St Andrews and of the presbytery of Edinburgh, both before the revolution and immediately after it, that the bailies of South Leith were *ex officio* members of the kirk session of South Leith ([17]).

In these circumstances, it is scarcely surprising that burgh magistrates and burgh councillors should regularly have been appointed as elders in their kirk sessions, or indeed that they should often have been described by their civil titles. In St Andrews, the list of burgh elders was normally headed by the provost, five bailies and the dean of guild; the treasurer was sometimes added. It seems likely that the membership of this part - and it must have been an influential part - of the session changed when the dignitaries concerned laid down their offices rather than when elections to the session were held. Aberdeen presented a very similar picture, but the extreme case was to be found in the small southern burgh of Dumfries. The clerk to the kirk session described the first thirteen of his nineteen elders as the provost, the three bailies, the late provost, the dean, the treasurer, the four late bailies, the convener and the late treasurer, of the burgh. It is possible that the other six - who were merely described by their occupations - were also councillors; whether they were or not, it is evident that church and state were one in Dumfries ([18]).

By and large the burghs are better documented than the countryside, and none more so than the Canongate, the small town which had grown up to service first the abbey and then the palace of Holyrood. The regality jurisdiction under which the burgh was governed had resided in the succession of abbots, commendators and lords of erection who had enjoyed the fruits of the abbey. It implied the right, passed on to the Town Council of Edinburgh in 1639, to appoint a baron bailie who exercised a criminal jurisdiction in the burgh and the neighbouring barony of Broughton. But this jurisdiction had long been contested by the inhabitants of the Canongate and its significance should not be exaggerated. The ordinary affairs of the burgh were regulated by a council consisting of two resident bailies - who were not appointed by Edinburgh until 1652 - a treasurer, six ordinary councillors and the deacons of the six incorporated trades ([19]). This Council was strikingly similar to - and at times almost as independent as - the government of a royal burgh.

The leading citizens of the Canongate tended to fall into two well-defined groups. The first consisted of middlemen who purchased imported luxuries from Edinburgh merchants and sold them to the Court. The second comprised the incorporations among which the manufacture of luxury items was prominent. The two groups were distinct and the first was definitely senior to the second. The magistrates and the councillors tended to be drawn from the first, while the trades were separately represented through their deacons. This order of precedence was also observed in the kirk session.

The membership of the session can be assessed accurately enough; indeed no less than 96% of the elders and deacons have been definitely identified and the remaining 4% have been ignored in the calculations which follow. Altogether 142 elders and deacons were appointed a total of 311 times during the course of the fourteen elections held between 1630 and 1651 ([20]). Just over three quarters of these appointments were accounted for by craftsmen from one or other of the six incorporations. It is almost certain that all of these were masters; there is no evidence that any of them were journeymen.

The remaining quarter of the session is not without interest. It included a small group of lesser tradesmen from outside the incorporations; these were all deacons and none of them ever became elders. Another group, also very small, consisted of lairds and professional men; these were all elders and, as far as one can tell, only one of them had ever been a deacon. But there was also a more numerous group - some 16% of the whole - which was drawn from the plutocracy of the burgh. These were the middlemen who sold imported luxuries, the maltmen and the skinners who were also outside the ranks of the incorporations. This group accounts for only 9% of the deacons, but 17% of the deacons who later became elders and 29% of the elders who had never been deacons. Like the lairds and the professional men, they were definitely concentrated in the upper reaches of the session. It may be added that the testaments confirm the impression that the elder was a lot wealthier than the deacon. His domestic establishment was five times as valuable; his inventory, essentially his stock of goods, was about three times as great; his moveable wealth, that is his goods together with the net value of his debts, was again three times as great.

But it is possible that wealth was not the real point. For no less than three quarters of the elders, compared with a mere 4% of the deacons, served in one capacity or another on the council of the Canongate, which was incidentally a smaller body than the kirk session. It may be added that about half of the first-time elders were either magistrates or ordinary councillors and that about half of the deacons who later became elders were also, at one time or another, the deacons of their various incorporations. To generalise, the deacon - using the term in its ecclesiastical sense - tended to be an ordinary master craftsman, the deacon who became an elder tended to be the deacon - using the term in its craft sense - of his incorporation; the first-time elder tended to be a wealthy magistrate or councillor from outside the ranks of the incorporations. Indeed, the eldership represented the dominant elements in the burgh almost as faithfully as did the burgh organisation itself ([21]).

It might be objected that Canongate was too sophisticated to be typical. If this was so, the tiny seafaring town of Queensferry furnished a total contrast. The town had served the great abbey of Dunfermline since the Middle Ages and was erected into a royal burgh in 1636. By this time, it was a small port fishing the waters of the Forth and importing wine and timber for a small hinterland recently won from the rival burgh of Linlithgow. In 1642, shortly after the arguments about its status had finally been resolved, the town clerk entered a new burgess roll into his minutes. It contained less than forty names and, though it was plainly incomplete, the active burgess community probably did not exceed fifty. The government of the burgh was conducted by two bailies, a treasurer, a town clerk and a council of about twenty, two thirds of whom were 'seamen' - that is skippers, shipowners and merchants - and one third 'landmen', most of whom were craftsmen working in the town. At Michaelmas each year the old council elected the new and the two together appointed the magistrates and the clerk. As was inevitable in a small town, the same names constantly recur and it is reasonable to infer the existence of a fairly well defined burgh oligarchy, though only with the proviso that it was almost as large as the burgess community itself. The government of the parish was strikingly similar. In June 1643, a new session of twenty-eight was elected by its predecessor, itself elected in 1640. The list of elders was headed, as it had been in all of the four elections held since the parish had been disjoined from Dalmeny in 1635, by the two bailies then in office and by sixteen of the councillors who had been elected in the previous October; two more had acted as proxies in the same election; four others had served on previous councils. The remaining four may not have been burgesses in 1643, although their surnames suggest that they may well have been burgesses in the making. Whether they were or not, it is clear enough that the kirk session was merely the burgh oligarchy in a different guise. In Queensferry, as in Canongate, Dumfries and surely in many other small towns, church and state were close enough. The one helped, and for the most part did not hinder, the other ([22]).

In most burghs, the kirk session often seemed to identify with the civil power, but seventeenth century Scotland was not an urban country. In the countryside, the pattern was quite different. Elders, or at least active elders, tended to be tenant farmers or feuars; they were seldom cottars and never servants; some were small landowners, but very few were magnates. The typical elder was a man of some local consequence, but he was outside the power structure of a feudal state. The godly tended to be of fairly low degree; church and state kept their Melvillian distance. But it is arguable that this situation had emerged naturally enough from the facts as they actually were. Many of the baronies of Scotland were held by absentees and, where this was so, the power of everyday jurisdiction was exercised by a resident bailie, who might well be a local farmer, and an assise which almost invariably consisted of farmers. In these circumstances, the kirk session closely resembled a baron court with a minister in the chair instead of the bailie.

But many parishes had resident lairds and, even here, they seem to have taken little interest in the ordinary affairs of the session. They duly invaded the church in the late thirties; but, election meetings apart, the effort was not sustained. The session was left to the farmers, and its leadership passed, almost by default, to a minister who had probably emerged from a similar background. Indeed the minister's dominance was of a different kind. He was better educated, more sophisticated and more articulate than the elders around him. His pulpit was as lonely as it was commanding. It may well be that the petty power struggles of the parish were usually resolved by the elders; but they in their turn normally accepted the ideological authority of the minister. And this was vital. A thousand kirk sessions, low-born as they were and zealous though they may have been, were impotent in themselves; it was the minister who linked them into the rest of the structure. It is arguable that the kirk session reflected local feeling more faithfully than any of its civil rivals; but, in the middle years of the seventeenth century, this was not its main function. It fuelled the revolutionary engine that was the kirk.

12

Time Server And Better Sort

DAVID Calderwood was an old Melvillian with bitterness in his soul and he had a poor opinion of the burgesses of Edinburgh. Recalling their ambiguous reaction to the affair of the Monday market in 1592, he remarked: 'Such has always been the religion of Edinburgh when they are touched in their particular'[1]. The burgesses would no doubt have replied that money was their business and that they had a lot of it to lose. But this is not perhaps the real point. Edinburgh was much more populous than the other burghs and it was growing faster than most. In the 1630s upwards of 20,000 people were crammed into an area of less than half a square mile. It was wealthy, crowded - and intensely vulnerable. Its site had been chosen for military reasons, but its prosperity had been founded on commerce; it was a trading city with no access to the sea; without Leith it was nothing. In the fifteenth century, it had been chosen as the capital of Scotland. It became the willing host of Parliaments, Privy Councils, Courts of Law and everybody who came to attend them. As its population grew, it became a great consumer centre and thus a manufacturing centre as well. Its crafts expanded, were incorporated and were striving for admission to a burgh oligarchy traditionally dominated by merchants engaged in foreign trade. The merchant prince in his turn was becoming a financier lending to the government and prospering yet more in the process. Too much depended on Leith; too much depended on the royal favour. The citizens of Edinburgh were necessarily concerned with 'their particular' and they looked after it well enough. A large population of bankers, merchants, craftsmen, noblemen, judges, lawyers, doctors and ministers looked down from their affluence on a journeyman proletariat, itself surmounting a mob of sturdy beggars drawn by the prospect of casual labour and kept by the prospect of plunder. If Edinburgh was more vulnerable than other Scottish towns, it was also more complex. It was as rich as it was poor, as dignified as it was lawless. It presented problems of government which the smaller burghs would scarcely have understood; it was at once a greater and a more elusive prize. Elder and magistrate were seldom entirely at one.

The conflict had indeed been present from the beginning. The privy kirk had necessarily been an insurrectionary body and Knox has told us that it merged imperceptibly into the 'public' kirk of the 1560s and furthermore that it brought with it an electoral system according significant powers to the congregation. The old session nominated twice as many elders and deacons as would be needed to serve on the new one. The congregation was then given the opportunity to reject

L

any of these and to substitute others of its own choice - 'to the end,' as Knox said, that none 'should complain that he was spoiled in his liberty in election'. This done, the congregation elected the session from the leet thus modified. Knox's final comment summarised the intentions behind a rather cumbersome process: '. . . if a poor man exceedeth a rich man in votes, he precedes him in place'. The earliest surviving kirk session records - which relate to the middle seventies - suggest that this system, or at least some close approximation to it, was actually put into operation ([2]).

The nature of the alternative was suggested by an entry in the council record dated as early as August 1560. The Incorporation of Tailors had sought the permission of the town council to replace their altar in St Giles with seats for the exclusive use of their members. The council, remarking that 'all titles to altars had been abolished', righteously rejected the idea and substituted another of their own. The 'Nobility, Provost, Bailies, Council, Elders and Deacons' - in that order of priority - would be 'first placed'. They would be followed by the rest of the burgesses '. . . providing always that neither the prentices or servants . . . or other common people take upon them the places or rooms of the said merchants and free craftsmen'. This was the voice of a merchant oligarchy which had embraced the new faith somewhat hesitantly and was now seeking to use it for its own purposes. The rich would precede the poor; the town council would dominate the kirk session ([3]).

Direct conflict between these two notions was postponed by the uncertainties of the day. The Queen Regent had occupied Leith with a French army and had threatened to create a new royal burgh there; at the same time, she played upon the grievances of craftsmen seeking permanent access to the oligarchy. She drove the merchant princes of Edinburgh to resentment and then strangled their defiance. They inevitably moved cautiously. During the crucial months of 1559 and 1560, they lurked hesitantly in the shadows, while lesser men made history. Two rival councils, opposite in their intentions but similar in their obscurity, struggled for power and then, their purpose served, lost themselves once more in the background. Once Leith had been saved, wealth and power became protestant and pro-English. They joined the Lords and Barons professing Christ Jesus and, by and large, they would be loyal ([4]).

No record has survived of the earliest elections to the kirk session of Edinburgh; but a fragment of 1574 shows that the system described by Knox was still operating in the immediate aftermath of the Civil War. But, despite the intervention of the congregation, two of the four bailies then in office - as well as the Clerk Register - were chosen as elders. Indeed the church plainly welcomed the protection of the magistrates, although there was no suggestion that they should be elected as a matter of course. It is no less evident that the elders of 1574 were relatively wealthy men. Six of the twelve were merchants and one of the others was a craftsman. All but one of the merchants were still paying tax in 1583, when their average payment was no less than eight times the average for the burgess community as a whole. The craftsman was Deacon of the Baxters and paid nearly five times the average. The remaining five were lawyers and two of them were advocates. They belonged to a profession that was seeking, probably in collusion with the merchants, full voting membership of the town council. Their bid would fail and they would eventually be tempted by the privy kirk; but, for the time being, they were still hopeful and still co-operative. It must have seemed that the kirk session was falling, as it would fall in so many burghs, to the oligarchy and the trend seemed to be continued in the elections of 1575 when the leet prepared by the previous session was suddenly reduced from twenty-four to twelve. The role of the congregation was now nearly - though not quite - a formality. The old session elected the new in a manner that was becoming common enough all over Scotland. Church and burgh were drawing closer together ([5]).

But protestantism meant more than Morton; it meant Melville too. The successors of Knox were outspoken radicals armed with a subversive ideology and violent congregations eager enough to sublimate their grievances. It seems quite likely that the new ministers were gradually constructing a different kind of kirk session to suit their purposes. It is impossible to identify most of the sessioners of the early 1580s, since the records have perished; but a few likely names - and a few unfamiliar faces - emerge from the list of laymen subsequently persecuted, along with the ministers themselves, by the Arran administration. Two of these, John Preston and John Blackburn, are known to have been elders. The first was the *doyen* of protestant Edinburgh. He was a merchant, prosperous rather than wealthy, and he had long years of devoted service on the council behind him. Like John Adamson and Alexander Udward, both of whom were probably elders, he can only be regarded as an oligarch. But Blackburn was a man of a different stamp. He had never been, and never would be, elected to the town council; he was a minor merchant, perhaps a shopkeeper, paying tax at less than the burgh average. Robert Mark kept a stall and was thus a merchant of a kind, but his tax payments were among the lowest in the town. John Bairnsfather, James Cathkyn, and his brother Edward were all craftsmen and were all almost as poor. William Archibald was so obscure that he has left no mark on the records of the town at all - and this is unusual. These men had two things in common. They had no connection with the oligarchy and they were all much less than wealthy. Some of them may have been deacons rather than elders; but, whatever they were, it is obvious that they were politically active - and this was new ([6]).

Indeed the Melvillian ministers and their plebeian sessioners were awakening the latent conflict between church and burgh. The fathers of the burgh, robustly protestant though most of them were, instinctively recoiled. The advent of Arran was timely. His previous associations may have been suspect, but he had broken the worst of them; his policy was at once protestant and erastian. The Black Acts quite specifically subordinated the kirk to the King in Parliament - to the ancient power structure of feudal Scotland. The capital, with a haste that seemed to betray its anxiety, followed the kingdom. At Michaelmas 1584 the Earl of Arran was elected lord provost of Edinburgh. A few weeks later the town council elected a new kirk session of its own choosing and decreed that the bailies, whether they were elders or not, should attend its deliberations. The civil magistrate would run the church. The session thus elected was, as might be expected, a gathering of the affluent. Six of the elders were merchants and two of them craftsmen and their average tax payment was six times the average for the burgh; indeed three of the merchants paid at more than ten times the burgh average. They included four previous magistrates and two previous councillors; both craftsmen had recently been the deacons of their Incorporations. The other four elders were lawyers; but the council was plainly trying to reproduce the kirk session in its own image ([7]).

In a sense, the contrast between the supporters of Arran and those of the ministers was less dramatic than this. There were still traces of the pattern established during the civil wars of the early seventies ([8]). A part of the burgh oligarchy had remembered Lennox and opposed Arran; but, as far as one can see, most of these had not been members of the Melvillian sessions of the early eighties. Like the Ruthven lords, they were content to admire the kirk from a safe distance. But the reign of Arran was brief and his collapse brought about an abrupt reversal. The ministers returned from England to find the town council discredited. Its new system of election lapsed and was replaced - at least as far as one can tell - by the system which it had so recently superseded. And it is reasonable to conclude that the sessions thus elected must have included Blackburn, Mark, the Cathkyns and others like them. At the same time, the burgh oligarchy - and especially perhaps its merchant component - was driven by the King's flirtation with the popish earls into an ambiguous half alliance with its Melvillian ministers; they at least were protestant. The kirk's famous ban on trade with Spain was taken seriously though eventually ignored. An entirely novel scheme for the augmentation of stipends through contributions levied by the church itself was considered and not actually denied. But the most striking of the ministers' proposals actually reached the Council Book. The oligarchy of Edinburgh, still dominated by its merchants, abjectly agreed to ban the Monday market, 'authorised to the Town by the Princes of ancient time', because the drovers supplying it cursed their way through the landward parishes on the sabbath. And then, to Calderwood's disgust, the act was frustrated by a mob of craftsmen who threatened to drive the ministers out of the town ([9]).

The strands of conflict were tangled enough. The oligarchy thought it could see an unholy compact between the King and the Pope; the crafts, jealous of the privileges recently written into the constitution of the burgh, imagined an alliance between merchant and minister to overthrow them; the King suspected a plot hatched by magistrate and Melvillian to reduce him to impotence and perhaps to murder him. They were all the victims of their illusions, but the events of 17th December 1596 had a crazy logic about them. As the pulpits incited rebellion and the bailies did nothing, the King, rescued by a counter mob organised by the Deacon Convener, threw everybody - including the Deacon Convener - into confusion by withdrawing his capital to Linlithgow. Edinburgh was touched on its particular now and the town council, whether it was guilty or innocent, was compelled to sue for peace and thus to leave the more obvious culprits unprotected. They included the ministers, the brothers Cathkyn, and Edward Hart, the bookbinder - and these were Melvillians in the truest sense of the term. But there were a dozen merchants as well and three at least were wealthy; one was a future councillor, another a future bailie, while the third was the father of an even wealthier bailie who would tempt the King's wrath in the 1620s. The oligarchy was well represented ([10]).

The local impact of the Melvillian defeat was softened by the simultaneous humiliation of the town council. Thereafter, as the council was forgiven and the ministers half forgiven, the balance of advantage swung slowly back towards the burgh; but no attempt was made to tamper with the electoral system until the way had been opened by the uproar which greeted the Articles of Perth. The Articles, however illogically, evoked the same emotional responses as had the antics of Huntly and Errol; but this time the King had more to offer. It seems unlikely that many of the councillors were anxious to enforce the Articles in Edinburgh; but they wanted to re-assert their power over the kirk session. The ministers, although they were now the King's men for the most part, would probably have resisted this; but they wanted a larger establishment and augmented stipends. The King himself wanted the Articles enforced in his capital and he was happy to pay the price. All the elements of a bargain were present and the sequel was almost predictable. At election time in 1618, and again in subsequent years, the 'old and new Council' swooped on the kirk session, rejected the 'better sort' and, as Calderwood complained, chose 'ignorants and time servers' in their places. The opposition was driven back into its last respectable refuge - the meetings held before communion in which the congregation could criticise its ministers - and thence underground into the conventicle. It eventually assumed a shape which church and burgh alike were bound to abhor ([11]).

The details of the bargain were not formally agreed until 1625, but its outlines had long been obvious. The Perth Articles would be enforced - and this pleased the King and his ministers. The establishment would be increased to eight and stipends would be augmented - and this pleased the ministers more than the magistrates, who would eventually have to levy a new tax to find the money. But the eight ministers would be distributed among four distinct parishes, each with its own quite separate kirk session. There would be no consistory - and this pleased the burgh. Again, each session would consist of two ministers, six elders, six deacons and the magistrates of the burgh, and each would be elected by its predecessor together with the 'Provost, Bailies and Council'. The system devised by the Arran regime was reborn - and this pleased the burgh even more. As an additional refinement, 'public conventions' at which the people could question their ministers were forbidden - and this pleased everybody outside the privy kirk. The essential purpose of the agreement was epitomised neatly enough in one of its codicils: 'The sessions of the church shall not meddle with any civil affair nor inflict any other censure but that which is ecclesiastical.' There would be no alternative government in Edinburgh. The fathers of the burgh could sleep easily and the Perth Articles, none too oppressively enforced, were a small enough price to pay. It is possible to believe that the town council smiled upon - and perhaps at - the posturings of Patrick Galloway, a minister who had once favoured the 'better sort', when he astounded his congregation by taking communion in an attitude so complex that it could plausibly be construed as sitting, kneeling or standing ([12]).

The Perth Articles had united two quite different elements in the opposition. There had always been a party within the oligarchy which was outspoken in its opposition. Thus, in 1620, Thomas Inglis, a past Dean of Guild paying tax at three times the burgh average, was banished from Edinburgh for his 'contumacy' over the Articles. John Dickson, who was much wealthier than craftsmen usually were and had four times been Deacon of the Fleshers, was exiled in 1624, when John Fleming, currently a merchant councillor, escaped only because he had prudently chosen to exile himself. But all these were overshadowed by William Rig, who had been banished in 1620 and banished, imprisoned and heavily fined in 1624. Rig was a merchant prince paying tax at no less than eighteen times the burgh average and he was in office as a bailie when his second offence was committed ([13]).

These men opposed the Articles with total sincerity, but they were neither instinctive conventiclers nor indeed were they revolutionaries in any meaningful sense. Fleming and Inglis were back on the town council well before 1637, while Rig, after receding into the background for a time, re-emerged as shire commissioner for Fife (where he had an estate) and speaker of the barons in the Parliament of 1641. He eventually turned out to be an orthodox covenanter. But there were other issues as well and on these Rig and his friends were equivocal. In April 1619 a meeting of the Edinburgh kirk session exploded into argument about the Articles. As the ministers gradually lost control of the argument, Alexander Clerk, who was present as a bailie rather than as an elder, demanded silence. John Mein, then a deacon, howled out his anger: 'You may not command me to silence in this place. . . . you are but a sessioner here, sir; you may not reign over us.' ([14]) This really had nothing to do with the Articles at all. It concerned the role of the magistrate in the kirk session, the relationship between the church and the burgh, and the council's part in the election of the session. Mein, whose connections with the oligarchy were remote, plainly felt no embarrassment; but Rig must surely have done so. He had been elected as an elder under the new system and, in 1624, he attended the session as a bailie. By Calderwood's definition, Rig was a 'time server'.

Calderwood tells us the names of seven of the 'better sort' passed over by the council in the session election of 1621. Four of the seven were doctors of medicine and the fifth was an apothecary. These were professional men with no secure access to the oligarchy; they resembled the lawyers. The other two, one of them the now notorious James Cathkyn, were booksellers, a trade that was relatively new, unincorporated and, at times like these, somewhat dangerous. None of the seven would ever sit on the town council and none was really wealthy. Only John Hamilton, the apothecary, paid tax much above the burgh average. It would plainly be possible to add others to Calderwood's roll of honour. John Mein, an inveterate conventicler, was a merchant but, as the Privy Council observed in the act of banishing him, a poor one - and the tax Rolls confirm their judgement. He eventually became a town councillor in 1649 - and the date is surely significant. William Simpson, who was exiled with Mein in 1624, may well have been another of the 'better sort'. He was a small merchant, 'living by his credit in vending wine' and paying barely more than the burgh average in tax; he would never serve on the town council. Nicolas Balfour, the widowed daughter of a Melvillian minister of Edinburgh, would obviously have been an elder if she had been a man and she made up for her ill fortune by entertaining conventicles in her modest house in the Cowgate. These were the true zealots and they used the opposition to the Articles for their own purposes ([15]). In true Melvillian style, they were seeking to elevate the kirk session above the burgh oligarchy. The bargain of 1625 united Crown, church and burgh against them and they were defeated. They retreated into their conventicles to await another pretext and they would not be disappointed. It is almost certain that Nicolas Balfour and Barbara Hamilton, the wife of John Mein, were among the 'matrons' who conspired with Henderson and Dickson to provoke the riot in St Giles.

The 'time servers' were men of a different stamp. Twenty-four elders were elected and, of these, fourteen were merchants and six were craftsmen. Several of the latter were guild brethren, which suggests that they were employers of labour who had ceased to practise their crafts themselves. Four fifths of the elders seem to have been leading members of the burgess community and the impression is confirmed by the fact that their average tax payment was about five times the average for the burgh as a whole. By contrast there were only four lawyers - a lower proportion than seems to have been customary during the previous century - and these were at once hand-picked and carefully distributed among the four sessions. It seems likely that they were there merely to provide legal advice.

It was almost as if the sessions of 1625 had been deliberately constructed in the image of the council itself. But, if this was so, the magistrates did not appoint themselves as elders; indeed one elder of the kirk is known to have resigned because he was subsequently elected a bailie of the burgh. Furthermore, only one of the twenty-four elders appointed had previously been a magistrate, though eight others had served on the council in one capacity or another during the previous ten years. The elders of 1625 can reasonably be regarded as junior members of the burgh oligarchy ([16]).

The annuity tax, authorised in 1634 to meet the mounting cost of ministers' stipends, also - if only accidentally - offers a much deeper insight into the place of the elders in Edinburgh society. The tax was based on house rents and was thus paid by the head of every household in Edinburgh. The new valuation roll, drawn up between 1634 and 1636, was virtually a census of householders with an indication of the rents paid by each of them. The south-east quarter of the burgh - broadly speaking the area bounded by the High Street, St Mary's Wynd, the Flodden Wall, the Horse Wynd and Conn's Close - contained 982 households, of which 660 - about two thirds - paid rents of less than £40 annually, and none of these included any of the elders elected to the session of the south-east parish from 1631 to 1638. At the other extreme, there were 26 heads of households paying rents of more than £200 annually and eight of these - about one in three - were elders. The wealthier the household, the greater was the chance that its head would be an elder (see Table IV).

In December 1637 the town council, which had recently joined the Supplicants, again elected a further series of kirk sessions. The names of most of them are

Table IV ([17])

*The Elders of the South-East Parish of Edinburgh, 1631-8, analysed by the
annual value of their houses*

Houses with an annual value of ($£$s)

	1-39	40-69	70-99	100-199	Over 199
Number of Houses	660	153	37	106	26
Number of Elders	0	3	4	27	8
Ratio of Elders to Houses	0/660	1/50	1/9	1/4	1/3

known, since the town clerk noted the names of those who - in the following October - attended the council to give their consent to its election of commissioners to the Glasgow Assembly. Three elders were absent, but the remaining twenty-one included twelve merchants, four craftsmen, three lawyers and two others who may have been lawyers. The average tax payment was £64, or rather more than three and a half times the average for the city as a whole. They included one former magistrate and six former councillors ([18]). The list is incomplete; but it seems likely that the sessions elected in December 1637 were somewhat less wealthy than their predecessors of December 1625 and that they contained a rather higher proportion of lawyers and a rather lower proportion of former councillors. The change, if it was real at all, was slight and its meaning ambiguous. It might be argued that the kirk sessions of Edinburgh were, under the stresses of revolution, reverting to an older pattern - that the 'time servers' were giving way to the 'better sort'. But the change, if change it was, might just as well have been a gradual process extending over the whole period. After all, the city fathers had contrived to reduce the kirk session to a subordinate role. It would hardly have been surprising if some of their friends had lost interest in it.

But, by the end of 1637, the 'time servers' and the 'better sort' were re-united. In the spring, the conventicles prepared themselves; in the summer, they acted; in the autumn, they were joined by the oligarchy; by the winter, Edinburgh belonged to the Supplicants. Indeed the burgh paused more briefly than usual. After the riot in St Giles, the bailies pulled in a few servants and then let them go again. No doubt they were questioned, but it is obvious that they were not pressed very hard. The secrets of Nicolas Balfour, Barbara Hamilton, John Mein and their growing army of supporters remained undisclosed. The oligarchy had silently declared its sympathies but not yet its allegiance. In September Sir John Hay, a brilliantly successful town clerk and now the Canterburian clerk register, arrived from Court with a letter demanding his election to the office of lord provost left vacant by the recent death of David Aikenhead. The council obeyed without any visible sign of dissent; but, a few days later, they took advantage of Hay's absence to submit a supplication against the Liturgy. Then, at the Michaelmas elections, they dutifully confirmed Hay in his office, apparently without serious opposition. The moment of truth came in mid-October when, with the mob outside and Hay within, they finally chose the Supplicants ([19]).

Hay soon disappeared never to return; but it is significant that Sinclair, his principal henchman, stayed on and then served out his term as old dean of guild in the following year. Indeed the elections of 1637 and 1638, unlike those of 1559 and

1648, produced no startling changes. The complex procedures of the Decree Arbitral ensured an essential continuity and this was apparent enough in both elections; but they also prescribed an element of discontinuity and this was no more apparent than it was in a typical election of the period. The number of new faces was about average; the proportion of old hands was also about average. Very few political careers ended with the ˙.iturgy [20].

The only real change was at the top. At Michaelmas 1638, Hay was replaː J by William Dick of Braid. It was an apt and a significant choice. His political career had begun in 1611 and he had served as bailie, treasurer and dean of guild. In one sense, he personified the oligarchy; in another, he outshone it. William Dick was a financier, a customs farmer, a manufacturer, a shipowner, a merchant, and a landowner with a string of estates spanning the Lothians. He lived and worked in the largest private house in the burgh and his tax payments were four times the next on the list and seventy times the average. His links with the Crown had been financial rather than political; he had lent money to the government and he had made money out of it; but he had never seriously tried to join it. He could pose as the patriot and he never hesitated to do so. From the beginning of the Bishops' Wars, his vast fortune was at the disposal of Leven's armies. He became the money lender of the Covenant.

But if Dick was a patriot, he was scarcely one of the 'better sort'. It is likely that he disliked the Articles of Perth, but he had played no public part in the opposition to them; it would be surprising if he had ever seen the inside of a conventicle. Old Edinburgh was the most intimate of cities and we must assume that he knew John Mein, but they can scarcely have moved in the same circles. The tax roll epitomises their differences. In 1634 Dick had paid £1,200; Mein had paid four. Mein kept a booth and sold all sorts of odds and ends besides Calderwood's tracts; Dick was a merchant prince [21]. Mein was a genuine revolutionary; Dick became a rebel to stop a revolution. Like the oligarchy, which he represented with such distinction, Dick had no thought of starting one and he must have found the early years reasonably encouraging. The bargain of 1625 was renegotiated in 1641 without decisively altering its meaning. There would now be six parishes instead of four and thus twelve ministers instead of eight. This plainly favoured the church, but the advantage was limited. As the number of sessions rose from four to six, the number of elders in each fell from six to four. Each would consist of four elders, four deacons, the lord provost and the bailies of the burgh. It may be doubted if the provost often came, but it is obvious that at least one bailie was expected to attend each meeting. For there were now six sessions and only four bailies. To meet the difficulty, the council allotted a separate meeting time for each session. The magistrate would always be there.

These provisions favoured the civil power and were obviously intended to do so; but, in Edinburgh as in Scotland as a whole, the settlement of 1641 was ambiguous. The closing passages of a fascinating act are worth quoting in full: 'and because the said sessions are appointed for trying the manners of the people and appointing of discipline both civil and ecclesiastical as occasion serves; therefore the Provost, Bailies and Council has, with consent of their ministers appointed that there shall be no bills read upon the said weekdays for contribution or supply, but that the same shall be heard upon the Sundays afternoon to be read and answered by the Provost, Bailies, Dean of Guild and Treasurer convening each sabbath day . . . with one or two of the sessions of the said parishes as shall be thought fitting.' The bargain of 1625 had quite specifically forbidden the church to interfere in civil affairs; the bargain of 1641, on the other hand, consciously confused the two jurisdictions. The phrase 'contribution or supply' is vague enough, but it is reasonable to assume that the magistrates were not to descend on the sessions merely to trifle with the poor money. They must at least have been concerned with the annuity tax and, quite probably, with national taxation as well. It is almost certain that the church, in Edinburgh as elsewhere, had been used, under the informal supervision of the magistrates, to raise the funds which had financed the Bishops' Wars and it seems quite possible that an arrangement of this kind was now being written into the constitution of the burgh. Taxes would be proclaimed and debated on the sabbath. The magistrates may well have thought that the courts of the church were becoming extensions of their own - and this was an error into which the Parliament was simultaneously tumbling (²²).

For the church must already have been pondering its reply. As early as February 1642, the six kirk sessions of Edinburgh were occasionally meeting as a single united body and their meetings were sufficiently formal to justify the employment of a clerk. The occasion of their only recorded early meeting was innocent enough; they merely consented to a decision by the council to divert a bequest for the poor into the funds of Trinity Hospital. But this was the thin end of a thick wedge. The council had previously contrived, from motives that are obvious enough, to keep the sessions apart. Now, perhaps in an informal corollary to the bargain of 1641, they were forced to give way and it is reasonable to assume, in the absence of positive evidence, that they were giving way slowly. It is fair to infer that the magistrates attended the meetings - as they would do in 1657 when the surviving record opens; it is fair to assume that the body thus constituted did not act as a court - as it would not be acting in 1657; it is doubtful whether it had any legal authority over its constituent parts - though it may have urged them, as it would do in 1657, to use their powers the more effectively. It was not, at least in the first instance, a consistory. But the wedge thickened as it was hammered. In 1648 the six sessions had, not merely a clerk, but a moderator as well. His name was Robert Douglas and he was a hammer indeed. Shortly afterwards, an argument between church and burgh, about the presentation of ministers and the rights of the kirk sessions in the election of burgh commissioners to the general assembly, brought matters to a head. The town council saw fit to deny that their negotiating with the six sessions acknowledged any 'power or jurisdiction' in their meetings. But the power was there whether the council chose to acknowledge it or not. The united sessions of Edinburgh, like the commission of the general assembly, had been created by stealth; but they were there nonetheless. Edinburgh had found its consistory and it is inconceivable that the magistrates - who supported the Engagement - could have attended its deliberations (²³).

The defeat of the Engagers at Preston was the defeat of the town council of

Edinburgh. At Michaelmas 1648 the Engager magistrates were forbidden to serve
out their terms on the council and the skinners were ordered to elect a new
deacon. Somewhat ironically, Laurence Todd was replaced as old provost by
William Dick who, whatever his sympathies, had avoided any direct link with the
Engagers. Like the Marquis of Argyll, he lingered on to become the hangman of an
all-powerful church. But he was soon to be joined by John Mein, who was elected a
merchant councillor in 1649. Mein had prospered during the forties and his tax
payments were now about double the average for the burgh; but he was still far
from wealthy and he had had no previous connection with the oligarchy at all. This
was perhaps the hesitant beginning of a new tendency. The council, given time,
might eventually have been persuaded to deliver itself to the godly of low degree;
but, in the meantime, the merchant princes were obliging - or impotent - enough
([24]). The consistory effectively ruled Edinburgh until Cromwell returned to pull
down the edifice he had helped to erect.

General Lambert restored the semblance of a normal government at the end of
1652 and thereafter the city fathers recovered rapidly. But they were not able, and
probably did not try, to repeat their previous intervention in the elections to the
kirk session. The session minutes of the north-east quarter, which resume in 1653,
merely show that the old session elected the new one in the traditional manner.
There is no evidence of intervention, either by the burgh on the one hand or the
congregation on the other; equally there is no indication that magistrates were
appointed as elders during their term of office or that they attended meetings in
their civil capacity. At some point between 1641 and 1653 - and probably during
the prelude to, or just possibly the aftermath of, the Engagement - the sessions of
Edinburgh regained their independence of the civil power.

An analysis of the eldership as it was during the radical days of 1649 would
plainly have been of the greatest interest. Unfortunately the loss of the relevant
church records, and the silence of the other sources, renders this impossible.
However, a list in the Council Record discloses the membership of all six of the
sessions as it was in June 1654, and this must serve as a substitute. In some respects
at least it is probably adequate, since the system of election was almost certainly
the same, while some at least of the elders of 1649 may well, to judge from the more
fully recorded experience of the thirties, have re-appeared four or five years later.
In any event, the comparison with the earlier lists of 1625 and 1637 is instructive
(see Table V).

Table V ([25])
Analysis of the Elders of Edinburgh, 1625, 1637 and 1654

	1625	1637	1654
All Elders	24	(21)	36
Merchants	14	(12)	16
Professional Men	4	(3, 4 or 5)	10
Served on Council in previous decade	9	(7)	4
Ratio of average elders' tax payment to average burgh tax payment	5/1	3.6/1	1.8/1

N.b. The figures for 1637 are based on an incomplete list of elders. The full total was twenty-four.

The total numerical strength of the kirk sessions, which had been so conspicuously kept down to twenty-four elders and twenty-four deacons in 1641, had been increased to thirty-six of each at some point - probably in the late forties - before 1654. The change, which probably reflected a real increase in the power of the kirk sessions, coincided with a change in their composition. The proportion of merchants fell; the proportion of professional men rose; the appearance of two doctors of medicine in 1654 must have recalled the 'better sort' of 1620. At the same time, the eldership had probably become much less wealthy and less closely connected with the burgh oligarchy. To put the same point in a different way: the session had become less dependent on the burgh and, in so doing, had come to be drawn from a different, and usually less prosperous, social background. It would be extravagant to identify the 'better sort' with the poor, for none of the elders of the period had ever known real poverty as the seventeenth century would have defined the term. None of them were journeymen and none were labourers; but none of them were merchant princes either. The elders of 1654 were small merchants, master craftsmen, lawyers, and doctors, together with a maltman. The last pursued a trade that had never been incorporated and was thus without political influence. Indeed the lack of real wealth or real power was the link which bound an otherwise diverse group together.

In a small burgh, where everybody knew everybody else and nobody was really wealthy, the kirk session was often the town council thinly disguised. But Edinburgh - larger, wealthier and more crowded as it was - seldom conformed to this pattern. During the Morton administration, bailies were sometimes elected to the session, but there was never any suggestion that they were there simply by virtue of their office. Later on, the town council sometimes participated in the elections and tended to reproduce an inferior copy of itself when it did so. But this was never accepted as the normal pattern. The church in Edinburgh preferred its own peculiar version of the ordinary Scottish system. The old would elect the new, but the rights of the congregation would seldom be entirely neglected. This suited Melvillian ministers well enough; but in a sense it suited Edinburgh too. The complex social structure of the capital demanded a channel of protest and it often found one in its kirk sessions and, failing them, in the conventicle. Indeed the official church sometimes assumed the character of a privy kirk. Its elders tended to be drawn from the outer fringes of the oligarchy or from outside it altogether. The 'better sort' were seldom the powerful sort.

13

The Privy Kirk

IN the autumn of 1651, when his revolution had succumbed to another with a longer sword, Samuel Rutherford found himself in doubt. He had always rejected the Cromwellian solution and he naturally lamented defeat. But, on another and perhaps more exalted level, he felt an odd sense of relief: 'The Lord hath done much to take out of the way all betwixt Him and us. There are not in our way now kings, nor armies, nor nobles, nor jurisdictions, nor strongholds, nor watchmen, nor godly professors. The fairest things and most eminent in Britain are stained and have lost their lustre; only Christ keepeth his greenness and beauty and remaineth what he was.' ([1]) Cromwell had smashed the old order and Rutherford naturally rejoiced; but he welcomed the downfall of the 'godly professors' - that is, the ministers and the now divided Commission - as well. He found comfort in the collapse of the state opposite to a state as well as the state itself. In a sense, Rutherford was merely luxuriating - for this was the privilege of the elect - in the mysteries of the invisible church; but he had always loved metaphor and he may have meant more. He had once scandalised a general assembly with the assertion that privy meetings were lawful in the sight of God; he would later attribute the defeat of his church to its preoccupation with power. The Scottish revolution, like all the others, was torn between the conflicting claims of organisation and innocence. Rutherford was yearning for the inspired simplicity of the privy kirk.

The privy kirk had always been the vehicle of insurrection. In the years before the Reformation, it had comprised a series of revolutionary cells operating entirely outside the ordinary machinery of church and state. It was quite different from the 'Lords and Barons professing Christ Jesus', who had merely conspired to use their authority within the existing order. It had created a new and necessarily informal apparatus of government different in kind from any of its predecessors. But it had operated in a society which was still basically stable and it had failed. Melville had been more fortunate in his time than Knox. He had often been able to work within the official church at a time when inflation had already begun to damage the foundations of feudalism. The privy kirk had gathered new strength and, in doing so, it had lost some of its informality; indeed it was becoming the property of a group of radical ministers seeking to seize the kirk. By a strange irony, the chaos of the conventicle came to serve the cause of a highly centralised professional church.

And yet the contradiction was no contradiction at all. The Melvillian ministers sought to subject a feudal state to a clerical church; the privy kirk operated outside the feudal system altogether. Each, in its different way, was eroding the existing order - and Samuel Rutherford was heir to both. The radical ministers of the 1640s more or less openly championed the cause of conventicles in the belief that they could control them. But most of the leading moderates did not want to forbid them. They looked back with a proper pride to their own insurrectionary past; they looked forward into a future that was still uncertain. The revolution - and it was their revolution as well as Rutherford's - was still insecure. They had liberated themselves from the bishops only to deliver themselves - bound but never gagged - to feudal masters only less imperious. It might be true that they were slowly easing the baron out of the presbytery and the Commission - that they were relegating him to the general assembly; but the relationship was uncomfortable and they could scarcely claim that the magnates of the mid-1640s were merely the civil arm of an all-powerful church. Conventicles might still be useful, and the moderates - perhaps quite consciously - kept them in reserve. The Engagement presented the radicals with their opportunity. As the moderates led the official church into a resistance that was outwardly passive, their radical colleagues connived at, and in a few cases actively fomented, direct action. The privy kirk was reborn (²).

The strongholds of the Whiggamores were disposed along a well-worn trail leading around the northern edge of the Southern Uplands from the city of Edinburgh to the Solway Firth. At the one end, it absorbed radical influences from London and the Continent; at the other, it received presbyterian zealots returning from exile in Ulster. Radical ideas travelled freely along it in both directions and they left sufficient evidence of their passage. It would be possible to trace an imaginary route entering Lanarkshire through the parish of Shotts - which had staged a famous revival in the 1630s - descending to the Clyde and spreading as it did so to embrace the broad acres of the Hamiltons, rising again to converge on upland Avondale - the parish of Auchengilloch and Drumclog - and skirting the foot of Loudoun Hill - that trysting ground of the privy kirk - as it passed across the Ayrshire border into the relative security of a different jurisdiction. Beyond the Irvine gap, it divided in two. One branch struck off northwards through Stewarton - which had been 'sick' until a radical minister had found a remedy - to the estuary of the Clyde. The other turned south through the Lollard lands of Kyle and thence, through relatively barren ground in Carrick, into Galloway, where Rutherford had had a conventicle of his own.

These areas had some features in common. They combined a moist climate with retentive soils difficult to drain and slow to warm in springtime. Favoured enclaves apart, they yielded grass more readily than grain; their character was essentially pastoral. The career of Barbara Gilmour, who returned from refuge in Ulster to marry an Ayrshire farmer and invent a famous cheese, epitomises their story. They differed quite fundamentally from the relatively self-sufficient communities of the arable east. All of them grew some victual and some of them enough to feed themselves in an average year; but a season of dearth would find them in the more abundant grain markets of the Lothians. Indeed their pastoral products had traditionally been drawn to Edinburgh and, through it, to more distant markets. Money had always played a fairly important part in their economies and, perhaps because of this, their rents had frequently been calculated in money rather than in kind. The occasional arable farm might pay in victual and some pastoral farms in wedders, butter or cheese; but a money rent was the general rule (³).

In the sixteenth century, money had been fickle. There is no reason to doubt that its value had declined as steeply in the pastoral west as it had done elsewhere. To judge from the conversion prices used in the accounts and rentals of the Hamilton estates in Clydesdale, the price of victual had risen almost tenfold, of wedders more than tenfold and of cheese almost ninefold between the early 1540s and the late 1640s. These impressions are substantially confirmed, though only over a shorter period, by the testaments of the parish of Avondale, which also suggest that the prices of farm animals had been rising at a similar rate. These calculations are fallible, but it is obvious - and sufficient for our purpose - that the increase, however gradual it may have been, was enormous (⁴).

In the arable shires of the east, where rents tended to be measured in kind, the customary relationship between landlord and tenant preserved itself; rents rose as prices rose. But these automatic adjustments did not operate in the pastoral regions, where the real value of rents could only be maintained if the landlord chose deliberately to increase them - and this could only look like rack renting. Long years of relatively stable prices had yielded a rigid rent structure with all the power of custom behind it. Church and state alike maintained, or at least professed to maintain, that stable rents were not merely normal but desirable in themselves (⁵). The sixteenth century had been conditioned by its past to regard inflation as a moral rather than an economic problem; indeed its very existence was obscured because the gradual upward trend of prices was lost in the ordinary fluctuations of dearth and abundance. It is arguable that landlords had the power - as they certainly had the legal right - to raise rents; but it may be doubted whether it immediately occurred to most of them to do so. It was not merely that rent increases provoked disorder or even that they flouted the received wisdom of the day. The landlord, at least if he was a tenant-in-chief, was himself a vital element in the structure of feudal Scotland. The guardian of custom was reluctant to abuse it. He was faced with an unhappy choice between relative poverty and absolute sin.

It may be thought that the tenant sometimes made up his mind for him. Recent research has strongly suggested that the Scottish farmer of the sixteenth century was less insecure than has usually been supposed. On the estates of the church and the Crown, some of the tenants, in the pastoral west as in the arable east, were rentallers with formal leases, granted for life and normally passed on to their heirs or assignees. Indeed the courts of the West of Scotland seem - or so one authority assures us - to have regarded rentallers as heritable proprietors. But the greater part of the kirklands and of the royal estates were feued either to the sitting tenants - whether they were rentallers or not - or to 'gentlemen' who, in their turn, sometimes, though not invariably, sub-feued them to sitting tenants. In these cases, the farmer became totally secure and there seems every reason to suppose that the ordinary husbandman was only less so. During the crucial middle years of the century - that is, at the time when inflation was becoming a serious problem - leases were getting longer rather than shorter and they were often renewed to the same tenant or his heir ([6]).

It seems probable, though the evidence has been less thoroughly explored, that a rather similar pattern developed on the lands of the civil magnates. For centuries, the barons had been granting estates heritably to cadets, bastards and deserving retainers for rents which, whether they were in money or in kind, were almost always nominal. The estates varied considerably in size. The new landed vassal might be a 'gentleman' owning several farms and operating them through tenants, or he might be a 'yeoman' owning the farm that he worked. These tenandry lands plainly bore a close resemblance to the feued lands of the temporalities. The superior had alienated the bulk of the income from the lands concerned, though not the jurisdiction inseparable from them. But he still administered the rest of his lands through his bailie and here the farmer was a husbandman with a limited lease or no lease at all. It is possible to believe that he was as secure in practice as he was vulnerable in theory; the parallel with the kirklands, so close in other respects, at least encourages us to believe that he may have been.

It will be argued that the pastoral tenants of the west were secure enough and that their security retarded the raising of their rents for so long that only a violent increase could restore the balance between landlord and tenant. The course of pastoral rents during the long years of the price rise has never been charted, partly no doubt because sixteenth and early seventeenth century rentals are rare. But later rentals are much more common - and this may not be entirely due to the growth of bureaucracy or to the accidents of survival. Customary rents, unlike racked rents, would not need a succession of rentals. It could be that rents did not begin to rise until the middle years of the seventeenth century. It may be worth testing this hypothesis through the unusually comprehensive collection of material available for the Hamilton lands in Clydesdale.

The barony of Hamilton itself, like some of the other estates in the Clyde Valley, included substantial areas of good arable land. A few of its farms paid most of their rents in victual, sometimes including a small proportion of wheat; others paid largely in dairy produce; indeed the total yield for the whole of the barony revealed a bewildering mixture of money and different forms of kind. An early rental, undated but almost certainly belonging to the middle of the sixteenth century, suggests that rather less than half the total, measured at the prices then prevailing, was paid in money. But it is significant that a later rental of 1592 records much the same money total and that nearly all the individual farms were still paying exactly the same rent in money and kind alike. A long series of early seventeenth century accounts seems at first glance to confirm this; but this was scarcely true. 'Augmentations', always large compared with the previous silver rents of the farms concerned, became a prominent feature of the accounts by the 1620s. They are always - and rather conspicuously - stated separately; it was almost as though the rent itself was still regarded as a fixed quantity that even the great Lady Anna could not presume to change. However this may be, it is evident that the effective money rents of some, though not yet of all, the farms in the barony were suddenly and vastly increased ([7]).

It might be objected that all this rests on a rental without a date and, perhaps more fundamentally, that it relates to an estate which was scarcely typical of the Whiggamore country. The barony of Hamilton, with its Clyde valley situation and its excellent cornlands, was too well endowed. Avondale, higher and wider as it was, is more to our purpose. The Water of Avon rose among the hills of the Ayrshire-Lanarkshire border and pointed somewhat north of east towards the Clyde, which it joined near Hamilton. It shared a common source with the Irvine and thus formed part of a natural line of passage linking middle Clydesdale with Cunningham and Kyle. The barony of Avondale occupied the upper half of the basin drained by the Avon and its tributaries. The valley itself fanned out as it descended, but it formed a relatively small part of the whole. The north-west was higher and mossier. The south included a vast upland area, inhabited only round its edges, culminating in the rounded summits of Dungavel and Auchengilloch. Avondale was at once the refuge and the routeway of the privy kirk.

The character of the parish, which roughly coincided with the barony, was strikingly revealed by the testaments of its farmers. An examination of some seventy inventories, ranging in time from the 1570s to the 1650s and in place from the four corners of a large parish, suggests that, on the average, only about a quarter of the agricultural component consisted of grain - and a comparison with the Isles is instructive here. The proportion was higher than most of Shetland and the Western Isles, but somewhat lower than the Orkney average and markedly lower than the average for its best arable parishes. It is reasonable to conclude that Avondale was essentially a pastoral parish, but its broad totals concealed considerable local variation. In the valley farms of the east, the proportion was much higher - in one case over a half. But the percentage fell, with a regularity almost too good to be true, as the valley rose. In Newton, it was 45%, in Linbank 38% and in Rylands 28%. The valley of the Water of Glengavil, an upland tributary joining the mainstream from the south above Rylands, made the same point. In Halls, the proportion of grain was 20%; in Plewland, high among the hills of the south-west, it was less than 10% - and the mossy farms of the north-west yielded comparable figures ([8]).

It is obvious enough that the hill farms could not feed themselves and likely that the richer farms of the valley could sometimes make up the deficit. The basis for a regular local trade plainly existed and, at least in times of dearth, this expanded into a broader exchange of products between the pastoral west and the arable east. It is scarcely surprising that Avondale, strategically situated on a natural route as it was, should have boasted a burgh of barony, looking over its cornlands towards the Clyde, as early as 1450. In the 1670s, 61 owner-occupiers - the successors of the original inhabitants - were holding houses and yards from the superior at nominal rents. The yards of the burgh of Strathaven were naturally cultivated, but it was more than a mere farmtoun. It had an array of village craftsmen, four maltsters, several brewers and probably a few drovers as well; above all it had resident merchants of some little substance bringing in goods from distant sources. To judge from the hearth tax rolls of the 1690s, it contained nearly a third of the total population of the parish.

M

The barony thus constituted had been held by the Bairds, the Sinclairs, the Douglases, the Stewarts of Ochiltree, Hamilton of Finart, and his descendants of Crawfordjohn before finally joining the Hamilton empire early in the seventeenth century. It had survived the vicissitudes of forfeiture and favouritism; it had often been held by an absentee. The process of subinfeudation had begun early and it continued apace. By the middle years of the sixteenth century, the income from more than half of the barony had effectively been commuted for small annual payments which, insofar as they were made in money, would be further diminished by inflation. These tenandry lands had usually been granted to landowners, very like the 'gentlemen' of the temporalities, who operated them through husbandmen. Thus the £5 land of Newton was worked by tenants who paid their rents to Hamilton of Silvertonhill, a gentleman also holding other tenandries in Avondale and elsewhere. Similarly most of the upland farms of the north-west were held by Cunningham of Cunninghamhead, a baron in Ayrshire but a gentleman in Avondale, while Hamilton of Raploch had lands in hill and valley alike. Some of the other tenandries were smaller and it is possible that they were held by yeomen operating their own farms. But this was not the vital point. The tenants who worked the gentlemen's lands seem to have been almost as secure as the gentlemen themselves. Many of their testaments show them passing on their 'rights', their 'titles' and their 'kindness', as well as their 'possession', to their widows and their sons. The valuation rolls of the eighteenth century show that they eventually came to own their farms; but this again is almost immaterial. Their wills suggest that they had had most of the rights of ownership time out of mind. The tenandry lands of Avondale enjoyed - or perhaps suffered - a social structure that was stable to the point of rigidity; three people - the superior, the gentleman, and the farmer himself - had heritable rights in each acre of land ([9]).

The rest of the barony was farmed by husbandmen who paid their rents directly to the superior. Their wills were less specific and their titles were presumably less formal; but there can be no doubt that sons often followed fathers in their farms. The Hamiltons in Halls of Glengavil - two pastoral farms in the south-west of the barony - may have been an extreme case, but it seems certain that one and almost certain that both remained in the family from the 1540s to the 1670s ([10]). The rentals of the barony, which have survived well enough for the middle years of the seventeenth century, suggest that this was not uncommon. Thus Hookhead was shared between two Aytons and two Morrisons in the 1630s, one Ayton, two Morrisons and a Cochrane in the early fifties and one Ayton, two Morrisons and an Allason - still there twenty years later - in the 1670s. There are several exceptions, but such instances could be multiplied and, at least in one or two cases, projected backwards through the testaments into the later years of the previous century. The farmers of the rented lands may have been somewhat less secure, in fact as well as in law, than were their comrades in the tenandries; but they were reasonably secure nonetheless. And yet inflation pressed hard.

It would be as interesting as it is impossible to trace the impact of inflation on rents throughout the barony of Avondale. Unfortunately, the farmers of the tenandries paid their rents to a 'gentleman' rather than to the superior and none of the rentals has survived. The testaments of the farmers, though they survive in some quantity, do not entirely fill the gap. They fairly often list rent payments as debts owed by the deceased, but they are often vague about the precise identity of the farm concerned and about the period covered by the debt. It is difficult to be certain that like is being compared with like. Nonetheless, most of the figures for the first three decades of the seventeenth century seem low, with the possible exception of those relating to the hill farms of the north-west. It seems quite likely that Cunningham of Cunninghamhead was raising his rents at this time and that the rest of the gentlemen were not. This is debatable enough and it is fortunate that the rented lands are better served. Here the tenants paid their rents directly to a superior whose records have survived better than most. A rental and two sets of accounts span the decade between 1535 and 1545. These are followed, after a gap occasionally filled by the testaments, by another rental, undated but clearly belonging to the late 1620s or the 1630s, and by a fortunate fragment from the baron court book of 1642. A series of accounts and a rental cover the late 1640s and the early 1650s and the story is completed by a detailed rental of the 1670s and a collection of individual tacks of the 1690s. They are as eloquent as the privy kirk ([11]).

In the 1540s, the rented lands of Avondale had yielded £532 in money, 160 wedders (worth about £40 at contemporary prices), 200 stones of cheese (about £30) and 226 bolls of victual (about £165). It had paid the superior the equivalent of about £730 and, of this, the silver rent had amounted to nearly three quarters of the total. If these quantities had continued unchanged into the seventeenth century, inflation would have reduced the proportion to just over one fifth. It seems likely that something very like this actually happened. In the interim, one or two of the farms had been absorbed into the tenandries, while the cheese rent had been converted into money. With these reservations, the rents paid in kind remained more or less the same and the silver rent, originally the main element of the whole, remained almost exactly the same at rather over £500. But, in Avondale as in Hamilton, 'augmentations' had begun to appear; once more, they were listed separately; once again, they were huge in relation to the previous rent. By 1648, they amounted to two and a half times the silver rent, despite the fact that only some of the rents had been increased. The barony of Avondale was clearly in turmoil. In 1642, as the court books testify, tenants were threatened with eviction in Crawfordjohn and Lesmahagow as well as in Avondale and most of the cases arose out of augmentations sometimes demanded as an alternative to a huge grassum.

The details of the process are sometimes obscure, but the outlines are sharp enough. The rental of c1630 shows that many farms were still paying the rents of the 1540s, while some of the others were paying a lot more. Thus the four tenants of the valley farms of Hookhead had shared a rent of £33, paid entirely in money, in the 1540s and they were still paying exactly the same amount nearly a century later. On the other hand, the three tenants of the hill farm of Plewland near the head of Glengavil Water were paying a customary rent of £20 and 40 wedders (worth about £100 in the 1630s) and a 'new augmentation' of £200 as well. The impact was cushioned by the gradual increase in the value of the wedders, but it is evident that the silver component of the rent had been increased elevenfold at a single stroke. The contrast between old and new was even more blatant in Crookburn, a short distance down the valley from Hookhead. The tenant of the 10/- land was paying of 'old duty and new augmentation' nearly £27; his immediate neighbour was paying only the old rent of just over £10 for a farm which was, at least in terms of old extent, nearly three times as large.

A further group of augmentations seems to have been initiated in 1642. John Young was one of five tenants farming the £3 land of Hawkwood on the northern fringe of the southern hills and his customary rent, paid entirely in money, had been about £4. In May he was confronted with an augmentation of £40. He refused to pay, was evicted and thereafter disappeared from the story. His near neighbour, William Torrens, was offered the option of a huge grassum of £250 - about six times the new rent and sixty times the old one. In return, Torrens would continue to pay the old rent until he died, while his son would then be enrolled - but at the new rent - as his successor. Torrens accepted and defiantly lived on into the 1650s, thus postponing the actual increase into the days of Duchess Anne. He plainly had some difficulty in finding the ready money and this was no doubt fairly common; but it seems likely that most of the tenants, whatever their immediate difficulties, were able to pay the new rents. Indeed the customary rents were ludicrously low in terms of the withered pounds of the seventeenth century; a farmer's goods and gear were valued only at the time of his death - when he was beyond his best - but, even then, his rent liability was often only a tiny fraction of his total wealth. Threats of eviction were fairly common; actual evictions, or so it would seem, were relatively rare.

In a sense, the grassums of the thirties and forties served to prolong the old hereditary regime, though only into the next generation and, to this rather limited extent, they tended towards stability. But they were, in practice if not in theory, innovations in themselves. It is a reasonable assumption that grassums had always been exacted in Avondale as they had been on so many other estates. But they are not mentioned in any of the rentals or accounts and the testaments are almost as reticent. Many of them list rent payments, but only one lists a grassum. Thomas Morton in Overhouse of Glengavil owed £33 of 'mails, grassums and duties' for the year 1604. But the customary rent of his farm, together with a tiny fragment subsequently added to it, was only £36 if the wedder element is converted at the price used in the same testament ([12]). It is obvious that the grassum had - perhaps in some long-forgotten medieval augmentation - merged itself into the rent; there was no point in stating it separately. But Lady Anna's grassums, like her augmentations, were of a different order. They may not have caused the eviction of many of her tenants; but they evicted some of them and they can only have tormented the rest. Far from representing stability, they stimulated change.

A farmer who chose a grassum postponed the augmentation of his rent - and thus its appearance in the rentals - into the next generation. It nonetheless seems certain that nearly all the farms were affected in one way or the other at some time between 1625 and 1648 and almost certain that most of them were affected during the 1630s or the early 1640s. But the process was not completed until about 1670 and the total impact cannot be assessed before then. A crude comparison suggests that the total yield of the silver rent had risen from its customary level of about £500 to about £6,000. But this is misleading. The first figure excluded the wedder rent and the teinds; the second included both. The distinctions had disappeared in the interests of administrative convenience. The wedder silver was worth only about £450, but the teinds were more valuable. The parsonage was calculated in kind and had thus maintained its value; the vicarage, though measured in money, had once, as befitted a pastoral parish, been substantial and was still far from negligible. The calculations are difficult since several titulars were involved, but it seems likely that the teinds made up about £1,500 of the yield from the rented lands. The silver rent, properly so called, may have been worth about £4,000 in the seventies and, after further augmentation, nearly £5,000 in the 1690s. It was finally restored to its real value of the 1540s during the second half of the seventeenth century.

There is no reason to suspect that Lady Anna was consciously reacting to the price rise. As the manager of her son's estates, she faced the problem of meeting his expenses at Court; she quite simply needed the money. Her tenants, who had to find it, were similarly ignorant; they were farmers, not economists. The vast augmentations of the period can surely be justified, but they must have seemed irrational to everybody involved in them. The gradual transfer of wealth from landlord to tenant was abruptly halted and indeed violently reversed. A century or more of security of tenure was suddenly threatened. The basic assumptions of the customary society were questioned. Again the Lady Marquis almost certainly did not intend this. Like her son and her tenants, she was tangled up in an economic process that she did not understand. The evidence suggests that she was devoted to her dependants and it is interesting that there was no real trouble while she lived. Lady Anna - a diamond at her bosom, a pistol at her belt - was a woman of character and a convinced Covenanter. She shared some at least of the religious eccentricities of her victims; she was a true daughter of the west. But, within a year of her death in 1647, many of her tenants were in arms against her son (13).

It is arguable that the Hamiltons did not regain full control of their estates until Duchess Anne came into her inheritance. Augmentation by proxy was a dubious proposition in the pastoral west and it must surely have been fairly common. The parish of Mauchline, across the border in Kyle, consisted largely of the old ecclesiastical barony of Kylesmure. It was held by the Earl of Loudoun, whose ancestral estates were elsewhere and whose interests were in Edinburgh rather than Ayrshire. The Earl was a career politician and a Covenanter without conviction. His tastes were expensive and his debts a legend. He had wanted the Treasury and he had been disappointed; but, in 1641, he was made Chancellor and granted a pension that was large, though largely unpaid. Like the Duke of Hamilton, he needed money badly. His Countess by contrast was a zealot and the confidante of the radicals; she may well have sympathised with her vassals as Lady Anna did and as so many other noblewomen may have done. Whether this was so or not, it is clear that Kylesmure resembled Avondale in many respects. Many of its tenants had been rentallers paying a customary rent to the Abbey of Melrose. During the sixteenth century, most of them had become feuars - or, perhaps in a few cases, the sub-feuars of gentlemen - paying a mildly augmented annual duty which had duly depreciated with the passage of time. During the seventeenth century, they were the modestly affluent vassals of a superior who was nearly always elsewhere. The proper lands of Kylesmure had, on the other hand, remained unfeued; but the tenants, whether they had been rentallers or not, had probably been reasonably secure. And yet their rents had almost certainly been augmented; the parish valuation of 1649 shows a predominance of money rents that would scarcely have been possible if they had remained at, or even near, their customary level. It is plainly possible that rents had risen more gradually here than they had in Avondale; but it is almost certain that they had multiplied themselves. The proper lands of Kylesmure, together with the lands of any gentleman who had been free to raise his rents, were now being worked by husbandmen at rents which must have seemed extortionate. But most of the barony was worked by yeomen feuars who were still paying only a little more than the customary rent. Inflation had distorted the social structure in Mauchline as it had done in Avondale - and as it surely must have done in many other pastoral areas. It had enriched the vassals and then it had made some of them poor again ([14]). The argument from coincidence has its dangers, but it must surely be clear that the Mauchline Rising had some of the characteristics of a peasants' revolt. The farmers of Kylesmure listened more attentively to Mr. Thomas Wylie, the radical minister of Mauchline, than they did to the doubting Chancellor of Scotland.

The Mauchline Rising and its sequel two years later were the great spectaculars of the privy kirk, but both arose out of smaller beginnings. In each case, an armed congregation grew out of a multitude of local congregations - and so it had always been. The privy kirk had always been local in its origins and insurrectionary in its purpose; it had always supported informality against organisation, the congregation against the patron, the vassal against the baron and the 'poor' - who were sometimes fairly affluent - against the 'rich'. It manifested itself in a multitude of local quarrels each insignificant in itself - and the Glassford affair was one of these. It was first and foremost a dispute about the presentation of ministers and it arose out of the deposition of the Canterburian incumbent, Robert Hamilton, in the Glasgow Assembly. The Glassford men, who came to the assembly to testify against Hamilton, had stayed to find a successor. The minister of a neighbouring parish had suggested John Bell, a son of the minister of Stevenston who happened to be a friend of Robert Baillie. Baillie, in his turn, persuaded Argyll and Eglinton to ask Lord Sempill, the patron and sole superior of the parish, to present Bell. Sempill seems readily to have agreed and the presbytery followed suit. Thus far the story was familiar enough; magnate and minister were at one. All would perhaps have gone well if Sempill, already ailing and soon to die, had not lost his nerve. The Glasgow Assembly - and thus Hamilton's deposition - was doubtfully legal and a prudent patron chose to await the verdict of its successor. In the meantime, Hamilton had refused to leave his pulpit and the reader of the parish had responded by establishing a conventicle which was regularly attended by at least a part of the congregation. Then, in the aftermath of the legal assembly of 1639, Sempill's son presented Bell - and this proved less simple than he may have thought. The reader - whoever he was - had tasted power and he was loath to let it go again. The dissident congregation, brandishing the arms that they had loyally carried to Dunce Law and back again, loudly complained that they had not been consulted. Had not the *First Book of Discipline* proclaimed the right of the people to elect their minister? And were not the people bound in Covenant to the discipline of the kirk? The metaphor was not far to seek - indeed Rutherford might have used it himself: 'As the virgin forced in the field, if she cried was free from guilt, if silent was punishable for villainy; so they, if now they did not cry against this violence, were by God to be plagued.' And they howled.

It is easy to imagine the embarrassment of magnate and minister alike. They had used the privy kirk to get rid of Robert Hamilton - and this had been wonderful; but now it wanted to elect his successor - and that was absurd. The cause of patronage had few friends among the ministers; but the congregation was almost as unpopular - and even the radicals were bound by a recent agreement to forget a divisive issue for the time being. But the Glassford conventicle knew no such inhibitions and it went on. It would take the combined weight of the presbytery, the synod, the patron, the magnates of the west, David Dickson and a legal opinion - incidentally running to over 6,000 words - dashed off by Wariston himself - to instal young Bell in his pulpit. The entire resources of an already mighty church were used to crush the reader of Glassford - whoever he was. Wariston suffered a peculiar embarrassment. His reluctant consent to the agreement compelled him to deploy his legal learning in the service of a cause which he despised. He salved a rather sensitive conscience by begging Baillie, to whom the opinion was addressed, not to allow it to be used in the debate that was bound to follow as soon as the emergencey was over ([15]).

The barony of Glassford, which broadly corresponded with the parish, was shaped like an hour glass reclining along the northern and eastern edges of Avondale. The northern part of the barony, appropriately called the Muir, was high, rolling and mossy. Like the adjacent areas of Avondale, it was pastoral in character. The better lands were further south and, like the nearby valley lands around Strathaven, they were capable of arable cultivation. The barony was held by Lord Sempill, an absentee, who seems to have taken only a distant interest in it. The narrow waist had been feued to the Laird of Earnock, an absentee who, in his turn, had sub-feued it to the sitting tenants; but the rest was worked by husbandmen. There were some victual rents, presumably from the southern farms, but the parish valuation of 1649 suggests that most of the rents were paid in money and that they were already being augmented; a later rental of the 1680s shows that augmentation was then almost complete. The story of Glassford reflected the experience of the Hamilton lands which almost surrounded it.

The men who went to Glasgow to find a minister were described by Baillie as 'parochiners' and it seems unlikely that he was merely using the term in its general sense. He was surely referring to the leaders of the local community. These cannot have included Sempill or Earnock, whose main interests were elsewhere, nor Robert Hamilton whose church was almost empty. They were the reader - whoever he was - the feuars of Chapelton and Shawtonhill, the husbandmen of Glassford and the Muir. It is fair to assume that some of the farmers were elders and thus that they knew the reader fairly well. But, if the evidence given at the Glasgow Assembly is to be believed, Hamilton's kirk session had not met very often and it is certain that it did not officially meet after he had been deprived. For a long period, there was no ecclesiastical discipline in Glassford - and Lord Sempill was far away. It seems likely that the reader's conventicle grew out of a kirk session of farmers, but Baillie also mentioned 'poor men' - who might have been farmers - and 'silly cottars' - who plainly were not. A mob was a necessary part of any conventicle and it is obvious enough that this one included many cottars and indeed farm servants as well. But they were followers rather than leaders - and the Glassford affair was the Mauchline Rising in miniature ([16]).

Conventiclers seldom identified themselves, for fairly obvious reasons, and, in the middle years of the century, they were seldom actually prosecuted. The noisiest element in Scottish society was, by an odd irony, the least obtrusive. Baillie's rather hasty definitions are thus doubly valuable. He described the Clydesdale men, who formed the hard core of the Mauchline Rising, as 'yeomen'. The term still had a fairly precise meaning in the seventeenth century. A yeoman was a husbandman. He might, or he might not, own his farm; but, even if he did, he was not a gentleman, let alone a baron. He might well work his own farm; but he was not a cottar, still less was he a farm servant. The yeomen of Clydesdale, like the 'parochiners' of Glassford, were men of some substance; in other circumstances, they might well have been elders of the kirk. Baillie also tells us that the magnates were elsewhere and that only one or two gentlemen were present. By and large, landed power and landed wealth were missing. It is obvious enough that many cottars and village craftsmen must have come to Mauchline - indeed the hero who claimed the honour of wounding General Middleton seems to have been a blacksmith. But they were neither typical nor even numerically predominant. About two thirds of the 'slashing communicants' came on horseback - and the horse nearly always figured prominently in the testament of a pastoral farmer.

The moonlight communion on Mauchline Muir was the climax of a sequence which had begun in Clydesdale and, quite probably, on the Hamilton estates. It is almost certain that the Duke was able to raise his quota only by quartering regular soldiers on his farms. But the dissidents quite simply disappeared. Converging on Avondale, they crossed the Ayrshire border to a rendezvous on the rocky heights of Loudoun Hill. There they paused briefly and then moved forward to Mauchline, gathering strength from Cunningham and Kyle as they went. By this time, they had already, and as though by instinct, reached for clerical support. They found it in seven zealots from Ayrshire led by John Nevay, already a national figure and the most radical member of the Commission. At Mauchline, the ministers preached in relays for a day and a night to an armed congregation of 2,000 people. On the following day they began - almost as an afterthought - to elect officers, only to find that the initiative had suddenly been snatched from them. Middleton's cavalry appeared on a none too distant horizon and it was obvious that Callendar's foot were not far behind. The ministers, abruptly changing course, asked for terms, got them and spirited their Ayrshire followers away. But the Clydesdale men had nowhere to go. Some fled, perhaps to join their comrades in Galloway. The rest stood to fight a hopeless fight, were captured and hauled off to a court martial in Ayr. There Callendar, apparently on instructions from above, let them go again. The Duke, as Turner was to complain in a different context, was a poor 'justiciar'; or perhaps he merely hesitated to hang his own tenants. It was an anti-climax after so much melodrama ([17]).

The Mauchline Rising degenerated into farce. The 'slashing communicants' merely succeeded in making fools of themselves; but their colleagues in Galloway, whether or not they were joined by a contingent from Clydesdale, did better. Their task was quite simply to delay Monro's battle-hardened Ulstermen in their march to join the Duke in England. They were content to operate in small local groups which melted away as soon as they met real resistance, and it is significant that they were not unsuccessful. Monro, after haggling too long in Ulster, was forced to fight his way through Galloway as if it had been a 'hostile country' ([18]). The best troops at the Duke's disposal arrived too late for the battle. At Mauchline, on the other hand, an army without officers and with seven ministers for a general had drawn itself up for a formal engagement that it was bound to lose. The Whiggamores were guerrillas or nothing.

The direct military impact of the resistance to the levy was trivial; but its strategic consequences were considerable. It drew the nucleus of Hamilton's army, and thus eventually the whole of it, over into the west. It forced the Duke to take the western route into England and, in doing so, it funnelled his forces into the confined spaces of the Eden valley already foraged by Lambert and Langdale. Further south, the Engagers stumbled through a waste laid bare by the guerrillas of the Lancashire committee. Their great numbers, which the kirk had failed significantly to reduce, became an embarrassment. The Duke was forced to spread them over a wide area in the hope of feeding them - and still they arrived hungry. The Engagers were already half defeated when Cromwell burst through the Ribble Gap to surprise them. And the privy kirk, whether it knew what it was doing or not, is entitled to some credit for this.

Lambert and Cromwell stood to gain more than anybody else from the rising in the west and they may well have contrived it. A rather dubious Restoration source asserted that Colonel Strachan, who had served under Cromwell at Preston, had acted as an intermediary between Argyll and the New Model ([19]). The story was perhaps misleading rather than inaccurate. Argyll had no connection with the rising; indeed he discouraged it. Strachan, for his part, would eventually become the commander of the Westland army; his natural allies were the radical ministers and the Whiggamores themselves - and it is likely that he kept Lambert in touch with both. But, whether this was so or not, the Whiggamore movement plainly had an existence of its own and it can be explained only in Scottish terms. It belonged to the godly of low, but not very low, degree. It appealed to farmers and feuars; it was utterly rejected by their superiors. It was always anti-feudal and often quite consciously so. But so were the ministers themselves and so were most of their elders. It was, at least in its rural form, confined to areas which measured most of their rents in money and it might cogently be argued that it arose out of the dislocations of inflation. But this again is only half of the truth. It distinguishes the Whiggamores from their more passive comrades along the eastern seaboard; but it fails to distinguish them from the peasants of the other pastoral regions. Rents were commonly calculated in money in many parts of the Borders and along most of the Highland line. There were conventicles in both areas, but neither gave the radical cause any significant support. The Whiggamores became a popular movement only along the long trail, deeply rutted by the traffic in radical ideas, which linked Edinburgh with Ulster. In the west and south-west, radical idealism met social discontent and the mixture was explosive enough.

The Whiggamore movement was regional rather than national in its character and it is easy to exaggerate its importance. On the other hand, it has its place in a tradition which goes back to the Reformation and indeed beyond it. In the seventeenth century, it had powerful friends determined to preserve it; the old alliance with the Melvillian ministers was renewed in the 1640s. The Mauchline seven gave the rising of 1648 a coherence which it had previously lacked. Behind them, James Guthrie, Patrick Gillespie and Samuel Rutherford carried its voice into the inner councils of the kirk. Their orthodox colleagues could deplore the privy kirk; but they could never disown it, still less could they suppress it. For it was merely doing what they were too hidebound to say they were doing. The Whiggamores were the red guards of the Scottish Revolution. They constantly reminded it of its origins; they were its conscience.

14

Minister And Magnate

SAMUEL Rutherford, the philosopher of the state opposite to a state, observed, in a letter written to the ever attentive Marion McNaught during the early 1630s, that 'our blessed Lord Jesus', unable to 'get leave to sleep with his spouse in this land', was 'going to seek an inn where he (would) be better entertained'. It had not always been so. The inspiring message of Calvin, conveyed from Geneva through the ministry of 'worthy Mr Knox', had begun its work well. The privy kirk had distilled the purest essence of reformation; but its translation into a public kirk - vital though it was - had been unhappy. 'Irreverent bishops' had come in and done their popish worst. The servants of Christ had been 'banished, deprived and confined'; instead of a pulpit, they got a 'stool and a cold fire in the Blackness'; at the same time the 'nobility' were 'spoiling them of the tithes and the kirk rents', leaving 'Him a poor naked Christ'. The reformed church, as Rutherford believed it to have been conceived, had simultaneously been challenged from two opposite quarters. It had been infiltrated by the Crown and robbed by the magnates. Rutherford utterly rejected the Reformation as it had actually developed in Scotland ([1]).

Rutherford had linked the church rents with the teinds. The entire patrimony of the old church formed the proper inheritance of the new one. The elaborate edifice sketched out in the *Second Book of Discipline* had rested on the assumption that the elder would be a salaried professional as the minister was. If the teinds belonged to the ministers, the temporalities must pay the elders and deacons. But this was now, in the middle years of the seventeenth century, all but impossible. The superiorities belonged to Lords of Erection who, in some cases at least, professed to be friends; in any event their yield, once huge, was now reduced by inflation to a pittance. The renegotiation of feu duties would alienate feuars who often genuinely believed that they were friends - and this was a revolution that even Rutherford could scarcely contemplate. The corollary was similarly inconceivable. The superiorities would have brought their jurisdictions with them. The bailie of regality would have become the hired official of the church. The Melvillian relationship between church and state would have been reproduced, if only in miniature, in the localities.

The radical ministers of the 1640s were engaged in a rather different, though no less revolutionary, enterprise. The *Second Book of Discipline* was second only to the Bible itself, and they were searching eagerly for a clerical church. They were bound to reject the structure erected by the Tables in 1638. It might have its virtues - for its baronial realities were decently concealed behind the principles of a better church; but the feudal elders, who had elected themselves to the Glasgow Assembly, must be supplanted by low-born zealots willing to do as they were told. In the end - or so it may have seemed in the dreamier hours of the night - the church would belong to its ministers. It would become a church of truly 'spiritual', as distinct from merely 'ecclesiastical', persons. This was the glittering vision which lured Samuel Rutherford to his destruction.

On the face of it, Rutherford's dream was even more preposterous than Melville's. The *Second Book of Discipline* had constructed a vast pyramid solidly founded in teind and temporality; the new revolutionaries sought to build a church no less powerful on the fragile foundation of an entitlement to a part of the teinds. It is easy - and perhaps a little too easy - to dismiss the enterprise as foolish. It sought the subjection of the mighty in the interests of the merely articulate; it assumed that the sword could be blunted by the keys; it tried to dictate to the English before it had conquered in Scotland. It could plausibly be argued that it would have been defeated by the Engagers had not Cromwell defeated them first. The triumph of the clerical church between Preston and Dunbar was not - or so it might be maintained - a true reflection of the balance of forces within Scotland itself. All this is true as far as it goes, but it surely does not go far enough.

Feudal Scotland had been conditioned by the centuries to fight itself, and three decades of relative peace had done little to change its nature. The Canterburian church, itself a force for social change, had been rejected by the feudal classes as a whole and this had been the main cause of its sudden collapse. But the Lords of the Council had taken one course and the Lords of the Covenant another. The revolutionary movement itself maintained the semblance of unity while the Bishops' Wars were actually in progress, but its baronial component split in two as soon as they were over. The feud between Montrose and Argyll, stripped of the emotion which has often clouded its interpretation, was essentially an old-fashioned faction fight over the control of the executive. The renewal of war, the association of Montrose with the clans and the consequent breach with his party, combined to renew an appearance of unity which again barely survived the King's defeat. The revolutionary establishment again split in two. The greater part of the Argyll party opposed the Engagement, while sympathising with the principles behind it; the rest, in company with the former supporters of Montrose, supported it. The campaign itself richly illustrated baronial Scotland in the early stages of its decline. The regiment of the Marquis of Argyll not only took part but, to judge from the lists of prisoners, died almost to a man. At the height of the battle, Hamilton ordered the Scottish foot in one direction; Callendar, his second-in-command and once the principal lieutenant of Montrose, promptly ordered them back again. Cromwell enjoyed the confusion.

The magnates of the period included two great men, and each betrayed his order. Montrose, thwarted in the Lowlands, crossed the Highland line into a wilderness of his own choosing; Argyll, his principality ravaged by Montrose, became the hangman of a revolutionary church which he had once contrived to dominate. Both died as martyrs, but neither was a martyr in the cause he had originally embraced. There was a harsh justice in the fate of both. Their separate defections were perhaps the outward manifestations of a deeper malaise. The visible surface of feudal Scotland never seemed to change; the barons, great and small, dispensed private justice to anybody who lived on their lands. But there was turmoil beneath and it is arguable that the ministers - who had emerged from it - understood it as well as anyone. The feudal system of heritable jurisdiction was collapsing beneath its own contradictions.

The lands of the parish of Scone had once formed a part of the abbacy of Scone. Many, though not all, of them had been feued during the sixteenth century and they now yielded an income, reduced by inflation to about a third of the original value, to the Lord of Erection. The remaining two thirds accrued to the feuars who thus, collectively though not individually, drew more from the lands concerned than did the Lord himself. In this respect, Scone was far from being an extreme case, for a substantial estate - now the proper lands of the Lordship of Scone - had been left unfeued and had thus retained its value. In many other cases, the superior's landed income had literally been decimated and the residue had been divided among the feuars. But the jurisdiction, which was inherent in the superiority, had not been so divided. The feudal equation between landed power and landed wealth had, in the vast feued lands of the ecclesiastical temporalities, been distorted beyond recognition.

Rents were less inflexible than feu duties; but, in practice, they were rigid enough. The sixteenth century had inherited a relatively stable rent structure with the power of custom behind it. This was appropriate enough in the arable areas of the east, where victual rents adjusted themselves to the price rise. But, in the pastoral regions, money rents could only keep pace with prices if the landlord repeatedly increased them. In fact many did not do so. The price rise, though eventually vast, was usually gradual, relatively inconspicuous and hardly ever understood. The landlords of the sixteenth century lived in a society which treated inflation as a moral, rather than as an economic, problem. Archbishop Hamilton could agree with John Knox that racked rents, like high prices or excessive interest, were merely special cases of the sin of avarice. In any case, rents could only be raised as leases expired; they might go up every seven years, every nineteen years, once in a lifetime or once in a century. At best they could rise in steps, at worst in a single leap that could only seem oppressive. The evidence is all too sparse; but it seems likely that, in many cases, the leap was postponed until the middle years of the seventeenth century. If this was so, the violence of the western Whigs, like the relative quiescence of their comrades in the east, needs no further explanation. But the impact was broader and deeper than this. Inflation was nibbling away at the foundations of the customary society. It discriminated, apparently quite capriciously, between different areas, different classes and indeed different individuals within the same class. Rural Scotland could never be the same again.

Nor was this the only distortion. The temporalities were, in many cases, large and scattered; huge tracts of territory were distantly separated from the institution which they were designed to support. It is easier to believe than to prove that the

Archbishop of St Andrews seldom visited his substantial Lordship of Stow (valued at about £10,000 in 1649). It is hardly surprising that the Lordship had been feued in its entirety during the 1540s nor that the regality jurisdiction attaching to it should have been granted heritably to a nobleman from south of the Forth. During the seventeenth century it yielded an income, valued at less than £1,000 in 1649, to a superior who had effectively alienated power and wealth alike. It was almost as if the Lordship of Stow had escaped from the feudal system altogether.

The feuing of the temporalities was probably fairly closely reproduced on estates administered directly by the Crown; but, at least as far as one can tell, it found no exact parallel among the baronies and regalities of the secular magnates. In another respect, however, the parallel was close enough. The sixteenth century was the age of the 'baronial complex', of the gradual accumulation of previously separate estates into the hands of a relatively small number of wealthy magnates. Even the rather ordinary barony of Penicuik (valued at about £1,500) had once consisted of at least two quite separate baronies. By the end of the sixteenth century, the two were one; soon after the beginning of the seventeenth century, the barony thus unified passed from its ancestral holder to a judge, who built a mansion and left it to a son - Preston of Airdrie - who chose to live elsewhere. From him it went, in 1646, to the Countess of Eglinton, another absentee, whose heirs sold it, in 1654, to Sir John Clerk, an Edinburgh merchant grown wealthy on the sale of imported works of art. In 1646 a rental, drawn up in the baron court of Penicuik, discloses the fact that an estate without a resident proprietor was administered by its wealthiest tenant acting as its bailie. It may be added that the court, like the kirk session, met in the church (²).

It should be emphasised that Penicuik was in no sense exceptional. The Earl of Tullibardine held land in at least fourteen Perthshire parishes, the Earl of Perth in seven and Hay of Balhousie in five; altogether at least sixty-two Perthshire proprietors held land in more than one parish. One or two of these were feuars and one or two others were barons who held some of their lands on a feu charter; but the majority were substantial lairds with two or more baronies at their disposal (³). To put the same point in a different way, many baronies were held by absentees who seldom attended the baron court. The proprietor, or so it might be argued, came to regard the outlying estate as a source of income which could be left alone as long as its rents continued to flow. Effective control fell, if only by default, into the hands of a local bailie - often, as in Penicuik, a tenant or, as in many a temporality, a feuar - assisted for some purposes by an assise composed, as the kirk session was also composed, of husbandmen and feuars. In most of the temporalities and on many secular estates, the feudal system of heritable jurisdiction was slowly breaking down.

The growth of the baronial complex heralded the eventual decline of the feudal system as it is usually understood; but the immediate impact was rather different. Baronial power was concentrated in fewer and wealthier hands. The threat to the Crown seemed to increase. The last three decades of the sixteenth century witnessed a series of experiments, each attempting to create an alternative system of jurisdiction. They were all prompted by the arrogance of the magnates; they were all justified by the patent inadequacies of the heritable system. They were all initiated by the Crown and most of them involved the machinery of the church. These rather tentative experiments substituted the parish for the barony as the normal unit of local administration and the man in possession - whether baron, feuar or tenant - for the absentee magnate. They inevitably centred on the kirk session, if only because it was already a working parochial institution; but none of them regarded the kirk session as adequate in itself. It might be used to activate the Justices or even in emergency to nominate them; or it might become the nucleus of a more powerful organisation which could include all the resident proprietors of the parish. The role of these novel bodies is capable of a Melvillian or a Canterburian interpretation, for both used them for their own purposes: but they were not essentially ideological in origin. They emerged quite naturally out of the situation as it actually was. They were part of the seventeenth century's response to its own unhappy past. They were part of a wider movement, of which the revocation was the most important manifestation, to substitute the concept of the heritor for the concept of the baron.

It may be significant that the revolution, in the very act of its rejection of the revocation and everything that came with it, nonetheless accepted its methods. The local committees improvised to raise men and money consisted of, or at least were operated by, resident heritors rather than absentee magnates. The magnates were firmly in command of the Tables and they obviously controlled the elections to the early assemblies of the period; but a feudal superstructure rested on a foundation that was only incidentally feudal, if indeed it can be described as feudal at all. Had not the kirk session of Dundonald, duly augmented by its 'gentlemen', sworn a local covenant of its own devising to drive the sturdy beggar from the parish?

The wars themselves made deeper inroads into the resources of the feudal classes. The forfeiting of Montrose and his friends, followed as it was by the disgrace of the Engagers, had the effect of divorcing huge tracts of territory from their traditional masters. From 1649 onwards, it was not uncommon for heritors, kirk sessions, or the two together, to appoint magistrates, usually local heritors, to impose civil penalties on moral delinquents [4]. These 'civil magistrates' or 'kirk magistrates' could, with some justice, be regarded as the local hangmen of their local kirks; but their appointment could equally have been justified from a purely practical point of view. The traditional machinery, already compromised by absenteeism and the unforeseen consequences of the feuing movement, was now threatening to break down altogether.

The parish, ruled by an augmented kirk session, was gradually ousting the barony, with its baron court, as the typical unit of local administration, and there was inevitably a parallel tendency for the minister to supplant the baron as the leading member of the local community. The clerical church rested on an increasingly solid foundation of local fact. It is arguable that the collective decisions of the Commission of the General Assembly were often, especially after the death of Henderson, tactically immature. But, on another and perhaps more exalted level, the ministers were riding the crest of a wave. Rutherford's state opposite to a state would perish beneath the combined weight of the magnates, the New Model Army and, eventually, a resurgence of the Crown. It would divide and ultimately fall, but it was not without resource.

The clerical church was a complex entity always on the brink of division and yet remarkably slow to divide. The ministers often disagreed about the privy kirk, the teinds, the aristocratic elder and indeed about almost everything that was fundamental. It sometimes seemed that only fear of their adversaries, within the kingdom and without, held them together. But this is surely to misunderstand them. Ever since the Reformation, the church had been reacting against a society that had been decentralised to a fault; the response, whether in its Canterburian or its Presbyterian form, was almost inevitably monolithic. The leading ministers, despite their squabbles, were predisposed towards unity. The radicals among them differed from their more numerous moderate colleagues over means but seldom over ends; they conspicuously failed to develop a distinctive system of theology of their own. Moderate and radical both agreed that theory could only be translated into practice through a church dominated by indoctrinated professionals. They both agreed that the Covenants rather than feudal law formed the foundation of authority and they both went on to assert that Covenants could only be interpreted by the kirk. They both agreed that the church must determine the broad outlines of policy, although the state must survive in some form to enact and, if necessary, to enforce. The ministers would do the thinking; the magistrate would merely do the doing.

All this was common ground; the church must somehow conjure the godly society out of an evil world. Most of the ministers could agree that the feudal system was inadequate for their high purpose. They could only use it by dominating it - as Calvin had dominated the worldly oligarchy of Geneva - and this might be difficult. Most of them were at least open to the argument that it was intrinsically corrupt and that it must eventually be destroyed. And yet the Lords of the Covenant had played a vital part in the early years of the revolution and in the wars that had followed. The moderate ministers resented their dependence, but hesitated to break it. In the event, the decision was taken for them. The Engagers barely concealed their intention to dismantle the state opposite to a state, and the ministers' resistance, passive though it was, was resolute and all but unanimous. The defeat of the Engagers was the victory of Douglas and the moderates. The Parliaments of 1649 and 1650, impeccably feudal as they were, had the prestige of the centuries behind them - and they were too weak to overawe the church. It was a convenient arrangement while it lasted; fundamental decisions were unnecessary. But, if Cromwell had closed the argument at Preston, he re-opened it at Dunbar. Under the stresses of defeat, the moderates cautiously reverted to the attitudes of the past. They needed an army and this would be difficult without the magnates. Douglas and his colleagues grudgingly re-admitted the demoralised Engagers in the belief - not entirely unjustified - that they could now be controlled. As they had done during the forties, they deliberately held the revolution back until the external threat had been met. The

Remonstrants dismissed all this as dilatory or worse. The defeat at Dunbar was a sign of God's wrath. They must climb yet another step of Reformation; Argyll was only Montrose in disguise; the civil power must be made over to the godly of low degree; the church must rebuild the state in its own image. The radicals wanted to do at once what the moderates might have attempted when a better opportunity eventually presented itself. The differences between the two parties were real enough but they were tactical rather than fundamental. Feudal society, whether it was corrupt or merely inadequate, was plainly in decline. One way or the other, the ministers would win in the end. Was not history on their side?

But history was not. In the short run, baronial Scotland was suffering a crisis of morale and it almost seemed to defeat itself. In the longer term, it was, as it had so often done before, slowly adapting itself to a changing world. The silent revolution had served to blur the distinction between superior and vassal. Gentlemen might be as wealthy, and sometimes as important, as barons. They were all heritors now. Indeed some gentlemen were acquiring their superiorities and, where the Crown was willing, baronial jurisdictions as well. But this was no longer vital. The baron court, once the bastion of feudal power, was slowly degenerating into a convenient instrument of estate management. Land had once been valued for the power which it represented; it would now be valued for the income it would yield - and this would suit many of the magnates well enough. In some cases at least, the greater part of the estate had survived the twin perils of creeping inflation and irretrievable subinfeudation. Their rents, whether they were counted in kind or in money, eventually recovered and, with the gradual progress of improvement, overtook the real values of the distant days before the price rise. The sixteenth century magnate was becoming an eighteenth century landowner. Lady Anna had found the pastoral baronies of the Hamilton heritage devastated by inflation; Duchess Anne would leave them renewed and indeed transformed. She advanced into the next century with a serenity that her father could never have known.

The inhibitions of a feudal past were simultaneously fading away. Geneva and Canterbury had combined to demonstrate the virtues of centralised power, and the new magnates of the Restoration, building on both in the very act of rejecting both, found a focus in the Crown. The state opposite to a state was suddenly as powerless as the bishops once had been. Its heroes would live on in the legend of the kirk, but it could never revive. The church duly achieved its independence of the state, but only on terms which liberated the state from the church. In the 1690s a new church accommodated itself to a new society. The castle gave way, not to the cowshed, but to the mansion.

N

Notes

The following abbreviations have been used in the notes:

APS	*Acts of the Parliaments of Scotland.*
Balfour	*Historical Works of Sir James Balfour,* 4 vols., 1824-5.
BH	*Memoir of James and William, Dukes of Hamilton,* by G. Burnet, 1852.
BLJ	*Letters and Journals of Robert Baillie, 1637-62* (Ed. D. Laing), Bannatyne Club, 73.
BM	British Museum.
BR	Burgh Records.
CJ	*Journal of the House of Commons.*
CSPV	*Calendar of State Papers, Venetian.*
CSPD	*Calendar of State Papers, Domestic.*
Extracts	*Extracts from Burgh Records.*
FES	*Fasti Ecclesiae Scoticanae,* 8 vols., 1915-50.
Gordon	James Gordon, *History of Scots Affairs, 1637-41* (Ed. J. Robertson and G. Grub), Spalding Club, 1841.
HMC	*Historical Manuscripts Commission Report.*
HP	*Hamilton Papers* (Ed. S. R. Gardiner), Camden Society, 1880.
KSR	Kirk Session Record.
LD	*Large Declaration of Charles I,* 1639.
LJ	*Journal of the House of Lords.*
MC	Mark Napier, *Montrose and the Covenanters,* 1838.
NLS	National Library of Scotland.
Peterkin	*Records of the Kirk* (Ed. A. Peterkin), 1843.
PR	Presbytery Record.
PSAS	*Proceedings of the Society of Antiquaries of Scotland.*
RCGA	*Records of the Commission of the General Assembly* (Ed. A. F. Mitchell and J. Christie), SHS, 11, 25, 58.
'RMS	*Registri Magni Sigilli Regum Scotorum.*
RPCS	*Register of the Privy Council of Scotland.*
RR	*Relation . . . by John, Earl of Rothes, 1637-8* (Ed. D. Laing), Bannatyne Club, 37.
RSCHS	*Records of the Scottish Church History Society.*
Rutherford	*The Letters of Samuel Rutherford* (Ed. A. A. Bonar), 1891.
SHR	*Scottish Historical Review.*
SHS	*Scottish History Society.*
SR	Synod Record.
SRO	Scottish Record Office.
SRS	*Scottish Record Society.*
Stevenson	A. Stevenson, *History of Church and State in Scotland,* 1753.
WD	*Wariston's Diary* (Ed. G. M. Paul and D. H. Fleming), *Scottish History Society,* 61, II 18, III 34.

Chapter 1

1. T. Ian Rae, *The Administration of the Scottish Frontier,* 1966, pp. 15, 17.

2. Mark Napier, *Memorials of Montrose*, Maitland Club, 1848-50, I, pp. 268-71. Some authorities consider that this letter was written by Lord Napier, a close friend of Montrose.

3. Ian B. Cowan, *The Parishes of Medieval Scotland*, SRS, XCIII, p. 226.

4. Cf. Gordon Donaldson, *Thirds of Benefices*, SHS, 3rd Series, XLII, p. xv.

5. S. G. E. Lythe, *The Economy of Scotland*, 1960, pp. 109-11.

6. *Extracts, Edin., 1528-1603* (first five volumes of series), *passim*.

7. *Rentale Sancte Andree* (Ed. R. K. Hannay), *SHS*, 2nd Series, IV, 1913, *passim*.

8. Fiars Prices: Fife Sheriff Court Records. I am most grateful to Mr John Moore for allowing me to use his transcript of the price information from these records. Mr Moore is engaged in a full-scale study of Scottish prices and he may eventually arrive at a different figure. The writer's estimate is relatively crude.

9. Exchequer Papers, Valuation Rolls, Parish Totals, 1649. These rolls normally draw a distinction between rents paid in money and rents paid in kind.

10. *Reports on Parishes in Scotland*, Maitland Club, 1836. See, for example, the parish of Tranent, pp. 135-6; cf. Basil Skinner, *Lime Industry in the Lothians*, 1969, p. 10.

11. BR, Edin., Moses Bundles, 197, no. 7103, Valuation of lands and teinds belonging to Lord Holyroodhouse, 1627.

12. Particular Tax Rolls, Coupar, 1630; Culross, 1617; D. Easson, *Medieval Religious Houses of Scotland*, 1957, p. 63.

13. Margaret H. B. Sanderson, *The Feuars of Kirklands*, SHR, LII, pt. 2, 1973, pp. 117-36 (especially Tables I, II, III). Dr. Sanderson's work, as revealed in this article, as well as in conversation, has made a large contribution to the argument presented in this chapter and in Chapter XIII. I am most grateful.

14. See above note 9 (for money rents) and note 13; Margaret H. B. Sanderson, *Kirkmen and their Tenants on the Eve of the Reformation*, RSCHS, XVIII, I, 1972, p. 41.

15. See Chapter XIII.

16. J. Calvin, *Institutes of the Christian Religion*, IV. 1, 4. Cf. A. G. Dickens, *Reformation and Society in Sixteenth Century Europe*, 1966, p. 160.

17. *The Appellation of John Knox with his Exhortation to the Nobility and Estates of the Realm*, 1558, in *Works of John Knox* (Ed. D. Laing) IV, pp. 467-522; *Letter Addressed to the Commonalty of Scotland*, 1558, *ibid*, IV, pp. 523-538; John Knox, *History of the Reformation*, Ed. W. Croft Dickinson, II, pp. 277-8.

18. Cf. Gordon Donaldson, *The Scottish Reformation*, 1960, Chapters III to VII.

19. D. Calderwood, *History of the Kirk of Scotland*, Wodrow Society, 1840-9, III, p. 544.

20. *Knox, op. cit*, II, p. 290; *APS*, II, pp. 86-9, 139-42.

21. *APS*, III, p. 576; IV, pp. 140, 232.

22. *The Kirk Session Record of Dundonald* (Ed. H. Paton) 1936, pp. 398-400.

23. *APS*, V, pp. 23-7; Sir James Balfour, *Historical Works*, II, p. 128.

24. *APS*, V, pp. 197-204.

25. *RPCS, 1625-7*, pp. 230-2. The immediate context related to teinds rather than to superiorities, but the point remains.

26. *APS*, V, p. 31.

27. *BLJ*, I, pp. 6-7.

28. Gordon Donaldson, *Scotland, James V - James VII*, 1965, p. 299; *Calderwood*, VII, p. 421.

Chapter 2

1. *RR*, pp. 1-3.

2. Gordon Donaldson, *The Making of the Scottish Prayer Book of 1637*, 1954, pp. 41-83.

3. Robert Wodrow, *Biographical Collections*, New Spalding Club, 1890, pp. 171-2; *BLJ*, I, pp. 16-7; *RR*, p. 198; *Gordon*, I, p. 5.

4. Henry Guthrie, *Memoirs* (Ed. 1747), pp. 10-15; James Spalding, *History of the Troubles . . . in Scotland and England, 1624-5* (Ed. J. Skene), Bannatyne Club, XXV, pt. I, pp. 77-8; *RR*, pp. 17-19.

5. *BLJ*, I, p. 98; *Guthrie, op. cit.*, p. 15.

6. 'An Advertisement of the Service Book, 1637' (Ed J. M. Henderson), *SHR*, XXIII, 1925-6, pp. 199-204.

7. *Guthrie, op. cit.*, p. 23; *Calderwood*, VII, p. 449; BR, Edin., Extent Roll for the Annuity Tax, 1635; see also *Life of Robert Blair*, Wodrow Society, 1848, pp. 150, 153.

8. *RR*, Appendix, pp. 198-200.

9. *RPCS, 1635-7*, pp. 483-4, 486-7, 489.

10. *RPCS, 1635-7*, pp. 445-6, 521; *RR*, pp. 5-7, Appendix, p. 203; *BLJ*, I, pp. 19-20.

11. *Rutherford*, pp. 519.

12. *Balfour*, II, pp. 232-3; BR, Edin., Minutes, 18.9.37, 4.10.37; *RPCS, 1635-7*, pp. 528-9, 699-716; *RR*, pp. 7-9, 18, 47-8; *BLJ*, I, pp. 13-14, 21-4.

13. *The Session Book of Dundonald, 1602-1731* (Ed. H. Paton), pp. 398-400, 521-2.

14. PR, Dalkeith, 14.9.37; *RPCS, loc. cit.*

15. *RPCS, 1635-7*, pp. 536-42; *RR*, pp. 13-20; *WD*, p. 270; *LD*, pp. 35-6; *Extracts, Edin., 1626-41*, p. 197.

16. D. H. Fleming, 'Scotland's Supplication . . . against the Book of Common Prayer', *PSAS*, LX, 1925-6, pp. 314-83; the original petition is among the Privy Council papers in the SRO; *Rutherford*, p. 539.

17. *RR*, pp. 23-30; *BLJ*, I, pp. 40-2; *WD*, p. 272; *RPCS, 1635-7*, pp. 544-5.

18. See above, note 16; Denmilne MSS, vol. XII, nos. 28, 37; Wodrow MSS, Quarto, vol. XXV, no. 12, vol. XXXI, no. 4.

19. *RR*, pp. 70-1, 80-1, 127; cf. David Stevenson, *The Financing of the Cause of the Covenants*, *SHR*, LI, pt. II, pp. 89-95.

20. See above, note 16; *Register of the Presbytery of Lanark* (Abbotsford Club, 1839), pp. 12-13.

21. PR, Kirkcaldy, 20.4.38; *BH,* pp. 53-4.
22. *WD,* pp. 279-80.

Chapter 3

1. I have used the text of the Negative Confession and the National Covenant as they are reproduced in *National Manuscripts of Scotland,* III, nos. 70 and 97.
2. *BH,* pp. 40-1.
3. *RPCS, 1638-43,* pp. 3-4.
4. *BLJ,* I, pp. 52-4; *RR,* pp. 69-78; *WD,* 320-1.
5. *The First and Second Book of Discipline,* 1622, pp. 71-96. The Act of the Assembly of 1580, declaring episcopacy unlawful, is also printed in this volume.
6. *RR,* pp. 100-2.
7. *WD,* p. 275; *BLJ,* I, p. 90.
8. *WD,* pp. 347-8.

Chapter 4

1. *BH,* pp. 56-64.
2. *BLJ,* I, pp. 124-5; Patrick Gordon of Ruthven, *Britain's Distemper,* Spalding Club, 1844, p. 208.
3. *RR,* pp. 143-167; *WD,* pp. 349-54.
4. *Stafford Letters* (Ed. W. Knowler), II, pp. 181, 186; Laud, *Works,* VII, p. 468; *CSPD, 1637-8,* pp. 574-5; *CSPV,* XXIV, pp. 435-6, 439; Breadalbane MSS, no. 738; *BLJ,* I, pp. 72, 86, 92.
5. *RPCS, 1638-43,* pp. 64-74; *HP,* pp. 26-32; *WD,* pp. 391-2; *BLJ,* I, pp. 103-4, appendix, p. 474.
6. *WD,* pp. 385, 393-9.
7. *RR,* pp. 83-4; *LD,* pp. 116; *BH,* p. 83.
8. NLS, Wodrow MSS, Folio, LXI, no. 81; *BUK,* III, pp. 947-8.
9. *LD,* pp. 129-31, 281-4; *WD,* p. 377; *BLJ,* I, Appendix, pp. 469-70.
10. *WD,* pp. 374-5; *BLJ,* I, pp. 98-9.
11. *WD,* p. 378.
12. *Peterkin,* pp. 109-111; NLS, MSS, no. 3840.
13. KSR, Kilconquar, 13.5.38, 9.9.38.
14. KSR, Falkirk, 22.5.38 - 25.9.38; Regality Court Book of Falkirk, 9.12.38. I am most grateful to Miss Doreen Hunter of the Scottish Record Office for allowing me to use her indexed transcript of these records.
15. KSR, Stow, 30.9.38.
16. KSR, Pencaitland, 9.9.38 - 16.9.38; KSR, Bothans, 18.9.38; PR, Haddington, 12.9.38 - 21.9.38.
17. PR, Kirkcaldy, 24.9.38; PR, Perth, 26.9.38; *Rental of Perthshire, 1649, Contrasted with 1835,* 1838, *passim; Retours,* Perthshire, *passim.*
18. *Presbytery Book of Strathbogie* (Spalding Club, VII), pp. 18-19; SP (Domestic), 399, no. 17.

19. *BLJ*, I, p. 104; *WD*, p. 394; PR, Paisley, 21.9.38.
20. *LD*, pp. 239-41; *Peterkin*, pp. 135-6; *BLJ*, I, pp. 131-3.
21. *Peterkin*, pp. 135-6; *BLJ*, I, pp. 131-3; PR, Peebles, 2.8.38 - 1.11.38.
22. PR, Elgin, 25.10.38; 13.12.38 - 14.2.39.
23. *Peterkin*, pp. 109-11, 135-7; *Spalding*, I, pp. 114-6.
24. NLS, MSS, no. 3840, f.61; *Gordon*, II, p. 5.
25. BR, Edin., Minutes, 13.10.38; *Extracts, Edin., 1626-41*, App. XV, pp. 321-4; *Extracts, Glasgow, 1573-1642*, pp. 393-5; NLS, MSS, no. 3840, f.61.
26. *Extracts, Aberdeen, 1625-42*, pp. 141-3; *Extracts, Stirling, 1519-1656*, pp. 177, 181.
27. *Peterkin, loc. cit; Gordon*, II, p. 5.
28. *Peterkin, loc. cit.* Biographical information has largely been drawn from the *History of Parliament*. I am most grateful to Dr. John Imrie, Keeper of the Records of Scotland, and Professor Gordon Donaldson, for allowing me to see this invaluable volume before publication.
29. See above note 28; *Retours, passim.*
30. See Chapter VIII.
31. *BLJ*, I, p. 121; *WD*, pp. 400-1.
32. *HP*, pp. 59-60; *BLJ*, I, pp. 123-4. The following account of the assembly is deliberately brief. It is based on the official record (*Peterkin*, pp. 128-93), Baillie's narrative (*BLJ*, I, pp. 118-76), Gordon's rather derivative account (II, pp. 5-17), Wariston's regrettably brief remarks (*WD*, pp. 400-404), the notes kept by Robert Douglas (NLS, Wodrow MSS, Octavo, X, no. 2) and on the anonymous account in the Edinburgh City Archives (City Muniments, V, 63-108).
33. *Peterkin*, pp. 128-35; *BLJ*, I, pp. 123-31.
34. *Peterkin*, pp. 135-7; *BLJ*, I, pp. 131-5; BR, Edin., City Muniments, V, p. 63.
35. *Peterkin*, pp. 140-7; *BLJ*, I, pp. 141-4.
36. *Peterkin*, pp. 151-2; *BLJ*, I, pp. 137, 147-8.
37. *WD*, pp. 402-4; *BLJ*, I, pp. 155-9; *Peterkin*, pp. 166-8, 186-9.
38. *WD*, p. 401.
39. Breadalbane MSS, no. 763; *Instruction for Defensive Arms (Stevenson*, II, pp. 686-95); *Diary of Johnston of Wariston, SHS*, XXIV, 1896, *passim.*
40. *Miscellaneous State Papers*, II, pp. 113-21; *Gordon*, II, p. 171.
41. *Peterkin*, pp. 204-5, 208; *RPCS, 1638-43*, pp. 131-2; *APS*, V, pp. 276, 291-9, 371; *BH*, pp. 189-92, 197-200; *Diary of Sir Thomas Hope of Craighall, 1633-45*, Bannatyne Club, p. 104.
42. *MC*, I, p. 362; the meeting was described in a letter, 20.4.41, from Wariston to Balmerino.
43. *APS*, V, pp. 282, 291-2, 298-9.
44. *BLJ*, I, pp. 360, 375, 378; *APS*, V, p. 317.
45. *APS*, V, pp. 311-3; cf. David Stevenson, 'The Financing of the Cause of the Covenants', *SHR*, LI, pt. 2, pp. 89-95.
46. *APS*, V, pp. 335, 340-1; *BLJ*, I, p. 396.
47. *BLJ*, I, p. 385; *Nicholas Papers*, I, p. 24.

Chapter 5

1. *Testimony left by Samuel Rutherford* (Ed. 1726), pp. 6-7.

2. *Rutherford,* p. 56; cf. Gordon Donaldson, 'The Emergence of Schism in Seventeenth Century Scotland', *Studies in Church History,* vol. 9, 1972. I am most grateful to Professor Donaldson for allowing me to see this article before publication. It has had a considerable influence on this chapter.

3. *BLJ,* I, pp. 248-55; Wodrow MSS, Quarto, XXVI, no. 7; *BH,* p. 39; PR, Stirling, 11.7.39, 25.7.39; KSR, Stirling, 22.7.39, 12.8.39.

4. *Stevenson,* III, pp. 889-92.

5. *BLJ,* I, pp. 369, 371.

6. *Rutherford,* pp. 611-2.

7. *BLJ,* I, pp. 254-5.

8. Wodrow MSS, Folio, LXV, no. 3.

9. *RMS,* IX, nos. 1035, 1255.

10. *APS,* V, pp. 340-1.

11. *BLJ,* I, pp. 305-6; *Arguments for the Commissioners of Scotland . . . persuading Conformity of Church Government,* BM, Thomason Tracts, E157 (2); *Correspondence of the Earls of Ancrum,* I, p. 105; *WD,* pp. 351, 375; Wodrow MSS, Quarto, XXVI, no. 7, ff. 104v-105r.

12. *APS,* V, pp. 340-1.

13. *Hardwick State Papers,* III, pp. 22-35.

14. *BH,* pp. 250, 253-4, 257.

15. *HMC, Hamilton Papers,* Supplement, p. 65; *BH,* pp. 263-7.

16. *RPCS, 1638-43,* pp. 374-6.

17. *BLJ,* II, p. 90; *APS,* VI, pt. 1, pp. 53-59.

18. *BLJ,* II, p. 90.

19. *BH,* p. 307; *BLJ,* II, p. 90; *APS,* VI, pt. 1, pp. 41-3.

20. *CJ,* III, pp. 224-5, 237, 241; *LJ,* VI, pp. 219-20; J. Lightfoot, *Works,* XIII, pp. 10, 14-5.

21. L. Kaplan, 'Presbyterians and Independents in 1643', *EHR,* LXXXIV, pp. 244-56.

22. *Acts and Ordinances of the Interregnum,* Ed. C. H. Firth and R. S. Rait, 1911, I, pp. 749-54, 789-93, 852-5. Cf. J. H. Hexter, 'The Problem of the Presbyterian Independents', reprinted in *Reappraisals in History,* 1961, pp. 163-84; *BLJ,* II, p. 362.

23. *Peterkin,* p. 475.

24. *LJ,* VII, p. 392.

25. S. R. Gardiner, *Constitutional Documents of the Puritan Revolution,* pp. 347-53.

26. *BH,* pp. 411-3; *APS,* VI, pt. 2, pp. 40-3.

27. *BLJ,* III, pp. 19-20.

28. *Peterkin,* pp. 472-3; *BLJ,* III, pp. 13-14.

29. *BLJ,* III; pp. 48-9; Turner, *Memoirs,* Bannatyne Club, 1828, pp. 55-7; see Chapter XIII. BM, Thomason Tracts, E461/9; this includes lists of prisoners taken during the Preston campaign.

30.   W. C. Abbott, *Writings and Speeches of Oliver Cromwell*, I, p. 678.

31.   *Balfour*, III, pp. 377-8, 395; *APS*, VI, pt. 2, pp. 47-8.

32.   *Balfour*, III, pp. 426-7; Robert Wodrow, *Analecta*, Maitland Club, 1842, II, p. 281.

33.   *Balfour*, III, pp. 391-2; *BLJ*, I, pp. 237-41; II, pp. 47-8, 450-60; *APS*, VI, pt. 2, pp. 261-2.

34.   *Balfour*, III, pp. 417-8; see Chapter VII.

35.   *BLJ*, III, pp. 94-5; *Peterkin*, pp. 530-1.

36.   *Balfour*, III, pp. 391-2.

37.   Sir John Scott of Scotstarvet, *True Relation*, *SHR*, XII, pp. 77-80; *RCGA*, II, pp. 290-5; *APS*, VI, pt. 2, pp. 446-7, 464-6; *Diplomatic Correspondence of Jean de Montreuil*, *SHS*, XXX, 1899, vol. II, pp. 438-40; Papers of the Committee of Estates, 18.8.49.

38.   *BLJ*, III, p. 122

39.   *RCGA*, II, pp. 200, 233, 239, 240, 263, 268; *BLJ*, III, pp. 112-3.

40.   *RCGA*, III, pp. 95-103.

41.   *RCGA*, III, pp. 295, 328.

42.   *Life of Robert Blair*, Wodrow Society, 1848, pp. 291-2; *RCGA*, III, p. 187.

Chapter 6

1.   *Rutherford*, p. 667.

2.   Records of the General Assembly, 1642-6; PR, Jedburgh, 1638-51; Haddington, 1638-50; Dalkeith, 1638-50; Linlithgow, 1638-51; Perth, 1638-51; Peebles, 1638-51; Stranraer, 1641-52; Ayr, 1638-51; Paisley, 1638-51; Glasgow, 1638-51; Dunoon, 1639-51; Cupar, 1646-51; Kirkcaldy, 1638-51; Dunfermline, 1646-51; Brechin, 1639-51; Garioch, 1639-51; Deer, 1649-51; Fordyce, 1640-51; Elgin, 1638-51; Dingwall, 1649-51; Biggar, 1644-51; Lanark, 1638-51; Strathbogie, 1638-51. I am most grateful to Richard Dell, Strathclyde Regional Archivist, for lending me his photocopies of the Glasgow Presbytery Record. Cf. David Stevenson, 'The General Assembly and the Commission of the Kirk, 1638-51', Appendix, *RSCHS*, XIX, pt. 1, pp. 76-7.

3.   Proprietors with a baronial jurisdiction have usually been identified from the *Retours* and the *Register of the Great Seal*. I am most grateful to Dr. John Imrie and Professor Gordon Donaldson for allowing me to use the galley proof and page proof copies of the unpublished *History of Parliament;* this invaluable volume has saved the writer a great deal of hard labour.

4.   J. Gordon, *History of Scots Affairs, 1637-41*, I, p. 62; *BLJ*, III, pp. 141-2.

5.   *BLJ*, III, p. 54.

6.   *BLJ*, II, p. 55.

7.   *Peterkin*, pp. 330, 359-60, 514; *RCGA*, III, pp. 445-6, 547-8, 551-2; *BLJ*, III, pp. 54, 134.

8.   *Peterkin*, pp. 330, 359-60, 399, 427-8, 477-8, 514, 549-50; *RCGA*, III, pp. 4-6, 449-502.

9.   *RCGA*, I, II and III, *passim*. Cf. Stevenson, *op. cit.* Dr. Stevenson and

myself have covered the same ground here. His figures do not exactly coincide with my own since he has organised them differently. The differences between them are fortunately trivial. It is fair to add that Dr. Stevenson attaches less importance to them than I do. He accepts the idea of a church dominated by its ministers only with reluctance.

10. *Balfour*, III, pp. 426-7.

Chapter 7

1. All the biographical material presented in the tables and the text of this chapter has, unless otherwise stated, been extracted from the *Fasti Ecclesiae Scoticanae*, 8 vols., 1915-50, *passim*. Hew Scott's earlier version of the *Fasti* has also been used. I am most grateful to Mrs. V. Eaves-Walton for lending me her copies of the *Fasti*.

2. Sir James Balfour, *The Scots Peerage*, vol. VIII, pp. 193-4.

3. *BLJ*, II, p. 91.

4. *BLJ*, III, Appendix, pp. xxi-xxii.

5. A. B. Birchler, 'The Influence of the Scottish Clergy on Politics', unpublished Ph.D. thesis, University of Nebraska, 1966.

6. Gordon Donaldson, *The Scottish Reformation*, 1960, p. 95.

7. *Rental of Perthshire, 1649, contrasted with 1835*, 1835, *passim*.

8. The proprietors concerned have been identified from the *Retours;* from *RMS*, vol. VIII, IX, X; and from the unpublished *History of Parliament;* see Chapter VI, note 3. Statistics for landed income have been taken from the earliest available valuation roll for the shire concerned.

9. BR, Edin., Extent roll, 1605; *Records of the Convention of Royal Burghs*, vol. II, p. 562.

10. *History of Parliament* (see Chapter VI, note 3); *Records of the Convention of Royal Burghs*, vols. II and III.

11. BR, Edin., Extent Rolls, 1567, 1605, 1608, 1615.

12. G. Brunton and D. Haig, *Historical Account of the Senators of the College of Justice*, 1832; *Faculty of Advocates in Scotland, 1532-1943, SRS*, pt. 145, 1944; *The Society of Writers to His Majesty's Signet*, 1936.

13. John Aiton, *The Life and Times of Alexander Henderson*, 1836, pp. 85-9; R. L. Orr, *Alexander Henderson, Churchman and Statesman*, 1920, p. 3; J. P. Thomson, *Alexander Henderson the Covenanter*, 1912, p. 15; *Exchequer Rolls*, XIV, pp. 182, 495, 502; XV, pp. 564, 568; *RMS*, VI, no. 1182; Valuation Roll, Fife, 1695, 1697, Parish of Creich.

14. *Reports on the Parishes in Scotland*, Maitland Club, 1836, *passim*.

15. See Chapter VI, pp. 90-2.

16. BR, Edin., Extent Rolls, 1615, 1627, 1628.

17. *BLJ*, III, p. 62.

Chapter 8

1. T. M'Crie, *Life of John Knox*, Ed. 1884, pp. 436-9; J. Aiton, *Life and Times*

of Alexander Henderson, 1836, pp. 661-4; *Register of Ministers . . . and their Stipends after the Reformation,* Maitland Club, 1830, p. 2; *BLJ,* I, p. 395; III, p. 12; *Extracts, Edin., 1626-41,* p. xliii.

2.   *Aiton, loc. cit.*

3.   *Rutherford,* p. 56.

4.   Gordon Donaldson, 'Accounts of the Collectors of Thirds of Benefices', *SHS,* 3rd series, XLII, p. xxiv; R. S. Bryden, 'The Finances of James VI', Ph.D., Divinity, Edin., 1925, pp. 119-20.

5.   Gordon Donaldson, *The Scottish Reformation,* 1960, pp. 93-4, 152-3; W. R. Foster, *The Church before the Covenants,* 1975, pp. 157-8.

6.   *Foster, op. cit.,* pp. 159-61.

7.   *APS,* IV, pp. 531, 605; V, pp. 35-9, 401-3; VI, pt. I, pp. 778-9, pt. II, pp. 287-8.

8.   *Balfour,* III, pp. 417-8.

9.   J. Connell, *A Treatise on the Law of Scotland respecting Tithes,* 1815; The Register to Supply Lost Records, 4 vols; The Sederunt Book of the Commissioners of Tithes, 1630-33; Miscellaneous Teind Papers.

10.   *Connell,* III, p. 44.

11.   BR, Edin., Minutes, 26.10.49.

12.   *Rental of the County of Perthshire, 1649, contrasted with 1835,* 1835; Exchequer, Valuation Rolls; Perthshire, Parish Totals, 1649.

13.   *APS,* V, 400-3.

14.   *Extracts, Edin., 1626-41,* pp. 74-5.

15.   BR, Edin., Minutes, 25.3.35, 26.10.49; Accounts of the Collectors of Kirk Rents, 1612-45, *passim.*

16.   *FES,* IV, p. 251.

17.   *Rental Perthshire, passim.*

18.   *Assessment of Wages Made by the Justices of the Peace in Edinburgh in 1656, SHS,* XXXI, 1899, pp. 405-11.

19.   *APS,* IV, p. 285; VI, pt. I, p. 221; VI, pt. II, p. 288.

20.   The figure is derived from the Extent Roll for the Annuity Tax, 1635, in the Edinburgh City Archives. The tax was paid by all householders.

21.   Ian B. Cowan, *Parishes of Medieval Scotland, SRS,* XCIII, 1967, p. 217.

22.   *FES,* I, pp. 37-141; *Extracts, Edin., 1604-26,* pp. 260, 261-6, 277, 289.

23.   The stipends given in this paragraph nearly all derive from the accounts of the burgh: Town Treasurer's Accounts, 1552-67, 1581-96, 1596-1612, 1612-23, 1623-36, 1636-50, 1650-66; Dean of Guild Accounts, 1552-67; Kirk Treasurer's Accounts, 1615-48, 1648-63; Accounts of Collectors of Kirk Rents, 1573-1612, 1612-45. The accounting system changed in 1634 and, since the volumes concerned do not survive, no record exists of payments actually made after that date. Intended payments can, however, often be discovered from the Town Council Minutes. See BR, Edin., 24.12.41. For Stipends paid from the Thirds, see *Register of Ministers, op. cit.,* p. 2; The Register for the Assignation of Stipends, 1590-1601.

24.   *Extracts, Edin., loc. cit; Extracts, Edin., 1626-41,* pp. 161-2; *RPCS, 1633-*

5, pp. 234-6; see Ch. XII.

    25.   *Extracts, Edin., 1626-41,* pp. 191-2.

    26.   *Extracts, Edin., 1626-41,* pp. 227-8, 243; *1642-55,* pp. 6-8, 13-14, 20, 26, 82; see also note 31 below.

    27.   *Extracts, Edin., 1642-55,* pp. 93-4; *Aiton, loc. cit.*

    28.   BR, Edin., 26.1.49, 20.2.50, 16.6.48; *APS,* VI, pt. II, pp. 225-7; *RCGA,* II, pp. 413-4; *Balfour,* III, pp. 417-8.

    29.   *Extracts, Edin., 1642-55,* p. 178; *APS,* VI, pt. II, pp. 225-7.

    30.   BR, Edin., 3.7.50, 23.6.54, 28.3.55.

    31.   Accounts of the Treasurer of Kirk Rents and Ministers' Stipends, 1657. These accounts are bound with BR, Edin., Kirk Treasurer's Accounts, 1648-63.

    32.   See above notes 18 and 20.

    33.   *Foster, op. cit.,* p. 167; Records of Testaments, all surviving records, 1610-59.

    34.   Fife Sheriff Court Records; H. Arnot, *History of Edinburgh,* Ed. 1788, Appendix, pp. 620-1 (for Midlothian); George Buchan-Hepburn, *General View of the Agriculture . . . of East Lothian,* 1794, Appendix.

Chapter 9

    1.   John Calvin, *Institutes of the Christian Religion,* 2.8.35, 4.11.1-2; I *Timothy,* V, 17; *Titus,* I, 4.

    2.   John Knox, *History of the Reformation* (Ed. W. C. Dickinson), II, pp. 277, 305, 309-12.

    3.   *Calderwood,* III, pp. 537-8, 544.

    4.   George Gillespie, *Assertion of the Government of the Church of Scotland in the Points of Ruling Elders,* 1641, p. 106.

    5.   KSR, Kinghorn, 10.5.42; St Cuthbert's, 17.2.42.

    6.   *Peterkin,* p. 321; *BLJ,* I, p. 337.

    7.   KSR, *Dundonald,* Kinnaird, Colinton, *passim.*

    8.   See list of kirk session records in Bibliography.

    9.   KSR, Penicuik, St Andrews, *passim.*

  10.   See Chapter Four, p. 39.

  11.   *Peterkin,* p. 46 (Act no. 25).

Chapter 10

    1.   Gilbert Burnet, *History of My Own Time,* Ed. 1897, I, pp. 53-4; James Guthrie, *Treatise of Ruling Elders and Deacons,* Ed. 1690, pp. 5-12, 76; *Gillespie, op. cit.,* p. 10; Robert Baillie, *Review of Doctor Bramhall . . . His Fair Warning,* 1649, pp. 66-7; *BLJ,* III, pp. 141-2; Alexander Henderson, *Government and Order of the Church of Scotland,* 1641, pp. 46-7; James Gordon, *History of Scots Affairs, 1637-41* (Spalding Club, 1841), III, p. 221. Gordon's comment actually refers to the similar act of 1640.

    2.   KSR, Kilconquar, ?.5.38, 9.9.38.

3. PR, Perth, 9, 16, 23.1.39; Haddington, 16.10.39; Dalkeith, September and October 1639; Ellon, April to August 1639.

4. PR, Haddington, 1638-46.

5. PR, Perth, 1650; Dalkeith, 1649; Linlithgow, 1649; Dumbarton, 1649; Dunfermline, 1647-49; Ayr, 1642, 1649, 1650.

6. *Rental of the County of Perth, 1649, compared with 1835,* 1835, pp. 10-34; SR, Perth, 1639-50; PR, Perth, 1650; SR, Fife, 1639-50; PR, Dunfermline, 1647-49; Cupar, 1647-50.

7. PR, Haddington, 1649; Dalkeith, 1649; Ayr, 1649; *BLJ,* III, pp. 141-2.

8. PR, Dumbarton, 1649; Paisley, 1649; *BLJ,* III, pp. 141-2.

9. As in previous chapters, proprietors have been identified and classified from the *Register of the Great Seal,* the *Retours* and the *History of Parliament.*

10. KSR, Fintry, 26.9.41; PR, Perth, 1650; PR, for all presbyteries mentioned in notes 5-8 above.

Chapter 11

1. *BLJ,* III, pp. 56-60.

2. Robert Baillie, *Review of Dr Bramhall . . . His Fair Warning,* 1649, pp. 66-7.

3. KSR, Liberton, 28.7.39, 6.3.42, 23.3.45, 17.2.49; Testaments, Edinburgh, 27.1.40 (Robert Preston of Craigmillar). Information about the proprietors of Liberton and of the other parishes studied in this chapter has been taken from the sources mentioned in Chapter VI, note 3. The Midlothian Valuation Roll of 1680 has also been used. Some inferences have also been drawn from the Poll Tax and Hearth Tax Rolls of the 1690s. Cf. G. Good, *Liberton in Ancient and Modern Times,* 1893.

4. KSR, Liberton, 26.4.40, 9.5.41.

5. KSR, Stow, ?.11.26, 28.10.27, 23.8.35, 12.5.37, 10.12.40, 6.3.42, 10.9.43, 6.10.44, 14.11.47, 4.11.49, 5.9.52; Valuation Roll, 1680.

6. Testaments, Edinburgh, 14.8.44 (Thomas Allen in Muirhouse); 21.11.32 (James Pringle, portioner of Cortilferry).

7. PR, Dalkeith, 2.11.48; Tax Survey, 1656 and Rental of Barony of Penicuik, 1654 (in Clerk of Penicuik Papers); Teind Valuation, 21.7.47 (in Register to Supply Lost Records, vol. I, pt. 2, p. 368); see also the general sources mentioned in note 3; cf. J. J. Wilson, *Annals of Penicuik,* 1891; I am most grateful to Dr. Duncan Thomson for pointing out the fact that Sir John Clerk was primarily an art dealer.

8. KSR, Penicuik, 7.5.54, 3.6.55, 6.12.57; see also note 7.

9. PR, Dalkeith, 2.11.48, 26.4.49, 7.11.49, 6.5.50.

10. KSR, Falkirk, 12.5.38; 4.2.40. *Register of the Great Seal,* IX, no. 171 (includes a list of the tenants of Lord Almond); Court Book of the Regality of Falkirk, 1638-42 (in SRO). I am most grateful to Miss Doreen Hunter for allowing me to use her indexed typescript of the Regality records.

11. KSR, St. Cuthbert's, 10.11.42-26.3.46.

12.   KSR, Cramond, 7.9.51, October 1652-December 1657; general sources in note 3; cf. H. Wood's admirable *History of the Parish of Cramond,* 1794, *passim.*

13.   KSR, Scone, 14.11.36, 16.12.38.

14.   KSR, Lyne, ?.1.49.

15.   J. Calvin, *Institutes of the Christian Religion,* 4.11.3.

16.   *Peterkin,* p. 109.

17.   BR, Edin., City Muniments, V, pp. 133-50.

18.   KSR, St Andrews, 1639-48; Aberdeen, 1638-40; Dumfries, 19.7.46.

19.   BR, Canongate, Acts of Bailies, II and III (in Edinburgh City Archives). I am most grateful to Miss Helen Armet for permission to use her notes relating to these volumes. Cf. J. Mackay, *History of the Burgh of Canongate,* 1900.

20.   KSR, Canongate, all elections held, 1630-51.

21.   Minutes of the following Canongate Incorporations: Bakers, Hammermen, Wrights and Weavers (in Edin. City Archives), Tailors (NLS) and Cordiners (SRO); see also note 19 above. N.b. Sessioners representing the Castle and the Abbey have been omitted from these calculations.

22.   KSR, South Queensferry, 23.8.35, 24.12.38, 3.5.40, 30.5.45. BR, South Queensferry (in Edin. City Archives) 1635-49 (Michaelmas Elections); October 1642 (Burgess Roll).

Chapter 12

1.   *Calderwood,* V, pp. 177-8.

2.   John Knox, *History of the Reformation* (Ed. W. C. Dickinson), II, p. 277; KSR, Edin., 7, 14, 22, 28.10.1574.

3.   *Extracts, Edin., 1557-71,* p. 71.

4.   Cf. Michael Lynch, 'The Two Edinburgh Councils, 1559-60', *SHR,* LIV, pt. 2, 1975, pp. 117-9. I hope I have not oversimplified Dr. Lynch's argument here.

5.   KSR, Edin., 1574-5; BR, Edin., Extent Rolls, June 1583.

6.   *Calderwood,* IV, pp. 65, 79, 122-4, 351, 425; *RPCS, 1578-85,* p. 692. BR, Edin., Extent Rolls for National Taxation, June 1583. I wish to thank Dr. Lynch for his kindness in allowing me to use his invaluable card index of Edinburgh burgesses for this period and for his patience in discussing the issues raised in this part of the chapter with me.

7.   *APS,* III, pp. 292-3; *Extracts, Edin., 1573-89,* pp. 353-4, 359, 362; BR, Edin., Extent Rolls for National Taxation, June 1583.

8.   *Calderwood,* IV, pp. 141, 200, 205; VIII, pp. 260, 269; *RPCS, 1578-85,* pp. 488, 678, 692, 695; see also note 6 above.

9.   *Extracts, Edin., 1589-1603,* pp. 69, 70, 73, 75, 95-6; *Records of the Convention of Royal Burghs,* I, pp. 402, 485-6; *History of King James VI,* pp. 254-6; John Spottiswood, *History of the Church of Scotland,* 1847, II, p. 432; *Calderwood,* V, pp. 172, 177-8.

10.   *Extracts, Edin., 1589-1603,* pp. 172-5; Extent Rolls for National Taxation, 1593.

11. *Calderwood,* VII, pp. 436-8, 454, 518, 544-5, 596-9.

12. *Extracts, Edin.,* 1604-26, pp. 260-66, 276-8, 283, 285-6, 289-90; *Calderwood,* VII, p. 547.

13. *Calderwood,* VII, pp. 355-6, 439, 456, 596-600; *RPCS, 1619-22,* pp. 249-50, 264, 299, 328; *RPCS, 1622-5,* pp. 503-4, 521-2, 541. Cf. David Stevenson, 'Conventicles in the Kirk, 1619-37', in *RSCHS,* XVIII, pt. II, pp. 99-114.

14. *Calderwood,* VII, pp. 361-4.

15. *Calderwood,* VII, pp. 348-9, 382-3, 433-4, 439, 449, 518, 580, 596-600; *RPCS, 1619-22,* pp. 249-50, 264, 299, 328; *RPCS, 1622-5,* pp. 503-4, 521-2, 541. Cf. *Stevenson, loc. cit.*

16. BR, Edin., Minutes, 26.12.25; Extent Roll for National Taxation, 1625; *Extracts, Edin.,* 1604-26 (for Michaelmas Elections).

17. KSR, Edin., SE Parish, 1631-8 (for December Elections); BR, Edin., Extent Roll for the Annuity Tax, 1635.

18. BR, Edin., Minutes, 13.10.38; Extent Roll for National Taxation, 1637; *Extracts, Edin., 1626-41* (Michaelmas Elections to Town Council).

19. BR, Edin., Minutes, 28.8.37, 18.9.37, 22.9.37, 4.10.37, 18.10.37; *Balfour,* II, p. 232; see Ch. II.

20. *Extracts, Edin., 1626-41, 1642-55* (for Michaelmas Elections to Town Council).

21. Extent Roll for National Taxation, 1634.

22. BR, Edin., Minutes, 24.12.41.

23. BR, Edin., McCleod's Bundles, 31A, no. 14; KSR, Edin., Six Sessions, 1657-62; *Extracts, Edin., 1642-55,* pp. 149, 156-8. See also the notebook in the Lee Papers (NLS, MS 3512) which has extracts, 1643-7, from an earlier volume of the session minutes which no longer survives. This volume would undoubtedly have clarified the issues discussed here; the notes unfortunately do not.

24. *Extracts, Edin., 1642-55,* pp. 169-74, 213; Extent Rolls for National Taxation, 1642, 1649.

25. See notes 16 and 18 above; BR, Edin., Minutes, 23.6.54; Extent Rolls for National Taxation, 1654-57; *Extracts, Edin., 1642-55* (for Michaelmas Elections to Town Council).

Chapter 13

1. *Rutherford,* pp. 663-4.

2. See Ch. V, pp. 59-63.

3. Exchequer Papers, Valuation Rolls, Ayrshire and Lanarkshire, Parish Totals, 1649.

4. See below, notes 7-11.

5. See Ch. I, pp. 3-6.

6. Margaret Sanderson, 'Kirkmen and their Tenants in the Era of the Reformation', *RSCHS,* vol. XVIII, pt. I, pp. 26-42. I should like to take this opportunity of thanking Dr. Sanderson for her help, so generously given, with the difficult question of the security of tenure on the estates of the magnates as well as those of the church.

7. Rentals and Accounts of the Barony of Hamilton, n.d. (mid-16th century), 1592, 1603-39. (The first is in the Tods, Murray & Jamieson papers, SRO; the other two are among the Hamilton Papers).

8. The testaments, 1573-1658, of 72 Avondale farmers, have been examined. They represent all the recorded testaments of farmers with surnames known to have been associated with the parish. There were, of course, others; the structure of the index unfortunately does not facilitate their discovery. For the comparison with the Isles see Frances Shaw, 'Insular Societies in their Economic Setting', pp. 168-174, Ph.D., Edin., 1974. I am most grateful to Dr. Shaw for her advice on the use of testaments.

9. See the testaments mentioned in note 8 above, the rentals mentioned in note 11 below and the 18th century valuation rolls for the parish in Exchequer Papers, Lanarkshire, 1667, 1722, 1742 (E901). See also *Directory of Landownership in Scotland, c1770* (Ed. Loretta R. Timperley), *SRS*, new series, V, pp. 206-8.

10. George Hamilton, *History of the House of Hamilton*, 1933, pp. 389-92.

11. Rentals, Accounts, Court Books and Tacks relating to the barony of Avondale (from the Hamilton Papers unless otherwise stated) as follows: Accounts, 1535; Accounts, 1542, 1544-5 *(Exchequer Rolls*, XVII, pp. 583-88; XVIII, pp. 59-64); Rental, c1540; Rental, c1630; Baron Court Book, 1642; Accounts, 1648-53; Rental, 1652-5; Rental, 1670-9; Tacks, 1642-1706.

12. Testament of Thomas Morton in Overhouse of Glengavil, 1612.

13. The preceding paragraphs owe a lot to Dr. Rosalind Marshall, her compendious knowledge of the Hamiltons and their archives and to her *Days of Duchess Anne*, 1974. I am most grateful.

14. Exchequer Papers, Valuation Rolls, Ayrshire, 1705, lists of heritors (E901).

15. *BLJ*, I, pp. 237-41; II, pp. 450-60.

16. *BLJ, loc. cit;* Rental of Glassford, c1680 (in Hamilton Papers); Summons for valuation of teinds of Glassford, 1636 (among Miscellaneous Teind Papers, SRO).

17. *BLJ*, III, pp. 48-50; *Diplomatic Correspondence of Jean de Montreuil, SHS*, XXX, 1899, vol. II, p. 497; *Packets of Letters from Scotland*, XII, pp. 1-2 (BM, Thomason Tracts); *Memoirs of his own Life and Times* by Sir James Turner (Ed. T. Thomson), Bannatyne Club, 184.

18. Gilbert Burnet, *Memoirs of the Lives and Actions of the Dukes of Hamilton*, (Ed. 1852), pp. 451-3; A Brief Account of the Scots Forces that came from Ireland into England, 1648 (Hamilton Papers). This MS. was obviously used by Burnet.

19. Henry Guthrie, *Memoirs*, 1747, pp. 270-3.

Chapter 14

1. *Rutherford*, p. 56.

2. J. J. Wilson, *Annals of Penicuik*, 1891, pp. 146-50; Rental of the Barony of Penicuik, 1646 (in Clerk of Penicuik Papers, SRO); see Ch. XI, note 7.

3. *Rentals of the County of Perth, 1649*, 1835, *passim*.

4.   KSR, Rothiemay, 7.2.50; Mortlach, 29.6.50; Dyce, 14.10.49; St Andrews (landward), 7.10.51; Newburgh, 11.9.53; Inveresk, 5.6.55; Edzell, 6.12.49; Blairgowrie, 1649-50.

List of Main Events

P

1644	Scottish Army crossed the Tweed
	Committee of Both Kingdoms established
1644-45	Campaigns of Montrose
1645	New Model Army formed
1645	Battle of Naseby
1646	Charles I surrendered to the Scottish Army
1647	Scottish Army left England
	Engagement concluded with Charles I
1648	Engagers, opposed by the Church, raised army to invade England
	Mauchline Rising
	Engagers defeated by Cromwell at Preston
	Whiggamore Raid
1649	Execution of Charles I; Charles II proclaimed King of Scotland
	Act of Classes passed by Parliament
	Patronage abolished
1650	Execution of Montrose
	Cromwell invaded Scotland and won Battle of Dunbar
	Western Army submitted its Remonstrance
1651	Remonstrants protested against the General Assembly
	Scottish Army defeated by Cromwell at Worcester

Bibliography

THIS bibliography attempts to list all the primary sources consulted by the author, together with those secondary sources which have, in one way or another, had a substantial influence on his approach to the subject.

A. Primary Sources, Manuscript.

1. *In the Scottish Record Office* (unless otherwise indicated).

(a) *Church of Scotland Records*

Register of the Acts of the General Assemblies, 1638-46 (CH1).

Minutes of the following Synods (CH2): Argyll (1639-45), Fife (1638-51), Moray (1638-51), Perth and Stirling (1639-51).

Minutes of the following Presbyteries (CH2): Ayr (1642-51), Biggar (1644-50), Brechin (1639-53), Caithness (1651-3), Cupar (1646-53), Dalkeith (1638-53), Deer (1649-53), Dingwall (1649-53), Dumbarton (1639-53), Dunbar (1652-3), Dunfermline (1647-52), Dunoon (1639-53), Elgin (1638-43), Fordyce (1640-53), Forres (1651-3), Haddington (1638-53), Inverness (1638-44), Irvine (1646-50), Jedburgh (1638-53), Kirkcaldy (1638-53), Lanark (1638-53), Linlithgow (1639-53), Paisley (1638-53), Peebles (1638-53), Stirling (1638-40), Stranraer (1641-52).

Minutes of the following Kirk Sessions (CH2): Aberdalgie*, Aberdeen (St. Nicholas), Aberdour, Aberlady, Alves, Alyth*, Anstruther Easter*, Anstruther Wester*, Arbroath*, Arbuthnot, Ardlach*, Auchterhouse, Auchtermuchty, Balmerino, Bathgate, Beath, Benvie*, Belhelvie, Blairgowrie*, Bolton, Botriphnie, Burntisland, Cambuslang, Canisbay, Canongate, Cargill*, Carluke, Carnbee*, Carnock*, Carrington, Ceres, Channelkirk*, Cleish, Colinton, Colmonell, Corstorphine, Cortachy and Clova, Covington, Cramond, Culross, Dairsie, Dalgetty*, Dalkeith, Dalmellington, Dron, Duddingston*, Duffus, Dumfries*, Dunbarney, Dunblane, Dundonald, Dunfermline, Dunino, Dyce, Dyke*, Dysart, Echt*, Edinburgh (Old) (Trinity), Edzell*, Elgin, Ellon, Errol*, Falkirk, Falkland, Ferryport, Fetteresso, Fintry, Glasgow (Barony), Gordon, Grange, Greenlaw*, Humbie, Hutton, Inchture, Innerleithen, Inverary (English), Inveraven, Inveresk, Inverurie*, Kennoway*, Kettins*, Kettle*, Kilconquhar, Kilmadock, Kilrenny*, Kilspindie*, Kinfauns*, Kingarth, Kinghorn, Kinglassie*, Kinnaird, Kinneff and Catterline*, Kinnoul, Kirkcaldy, Kirkden*, Kirkliston, Kirkmichael*, Kirkoswald, Lamington and Wandel*, Largo*, Lasswade, Lesmahagow, Liberton, Liff*, Livingston, Logierait*, Longforgan, Longformacus*, Lyne, Mains*, Markinch, Melrose, Menmuir, Mid-Calder, Moneydie, Monifieth*, Monikie*, Monimail, Mortlach, Newbattle, Newburgh, Newburn, Newton, North Leith, Oldhamstocks, Ormiston, Pencaitland, Penicuik, Petty, Prestonpans, Rattray, Rothiemay*, St. Andrews, St.

Cuthberts, St. Ninians, Saltoun, Scone, Scoonie, Shotts, Skirling, South Queensferry, Sprouston, Stow, Symington*, Tealing*, Thurso, Torryburn*, Tranent, Tweedsmuir, Tyningham, Wemyss, Yester.

N.b: The minutes of parishes marked with an asterisk are held by the Register General for Scotland in New Register House.

(b) *Teind Records.*

Sederunt Book of the Teind Commissioners (TE1).

Register to Supply Lost Records (TE8).

Miscellaneous Papers concerning Augmentations (TE5) relating to the following parishes: Abercorn, Aberfoyle, Aberlady, Abernethie, Abertarff, Aboyne, Alford, Alva, Alvah, Ardrossan, Ashkirk, Auchindoir, Auchreddie, Auchtermuchty, Avoch, Ayr, Ayton, Balfron, Belhelvie, Ballingrie, Balmerino, Banchory-Ternan, Barry, Bonhill, Bothkennar, Botriphnie, Burntisland, Calder Cleir, Cambusnethan, Canonbie, Cargill, Caerlaverock, Carmunnock, Carstairs, Castleton, Cavers, Channelkirk, Chirnside, Closeburn, Cockpen, Collessie, Conveth, Coulter, Crichton, Cumbrae, Cumnock, Dalgetty, Dolphinton, Dron, Drumelzier, Dull, Dunfermline, Dunlop, Dunning, Durris, Durisdeer, Earlston, Eccles, Ecclesgrieg, Ecclesmachan, Ellon, Eyemouth, Falkirk, Findogask, Forgandenny, Fordoun, Fyvie, Gamrie, Gartley, Glasgow (Barony), Glencorse, Glenholm, Hownam, Humbie, Hutton, Inchinnan, Innerwick, Inverchaolain, Inveresk, Inverkeillor, Inverkeithing, Inverkip, Kennethmont, Kettins, Kilbride, Kilbucho, Killearn, Killellan, Kilmalcolm, Kilmarnock, Kilrennie, Kinross, Kinclaven, Kingoldrum, Kinnoul, Kintore, Kippen, Kirkbride, Kirkcaldy, Kirkcowan, Kirkcudbright, Kirkmichael, Kirkoswald, Lamington, Langton, Largs, Lauder, Legerwood, Lenzie, Leuchars, Livingston, Logie, Longformacus, Maderty, Mains, Makerstoun, Maybole, Mertoun, Minigaff, Monikie, Monkland, Morebattle, Morton, Moulin, Muirkirk, Murroes, Muthill, Neilston, Newbattle, Newburn, Newton, Newtyle, Nigg, Ochiltree, Orwell, Oxnam, Paisley, Parton, Pittenweem, Penpont, Perth, Peterhead, Redgorton, Rhynie, Rosneath, St. Quivox, Saltoun, Scone, Soutra, Sprouston, Stewarton, Stobo, Stow, Stoneykirk, Strathmiglo, Symington, Tarbolton, Tibbermore, Torphichen, Tullich, Twynholm, Tynron, Walston, Wardlaw, Westruther, Wilton.

(c) *Exchequer Records, Tax Rolls.*

Valuations (parish totals), 1649, for the following shires (E901): Midlothian, West Lothian, Selkirk, Roxburgh, Berwick, Dumfries, Kirkcudbright, Wigtown, Ayr, Renfrew, Lanark, Dumbarton, Stirling, Clackmannan, Fife, Forfar, Kincardine, Aberdeen, Banff, Elgin, Nairn, Inverness, Sutherland.

Valuations (nominal rolls) for the following shires (E901): Haddington, Forfar, Lanark.

Particular Tax Rolls for the following lordships (E60): Coupar-Angus, Culross, Scone.

Hearth and Poll Tax Rolls for the following parishes (E69, 70): Cramond, Liberton, Penicuik, St. Cuthberts, Stow.

(d) *Miscellaneous.*

Clerk of Penicuik Papers (rental, valuations, court books, tax rolls) (GD18).

Breadalbane Papers (GD112).

Tods, Murray & Jamieson Papers (Rental of Barony of Hamilton) (GD237).

Papers of the Committees of Estates (PA11).

2. *In the Manuscript Department of the National Library of Scotland.*

Wodrow Collection (especially Folio and Quarto series).

Denmilne Collection.

Lee Papers (notes from kirk session records; burgh commissions to Glasgow Assembly).

Balcarres Papers.

Advocates Collection (list of patronage; anonymous notes from kirk session records; minutes of south-east parish of Edinburgh).

Teind Valuation (probably for the King's Annuity), c 1635.

3. *In the Edinburgh City Archives.*

Minutes of the Town Council.

Register of Burgesses.

Town Treasurer's Accounts.

Kirk Treasurer's Accounts.

College Treasurer's Accounts.

Bailies' Accounts.

Accounts of Collectors of Kirk Rents.

Extent Rolls of the Burgh.

Minutes of the Hammermen of Edinburgh and the Baxters, Hammermen, Wrights and Weavers of Canongate.

Teind Rental for the parish of St. Cuthberts.

Papers relating to dispute between the burgh of Edinburgh and the kirk session of South Leith.

4. *In Glasgow City Archives.*

Minutes of the Town Council.

Minutes of the Presbytery of Glasgow.

5. *Hamilton Papers* (held at Lennoxlove, seen through National Register of Archives): Rentals (E1), Accounts (F1), and Tacks (E2) relating to various Hamilton Estates.

B. **Primary Sources, Printed.**

Acts of the Parliament of Scotland.

Register of the Privy Council of Scotland.

Registrum Magni Sigilli Regum Scotorum.

Retours.

Laing Charters (Ed. D. Laing).

Records of the Kirk (Ed. A. Peterkin), 1843.

Calendar of State Papers, Domestic.

Acts and Ordinances of the Interregnum, 1642-60, (Ed. C. H. Firth and R. S. Rait), 3 vols.

The Scots Peerage, (Ed. Sir J. B. Paul), 9 vols., 1904-14.

Fasti Ecclesiae Scoticanae, 8 vols., 1915-50.

Senators of the College of Justice, (Ed. G. Brunton & D. Haig), 1832.

Rental of the County of Perth, 1649, contrasted with . . . 1835, (Ed. W. Gloag), 1835.

The Session Book of Dundonald, (Ed. H. Paton), 1936.

Calvin, *Institutes of the Christian Religion.*

J. Knox, *History of the Reformation*, (Ed. W. C. Dickinson), 2 vols.

Letters of Samuel Rutherford, (Ed. A. A. Bonar), 1891.

W. C. Abbot, *Writings and Speeches of Oliver Cromwell*, 4 vols.

A. Stevenson, *History of the Church of Scotland*, 1753, 4 vols.

G. Burnet, *Memoir of James and William Dukes of Hamilton*, 1852.

Historical Works of Sir James Balfour, 4 vols., 1824-5.

The Large Declaration of Charles I, 1639.

J. Connell, *A Treatise of the Law of Scotland respecting Tithes*, 1815, 3 vols.

Abbotsford Club:

7. *Selections from the Minutes of the Presbyteries of St. Andrews and Cupar, 1641-8*, (Ed. G. R. Kinloch).

8. *Selections from the Minutes of the Synod of Fife, 1611-87*, (Ed. G. R. Kinloch).

16. *Selections from the Registers of the Presbytery of Lanark, 1623-1709*, (Ed. J. Robertson).

Bannatyne Club:

25. *History of the Troubles . . . in Scotland and England, 1624-45*, by J. Spalding, (Ed. J. Skene).

28. *Memoirs of his own Life and Times, by Sir James Turner, 1632-70*, (Ed. T. Thomson).

37. *A Relation . . . by John, Earl of Rothes, 1637-8*, (Ed. D. Laing).

52. *Diary, 1650-67, of John Nicoll*, (Ed. D. Laing).

73. *Letters and Journals of Robert Baillie, 1637-62*, (Ed. D. Laing), 3 vols.

76. *Diary, 1633-45, of Sir Thomas Hope of Craighall*, (Ed. T. Thomson).

81. *Acts and Proceedings of the General Assemblies of the Church of Scotland, 1560-1618*, (Ed. T. Thomson), 3 vols.

93. *History of the Church of Scotland, by John Spottiswood*, (Ed. M. Russell and M. Napier), 3 vols.

Fasti Ecclesiae Scoticanae, (Ed. Hew Scott), 3 vols.

Grampian Club:

The Staggering State of Scottish Statesman, 1550-1650, (Ed. C. Rogers).

Maitland Club:

5. *Register of Ministers . . . and their Stipends after the Reformation*, (Ed. A. Macdonald).

34. *Reports on the State of Certain Parishes, 1627*, (Ed. A. Macdonald).

55. *History of the Kirk of Scotland by John Row.*

66. *Memorials of Montrose*, (Ed. M. Napier), 2 vols.

Scottish Burgh Records Society:

Extracts from the Records of the Burgh of Edinburgh, (Ed. J. D. Marwick and M. Wood), 8 vols., (1528-1665 only).

Extracts from the Records of the Burgh of Glasgow, (Ed. J. D. Marwick), 2 vols.,

(1573-1662 only).

Extracts from the Records of the Burgh of Aberdeen, (Ed. J. Stuart), 2 vols., (1625-1647 only).

Extracts from the Records of the Burgh of Stirling, (Ed. R. Renwick), 1 vol., (1519-1666 only).

Records of the Convention of Royal Burghs, (Ed. J. D. Marwick), 3 vols., (1597-1676 only).

Scottish History Society:

4, 7. *Register of the Kirk Session of St. Andrews, 1559-60,* (Ed. D. H. Fleming).

11, 25, 58. *Records of the Commissions of the General Assemblies, 1646-53,* (Ed. A. F. Mitchell and J. Christie).

17. *Charles II and Scotland, 1651-3,* (Ed. C. H. Firth).

18. *Scotland and the Commonwealth, 1651-3,* (Ed. C. H. Firth).

24. *Extracts from the Presbyteries of Inverness and Dingwall, 1638-88,* (Ed. W. Mackay).

26. *Wariston's Diary and Other Papers,* (Ed. G. M. Paul).

29, 30. *Correspondence of De Montreuil, 1645-8,* (Ed. J. G. Fotheringham).

31. *Scotland and the Protectorate, 1654-59,* (Ed. C. H. Firth).

40. *Negotiations for the Union of England and Scotland, 1651-3,* (Ed. C. S. Terry).

61, II 18, III 34. *Wariston's Diary,* (Ed. G. M. Paul, D. H. Fleming).

Series II, 4. *Rentale Sancti Andree,* (Ed. R. K. Hannay).

Series III, 1, 16. *Consultations of the Ministers of Edinburgh, 1652-60,* (Ed. W. Stephens).

Series III, 42. *Thirds of Benefices.* (Ed. G. Donaldson).

Scottish Record Society:

Burgesses and Guild Brethren of Edinburgh, 1406-1700.

Burgesses and Guild Brethren of Glasgow, 1573-1750.

Burgesses of the Burgh of Canongate, 1622-1733.

Directory of Landownership in Scotland, c. 1770.

Register of Marriages in the Parish of Edinburgh, 1595-1700.

Register of Apprentices of the City of Edinburgh, 1583-1666.

Registers of Testaments of Edinburgh, 1601-1700; Inverness, 1630-1800; Hamilton and Campsie, 1564-1800; Glasgow, 1547-1800; St. Andrews, 1549-1800; Brechin, 1576-1800; Dumfries, 1624-1800; Dunblane, 1539-1800; Lauder, 1561-1800; Lanark, 1595-1800; Orkney and Shetland, 1611-84; Stirling, 1607-1800.

Faculty of Advocates in Scotland, 1532-1943.

Parishes of Medieval Scotland.

Scottish Parish Clergy at the Reformation, 1540-74.

Records of the Church of Scotland.

Spalding Club:

4. *History of Scots Affairs, 1637-41, by James Gordon,* (Ed. J. Robertson and G. Grub).

7. *Extracts from the Presbytery Book of Strathbogie, 1631-54,* (Ed. T. Constable).

10. *Short Abridgement of Britain's Distemper, 1639-45,* (Ed. J. Dunn).

Wodrow Society:
4. *History of the Kirk by John Row,* (Ed. D. Laing).
7. *History of the Kirk by David Calderwood,* (Ed.T.Thomson and D.Laing),8 vols.
13. *Life of Robert Blair,* (Ed. T. McCrie).
Hamilton Papers, (Ed. S. R. Gardiner), Camden Society, 1880.
An Advertisement of the Service Book, (Ed. J. M. Henderson), *SHR,* XXIII, pp. 199-204.
Sir John Scott of Scotstarvet, *True Relation, SHR,* XII, pp. 77-8.
C. **Secondary Sources.**
J. W. Allen, *History of Political Thought in the Sixteenth Century,* 1928.
W. Baird, *Annals of Duddingston and Portobello,* 1900.
John Buchan, *Montrose,* 1928.
R. W. Cochran-Patrick, *Records of the Coinage of Scotland,* 2 vols., 1876.
I. B. Cowan, 'The Covenanters, a Review Article', in *SHR,* XLVII, pt. 1, p. 35.
I. B. Cowan, *The Scottish Covenanters, 1660-88,* 1976.
W. C. Dickinson and G. S. Pryde, *New History of Scotland,* 2 vols., 1962.
G. Donaldson, 'Emergence of Schism in Seventeenth Century Scotland', in *Schism, Heresy and Religious Protest,* 1972.
G. Donaldson, 'Foundations of Anglo-Scottish Union', in *Elizabethan Government and Society,* 1961, p. 282.
G. Donaldson, *Making of the Scottish Prayer Book of 1637,* 1954.
G. Donaldson, *Scotland - James V to James VII,* 1965.
G. Donaldson, *Scottish Kings,* 1967.
G. Donaldson, *Scottish Reformation,* 1960.
D. H. Fleming, 'Scotland's Supplication . . . against the Book of Common Prayer', *PSAS,* LX, pp. 314-83.
W. R. Foster, *The Church Before the Covenants,* 1975.
S. R. Gardiner, *History of England, 1603-41,* 10 vols., 1883-4.
S. R. Gardiner, *History of the Great Civil War,* 4 vols., 1894.
R. Gillespie, *Round about Falkirk,* 1879.
G. Good, *Liberton in Ancient and Modern Times,* 1896.
I. F. Grant, *Social and Economic History of Scotland before 1603,* 1930.
R. H. Groome, *Ordnance Gazetteer of Scotland,* 6 vols.
W. Haller, *Liberty and Reformation in the Puritan Revolution,* 1955.
W. Haller, *Rise of Puritanism,* 1938.
G. Hamilton, *History of the House of Hamilton,* 1933.
G. D. Henderson, *Religious Life in Seventeenth Century Scotland,* 1937.
G. D. Henderson, *Scottish Ruling Elder,* 1935.
J. K. Hewison, *The Covenanters,* 2 vols., 1913.
J. H. Hexter, *Reign of King Pym,* 1941.
J. H. Hexter, 'Problem of the Presbyterian Independents', in *Reappraisals in History,* 1961, p. 163.
C. Hill, *Economic Problems of the Church,* 1956.
L. Kaplan, 'Presbyterians and Independents in 1643', in *English Historical Review,* LXXXIV, p. 244.

M. Lynch, 'The Two Edinburgh Councils, 1559-60', *SHR*, LIV, pt. 2, pp. 117-39.

R. G. E. Lythe, *Economy of Scotland, 1550-1625*, 1960.

J. Mackay, *History of the Burgh of Canongate*, 1886.

R. Marshall, *The Days of Duchess Anne*, 1973.

D. Mathew, *Scotland Under Charles I*, 1955.

W. L. Mathieson, *Politics and Religion*, 2 vols., 1902.

W. Monter, *Calvin's Geneva*, 1967.

G. I. Murray, *Records of Falkirk Parish, 1617-1888*, 2 vols., 1887-8.

New Statistical Account of Scotland.

T. I. Rae, *Administration of the Scottish Frontier*, 1966.

R. S. Rait, *Parliaments of Scotland*, 1924.

D. Robertson, *South Leith Records*, 2 vols., 1911.

H. Rubinstein, *Captain Luckless*, 1975.

M. H. B. Sanderson, 'The Feuars of Kirklands', *SHR*, LII, pt. 2, pp. 117-36.

M. H. B. Sanderson, 'Kirkmen and their Tenants in the Era of the Reformation', in *RSCHS*, XVIII, pt. 1, p. 26.

M. H. B. Sanderson, 'Some Aspects of the Church in Scottish Society in the Era of the Reformation', in *RSCHS*, XVII, pt. 2, p. 81.

G. V. Selway, *A Midlothian Village*, 1890.

D. Shaw, *General Assemblies of the Church of Scotland*, 1964.

W. Sime, *History of Church and Parish of St. Cuthbert*, 1829.

A. Simpson, *Wealth of the Gentry, 1540-1660*, 1961.

T. C. Smout, *History of the Scottish People*, 1969.

T. C. Smout, *Scottish Trade on the Eve of the Union*, 1963.

T. Speedy, *Craigmillar and its Environs*, 1892.

D. Stevenson, 'Conventicles in the Kirk, 1619-37', *RSCHS*, XVIII, pt. 2, pp. 99-114.

D. Stevenson, 'The Financing of the Cause of the Covenants, 1638-51', in *SHR*, LI, p. 89.

D. Stevenson, 'The General Assembly and the Commission of the Kirk, 1638-51', *RSCHS*, XIX, pt. 1, pp. 59-79.

D. Stevenson, *The Scottish Revolution, 1637-44*, 1973.

Statistical Account of Scotland.

C. S. Terry, *Scottish Parliament, 1603-1707*, 1905.

H. R. Trevor-Roper, 'The Gentry, 1540-1640', in *Economic History Review, Supplement*, no. 1, 1952.

H. R. Trevor-Roper, 'Scotland and the Puritan Revolution', in *Historical Essays Presented to David Ogg*, 1962, p. 78.

C. V. Wedgwood, *King's Peace*, 1955.

C. V. Wedgwood, *King's War*, 1958.

J. Willcock, *The Great Marquess*, 1903.

J. J. Wilson, *Annals of Penicuik*, 1891.

T. Wilson, *Stow of Wedale*, 1917.

J. P. Wood, *Ancient and Modern State of the Parish of Cramond*, 1794.

A. S. P. Woodhouse, *Puritanism and Liberty*, 1938.

D. **Unpublished Theses.**

A. B. Birchler, 'The Influence of the Scottish Clergy on Politics, 1616-38', Nebraska, 1966.

D. J. Bryden, 'The Finances of James VI', Edinburgh, 1925.

W. R. Foster, 'Ecclesiastical Administration in Scotland, 1600-38', Edinburgh, 1963.

Frances Shaw, 'Insular Societies in their Economic Setting', Edinburgh, 1974.

D. Stevenson, 'The Covenanters and the Government of Scotland, 1637-51', Glasgow, 1970.

Index